You Can Paint Dazzling Watercolors in Twelve Easy Lessons

Yuko Nagayama

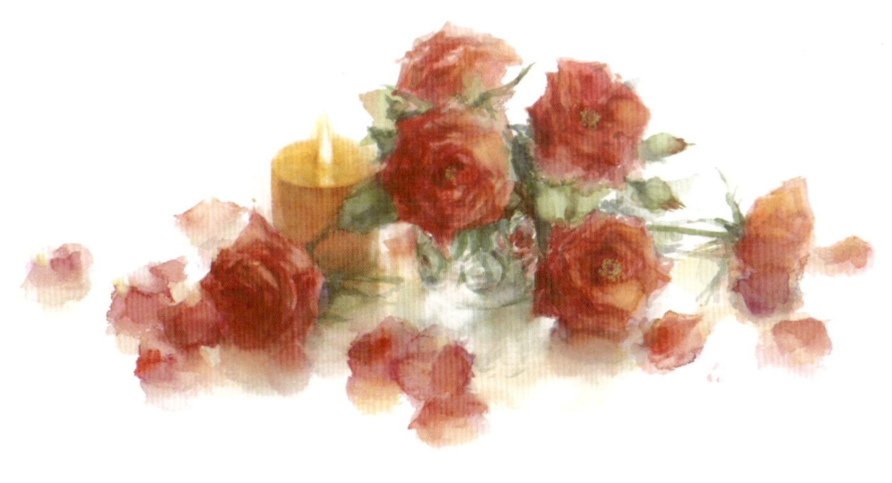

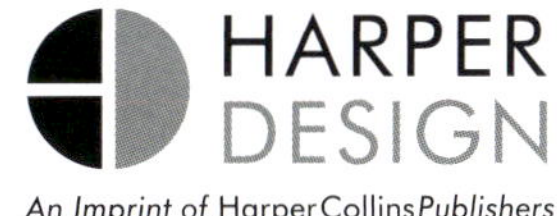

HARPER DESIGN

An Imprint of HarperCollins Publishers

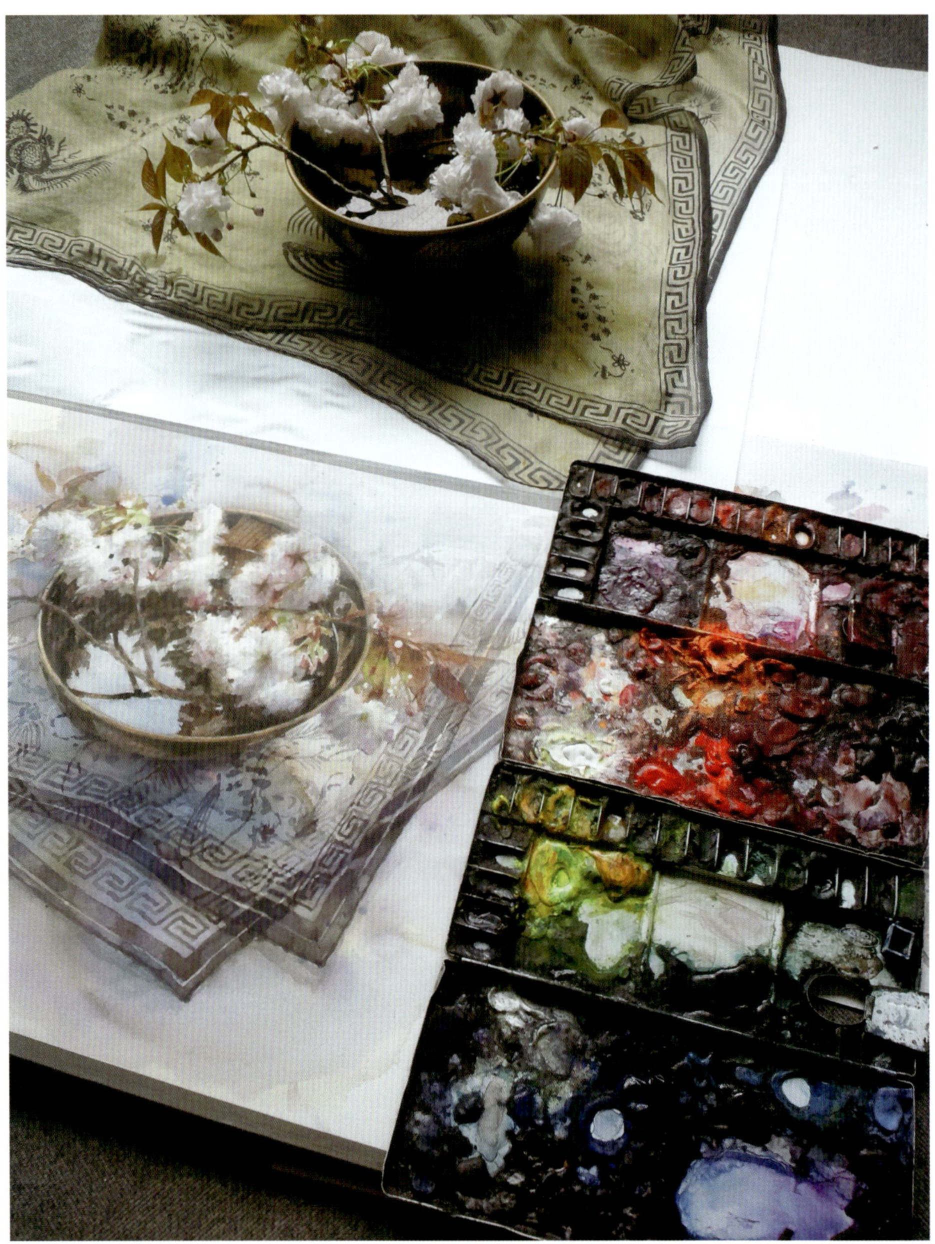

My studio on a spring day.
Please excuse the dirty palette.

Contents

Works from My Studio: Cherry Blossoms

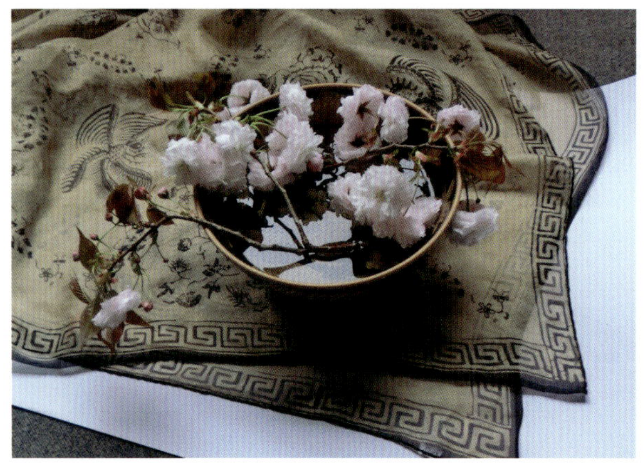

Arrange cherry blossoms in a basin, then begin to paint.

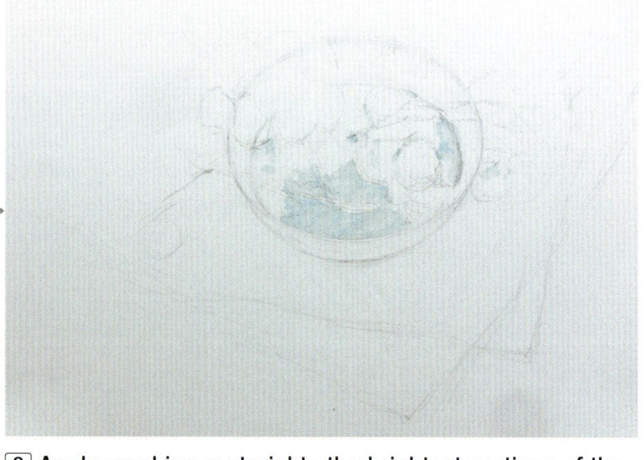

③ Apply masking material to the brightest portions of the water in order to leave that space white.

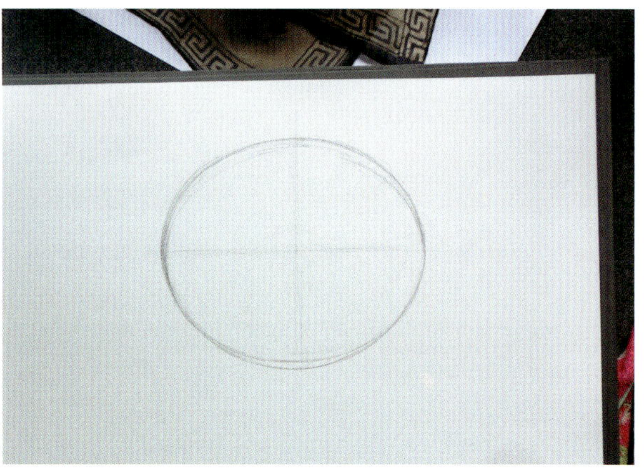

① Sketch using a pencil. For the basin, sketch out an oval by first drawing a vertical and a horizontal line.

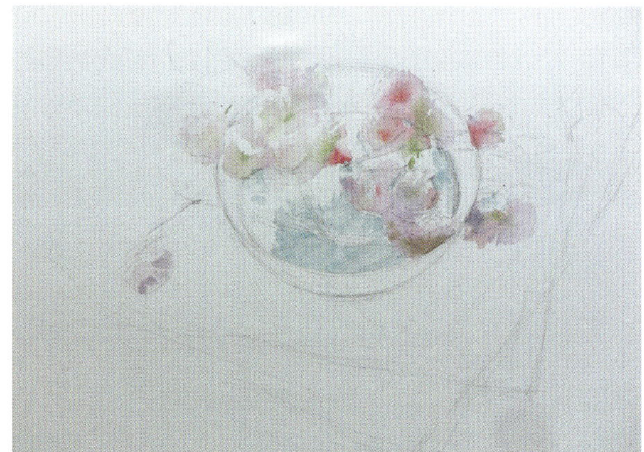

④ Paint the pale colors of the cherry blossoms first.

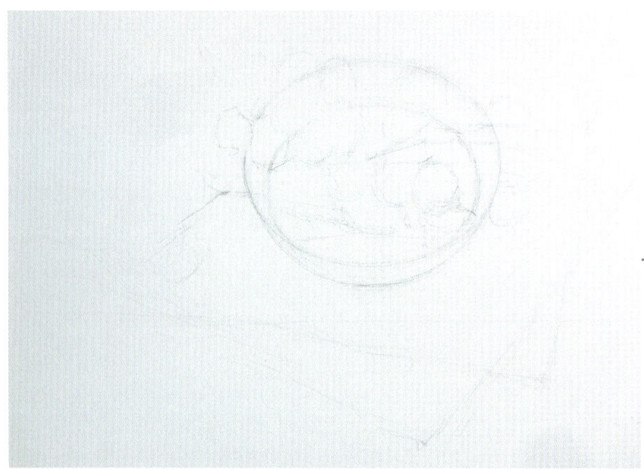

② You can complete the sketch by roughly adding in the position of the fabric and cherry blossoms.

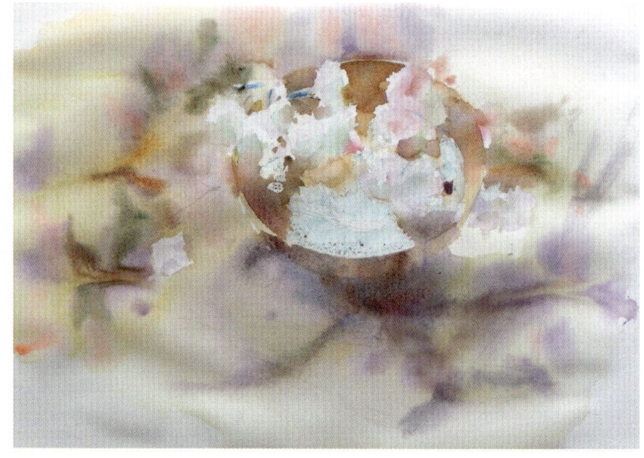

⑤ Add shading by using "unglazed porcelain" paint. For the fabric, spontaneously lay down different colors without fixating on any specific fabric colors.

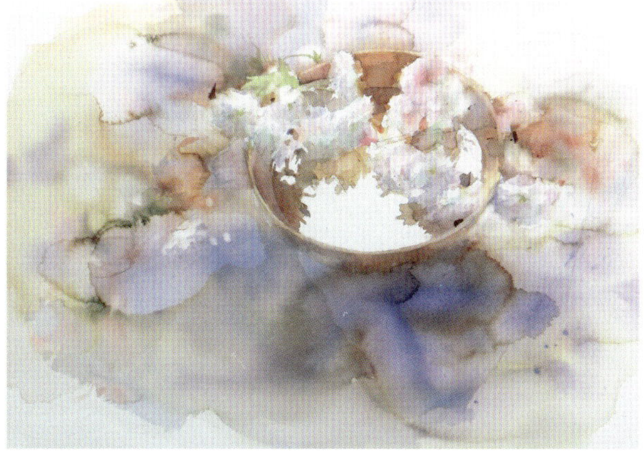

6 After the underpainting is complete, let it dry and then peel off the masking material.

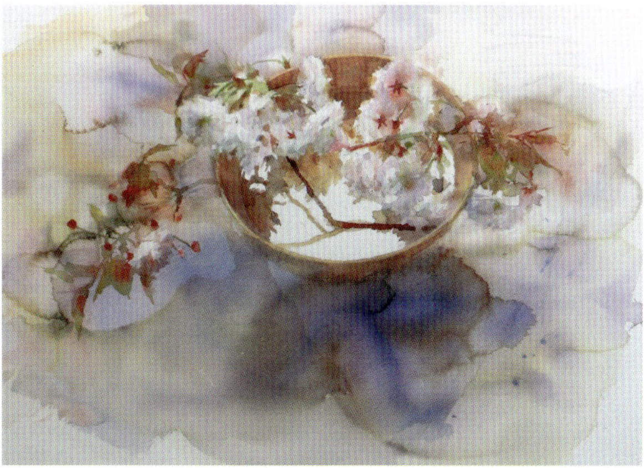

7 Add branch shadows to the surface of the water. Paint in darker colors to complete.

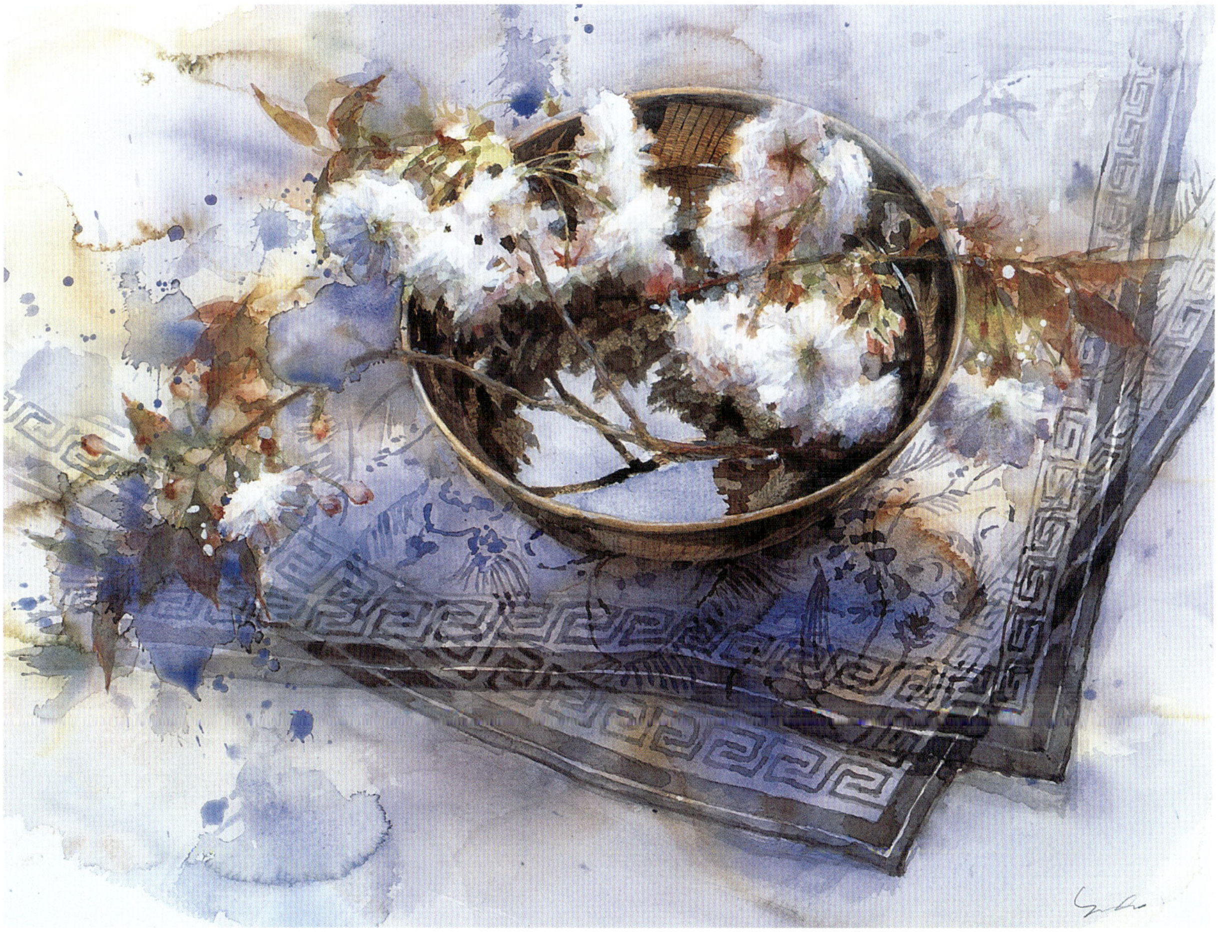

In late spring, double-flowered cherry blossoms sway leisurely on a branch. I put the double-flowered blossoms in a Vietnamese bowl on top of some fabric from Indonesia.

Sakura (Cherry Blossoms)
20.5 x 25.5 in (52 x 65 cm)

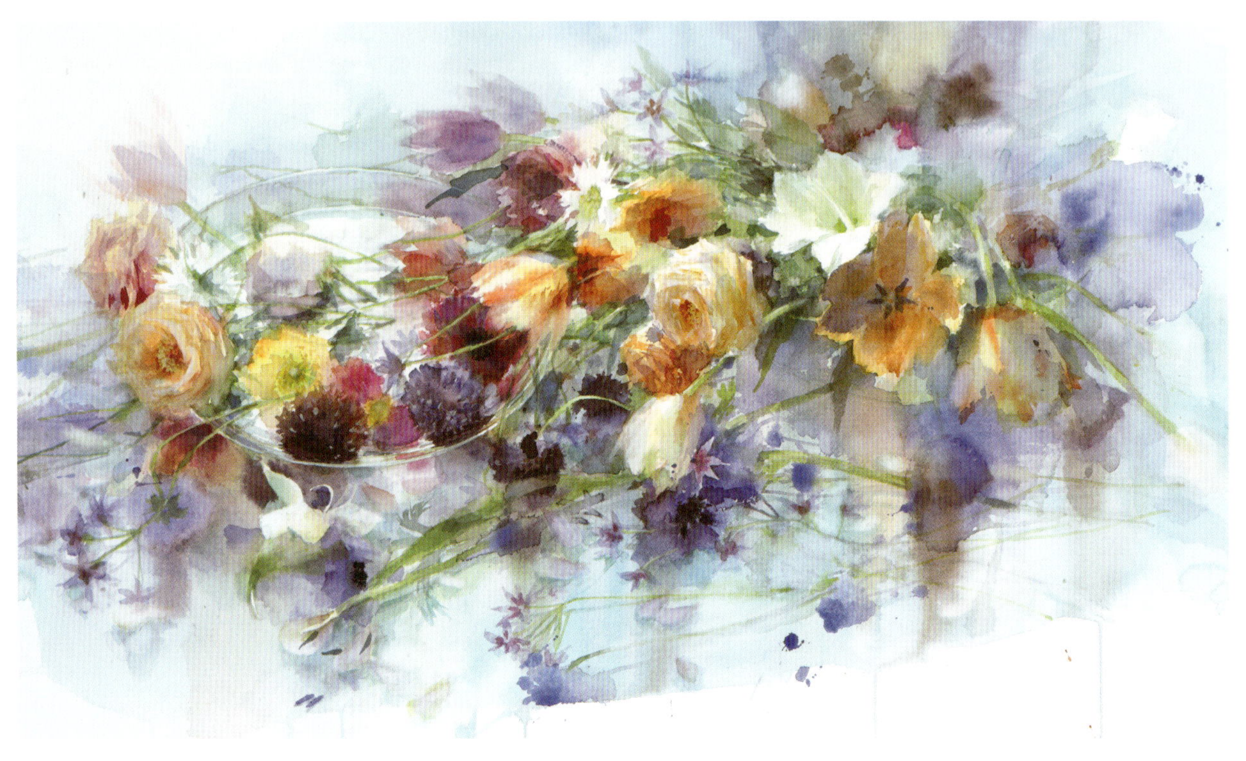

Ophelia

18.5 x 33.75 in (47 x 86 cm)

I painted this image by imagining a scene where Ophelia, a character from *Hamlet*, was floating along a brook.

Chapter 1

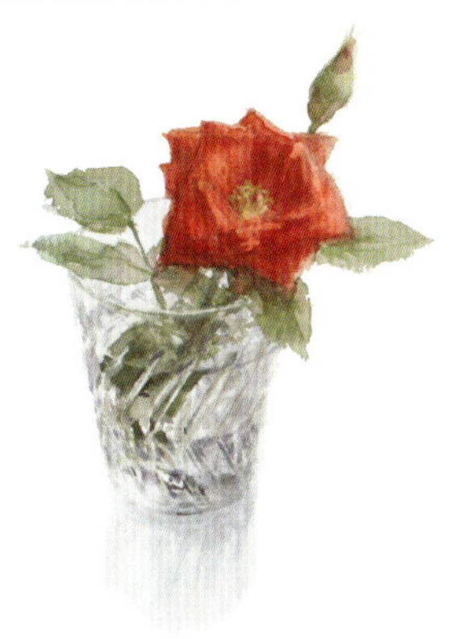

Colors and Materials

Paints

The lesson pages in this book include references for all colors used. Easy-to-obtain Holbein watercolors are given as examples, but please feel free to try out watercolors you already have on hand.

The photo below shows a palette with each well filled with paint. Squeeze the entire tube onto your palette rather than allowing the leftover paint to harden in the tube. You can let the paint dry in the wells of the palette so they will not be wasted. You can add water to reconstitute them later.

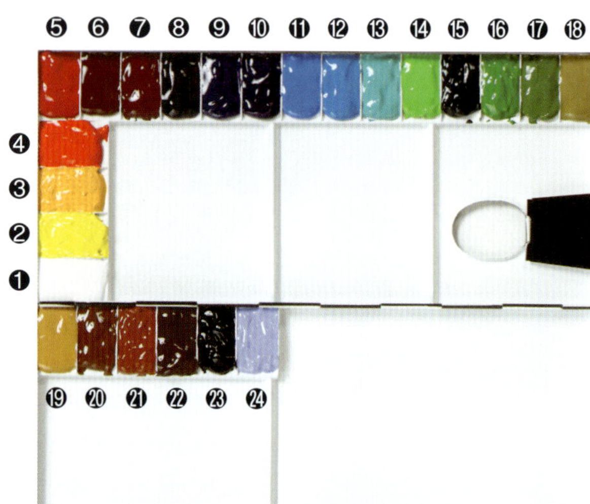

The picture above shows a set of paints on a palette. The main colors are from a Holbein set of 24, but I exchanged "Opera" and "Lavender" (for Ivory black and Jaune Brillant No. 2).

Gouache is an opaque water-based paint. You will see where I use white gouache in certain paintings to add highlights and other effects. You can also use Titanium White watercolor paint for a similar look.

From the left bottom corner of the palette:

❶ Chinese White
❷ Permanent Yellow Lemon
❸ Permanent Yellow Deep
❹ Vermilion Hue
❺ Opera
❻ Crimson Lake
❼ Rose Madder
❽ Mineral Violet
❾ Cobalt Blue Hue
❿ Ultramarine Deep
⓫ Compose Blue
⓬ Cerulean Blue
⓭ Cobalt Green
⓮ Permanent Green No. 1
⓯ Viridian Hue
⓰ Permanent Green No. 2
⓱ Terre Verte
⓲ Yellow Gray

From left on the lower half of the palette:

⓳ Yellow Ocher
⓴ Burnt Sienna
㉑ Light Red
㉒ Burnt Umber
㉓ Prussian Blue
㉔ Lavender

Note: Holbein's watercolor paint names are given for each color in the lesson pages but some are abbreviated.

Paint Color Name → Color Name Given in This Book

Vermilion Hue → Vermilion	Viridian Hue → Viridian
Cobalt Blue Hue → Cobalt Blue	Permanent Green No. 1 → Green No. 1
Permanent Yellow Lemon → Yellow Lemon	Permanent Green No. 2 → Green No. 2
Permanent Yellow Deep → Yellow Deep	

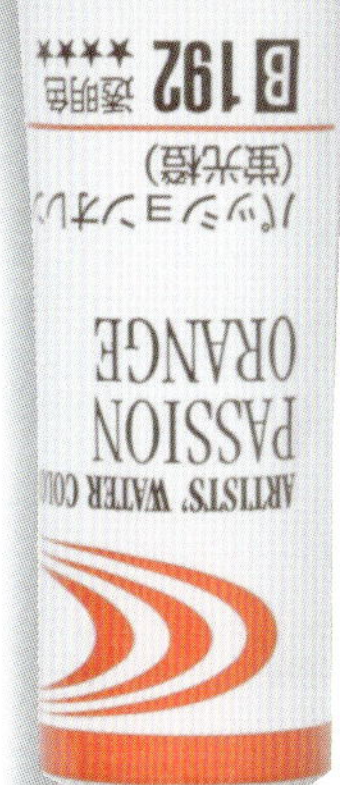

In addition to Opera and Lavender, these five colors are also used.

Kusakabe Passion Orange

Quite florescent. This color is used as the secret ingredient to depict bright light in landscapes and for vibrant flowers.

Schmincke Translucent Yellow

This shade can best be described as the color of mustard. This yellow also has a depth to it. It is used as a base color for landscapes and also to paint leaves by mixing with blue.

Winsor & Newton Manganese Blue Hue

This is a pale color whose tone dissipates when mixed with another color. It is an evanescent, but beautiful, color when applied by itself.

Schmincke Translucent Orange

An orange with distinctive depth. Described as "Chinese chili oil" because of its resemblance to that color.

Schmincke Mauve

Though this paint has the flavor of a mixed purple, it is a simple color that is vibrant while still having depth.

Paper

In this book, watercolor paper is used. For a sketchbook, I recommend the block type. I used sketchbooks from Arches and Hahnemühle.

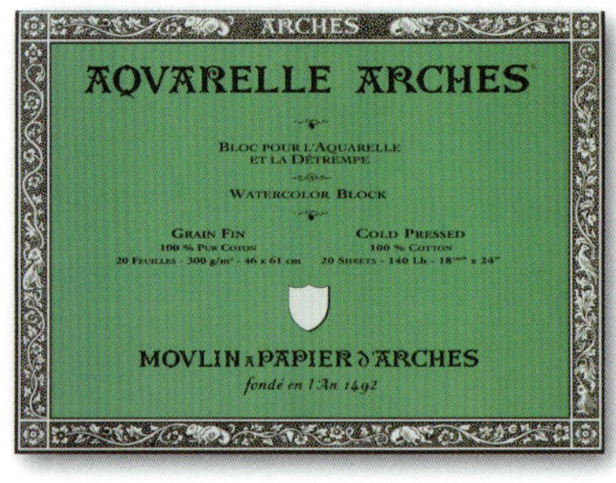

> ## Things You Need to Know
> ## You Cannot Paint on Damp Paper

This goes without saying, but watercolor painting uses water. Your paper will become damp if you store a closed sketchbook while the paint is still wet.

Block-type paper is amazing to draw on, but if you are not careful the precious paper will be ruined and a great deal of paper will be wasted. Let your paintings completely dry and then remove them from your sketchbook. Store the sketchbook where there is little moisture.

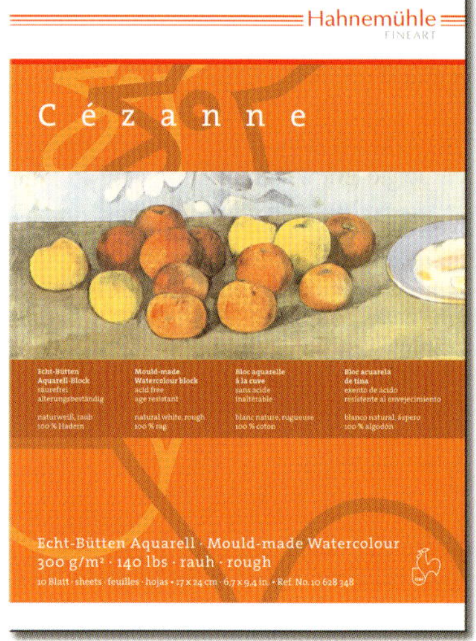

It is difficult to tell whether pure white paper is damp just by looking at it. After I had carefully performed my preliminary sketches and begun to paint, I found out that the paper was damaged and I was very disappointed. In order to prevent such problems, let's remember the following points:

1. Close your sketchbook after completely drying it with a hairdryer, etc. Or, make a habit of leaving it open and gaze awhile at your paintings after they are completed.

2. Do not use old paper. Do not buy a lot of paper when on sale and keep it as stock.

Brushes

In the beginning, I think it is easier to use brushes that you are familiar with. If you are a complete beginner, I think it would be best to use a small brush shaped for calligraphy. I use flat brushes or hake brushes for underpainting, because I want to avoid painting excessive details.

> ## Things You Need to Know
> ## Do Not Leave Brushes in Water

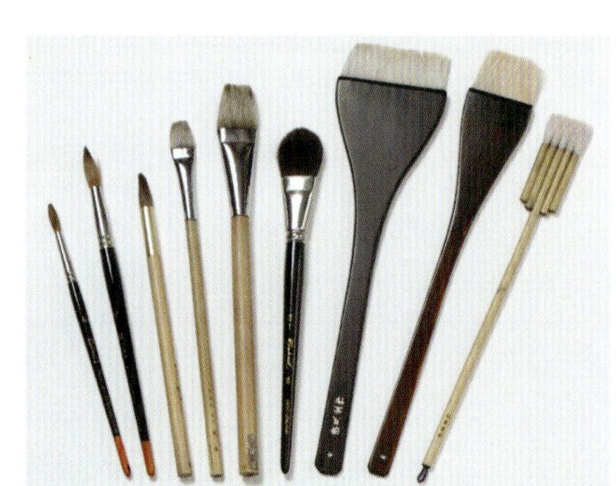

Just like sketchbooks will become damp, improperly drying brushes and storing them in a case will cause them to spoil, even the expensive ones. Some people say that brushes will lose their hair if you leave them in a bucket of water while you paint. Of course, this will damage them. Please make sure that you take your brushes out of your bucket.

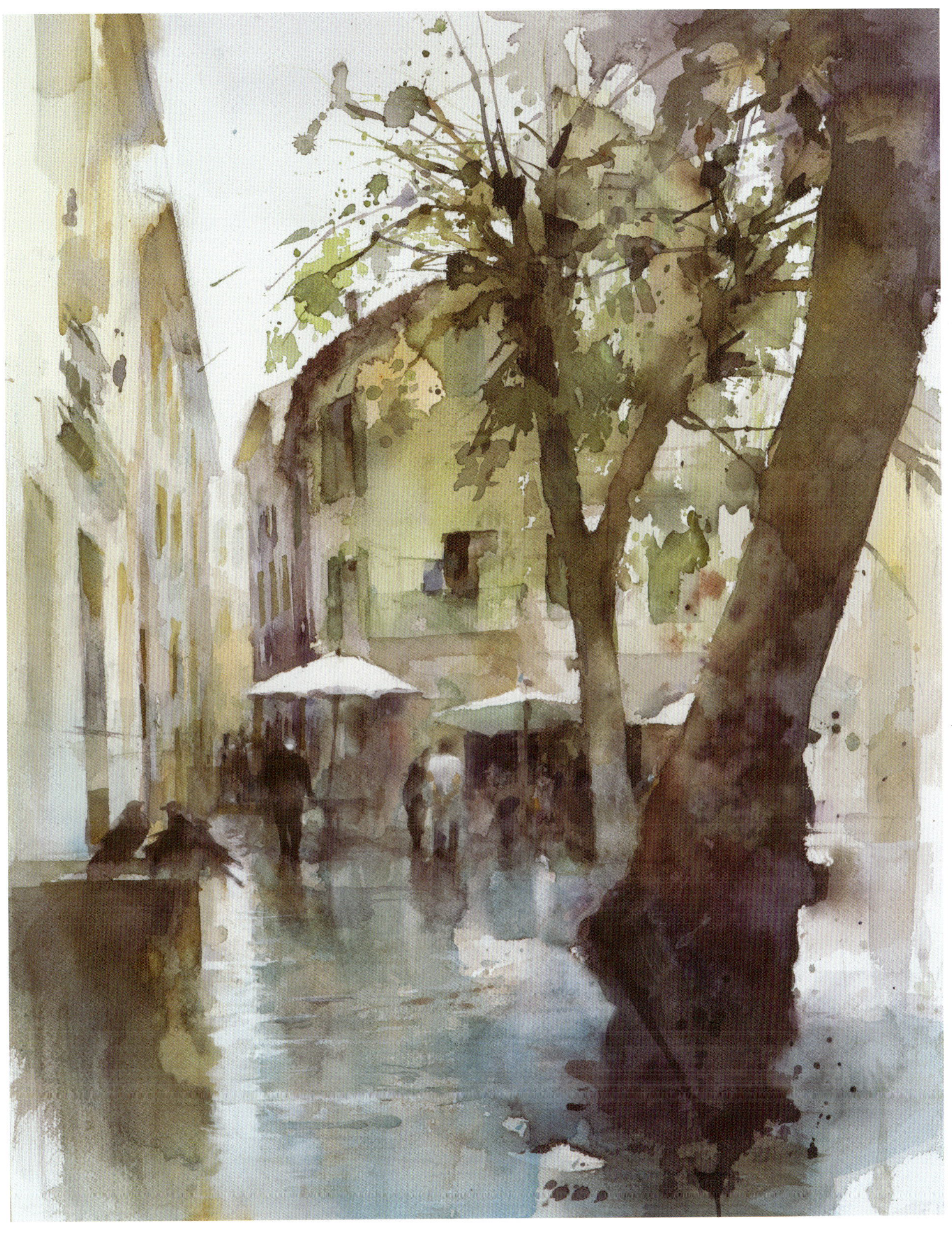

The square became lively again once the rain stopped.
Close to a fountain, I painted while surrounded by a
flock of pigeons.

Ame Agari (Saint-Paul-de-Vence)
22.5 x 17.25 in (57 x 44 cm)

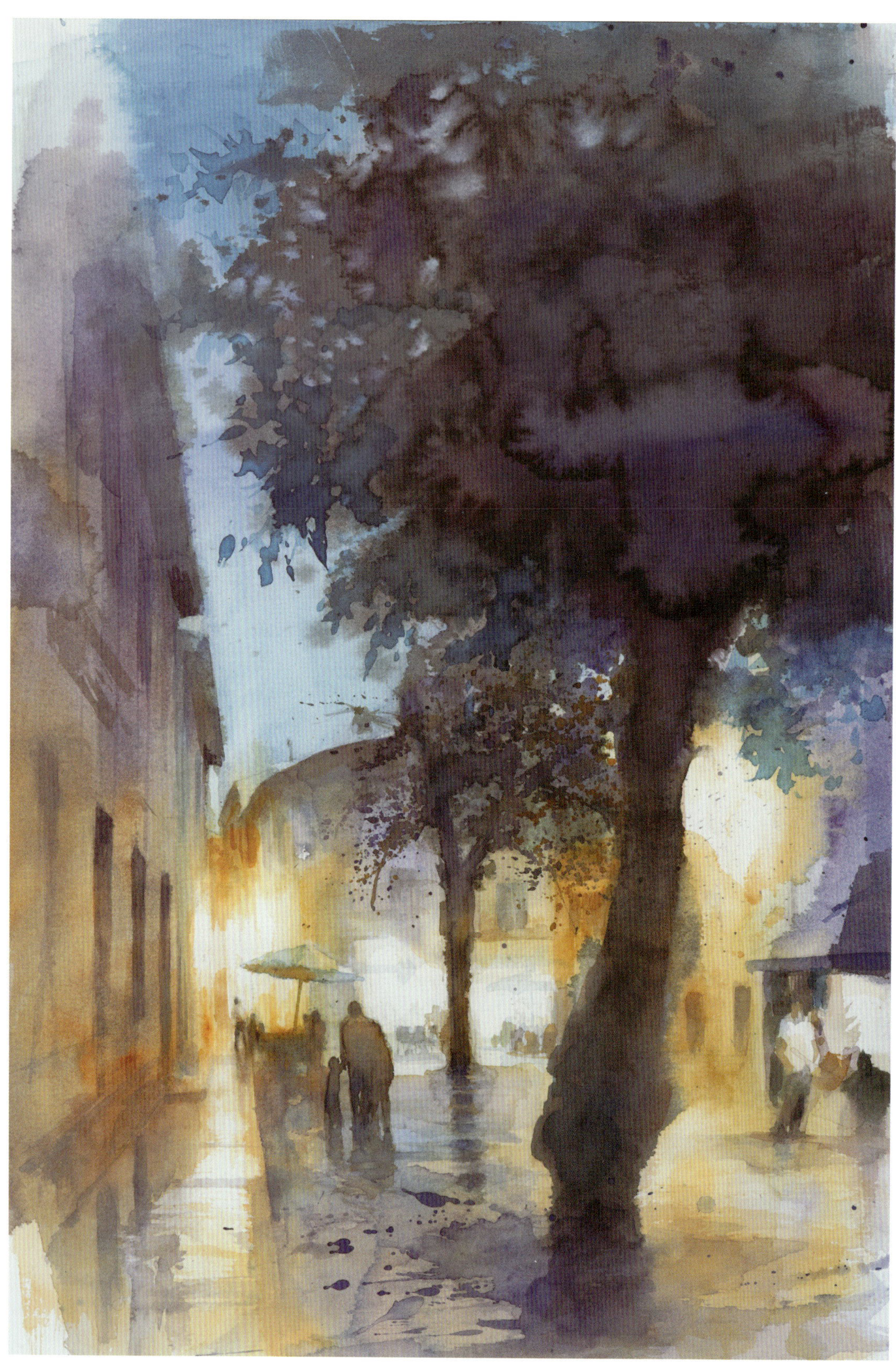

Yoru no Hiroba (The Square at Night)
21.75 x 14.5 in (55 x 37 cm)

I returned to the square I painted that day. The ambiance was devoid of florescent lights. Everything was quietly slipping into the night.

Chapter 2

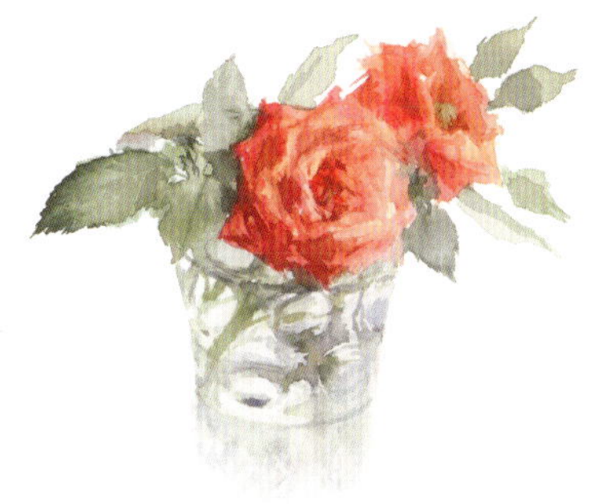

Backgrounds and Two Procedures

Roses 1: When to Leave Backgrounds White

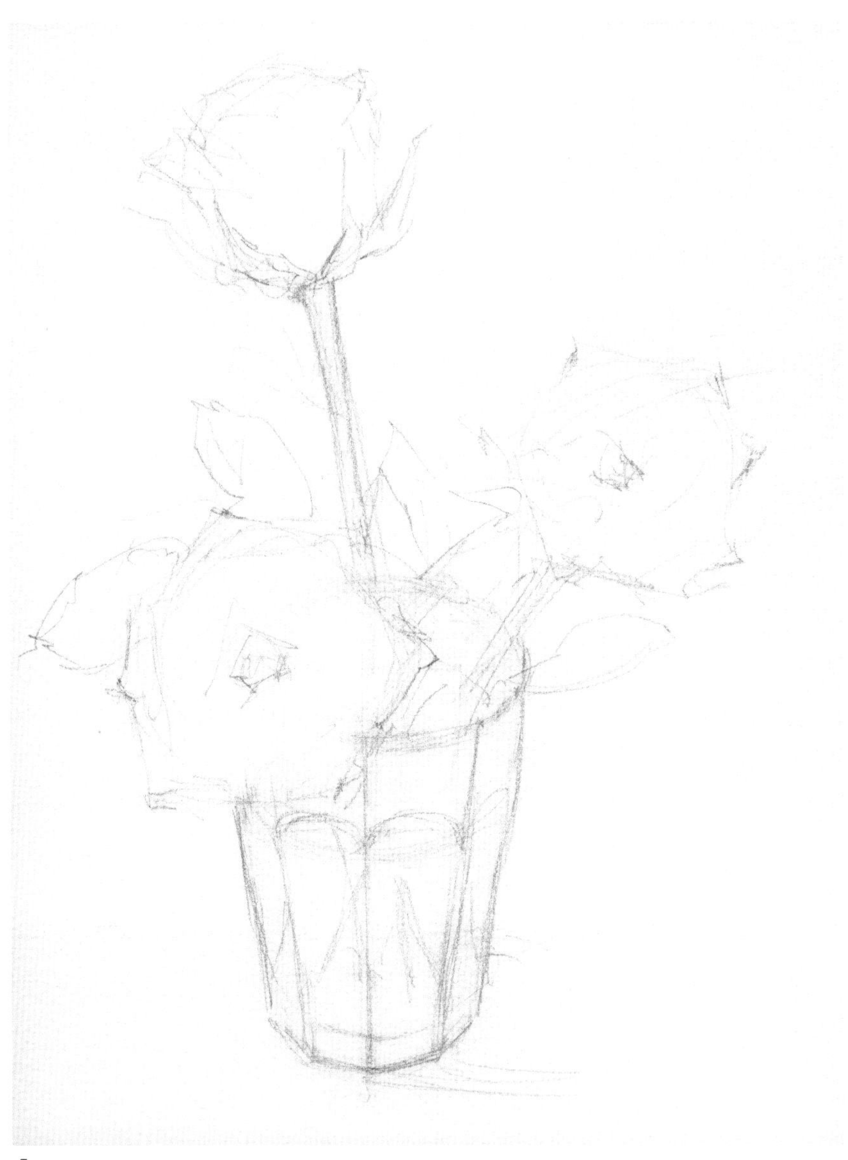

1

Roughly capture the shape. Draw the center of the roses, but omit each petal.

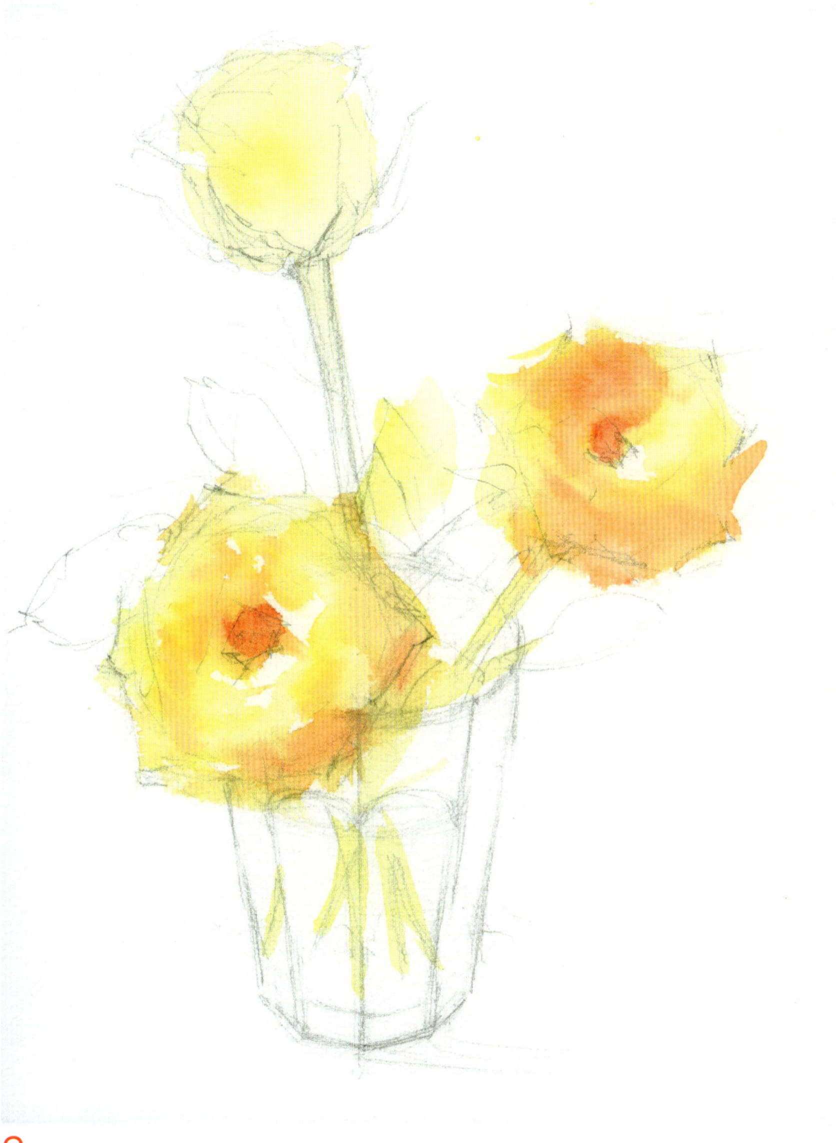

2

Shadows will emerge when you look at light, squint, and shade your eyes.

Note

It is important to look at the underpainting in both light and shade.

Use plenty of water in the beginning. Blot your brush well and, while the surface of the paper is still wet, drop in the darker color and blend.

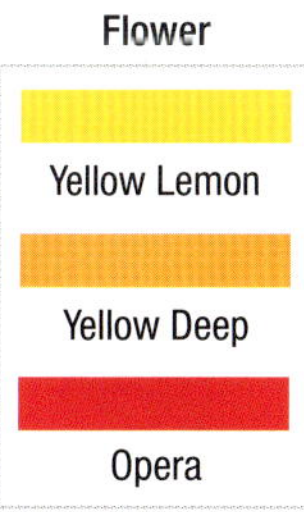

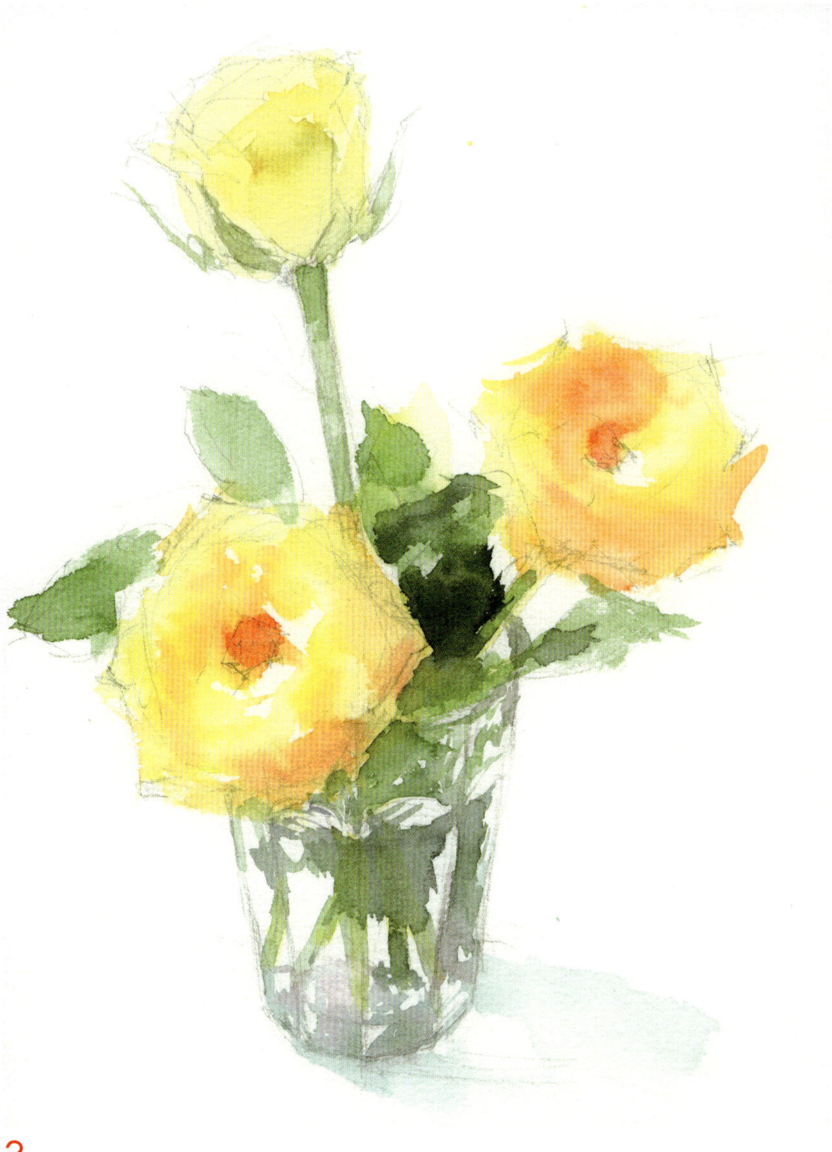

3

Paint the shadow of the glass at this point.

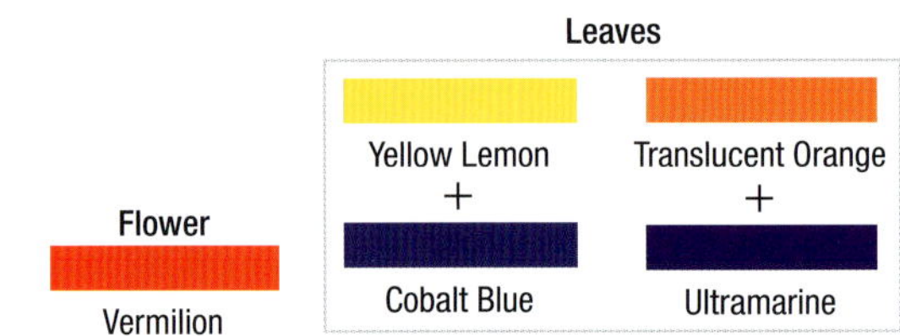

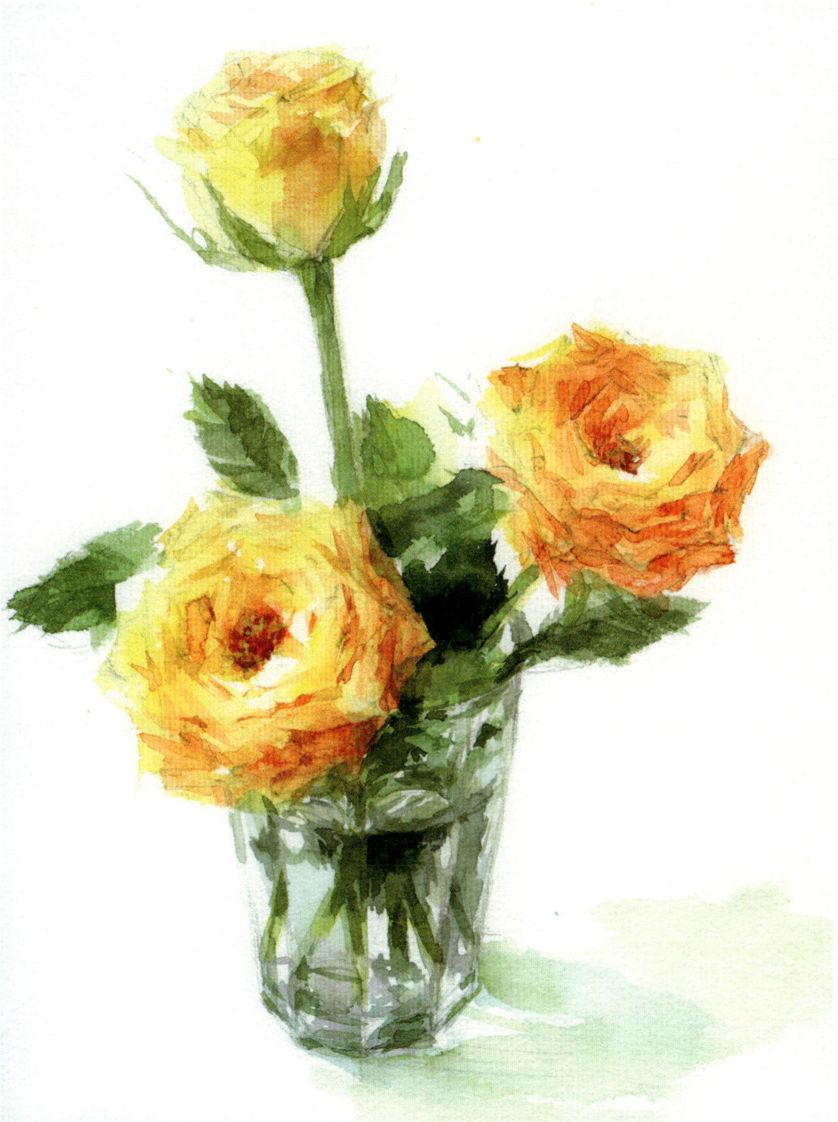

Complete

Once dry, paint the petals a different color from the underpainting. It is exactly this ability to layer colors that brings out the allure of watercolors.

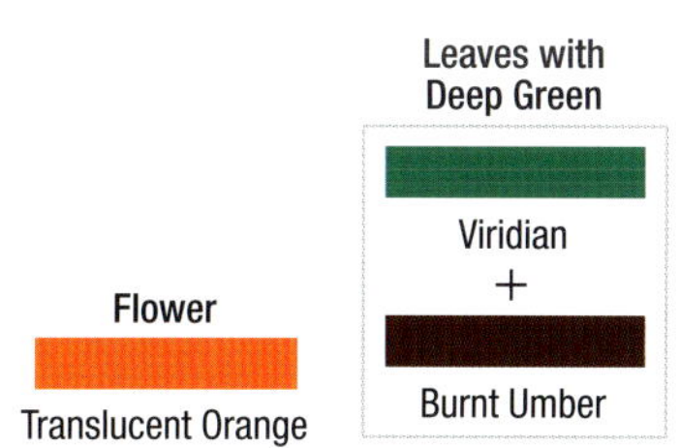

Background Colors and Drawing Procedures

Leaving the Background White

If you leave the background unpainted on purpose—because you are afraid of messing it up by painting it a certain color—you will find that, in truth, this technique is extremely hard to use.

"Leaving the background white" means, "to place a foreground object in a very bright place." In other words, the paper is filled with brilliant, dazzling light. The more the motif is placed to the rear, the more it becomes buried in light. Thus, you need to paint the rear section faintly. When you paint in a gloomy room, objects at the rear may actually look darker.

By painting exactly what you see in front of you onto a white surface you will find that the rear of the motif appears darker, which hinders the painting's perspective.

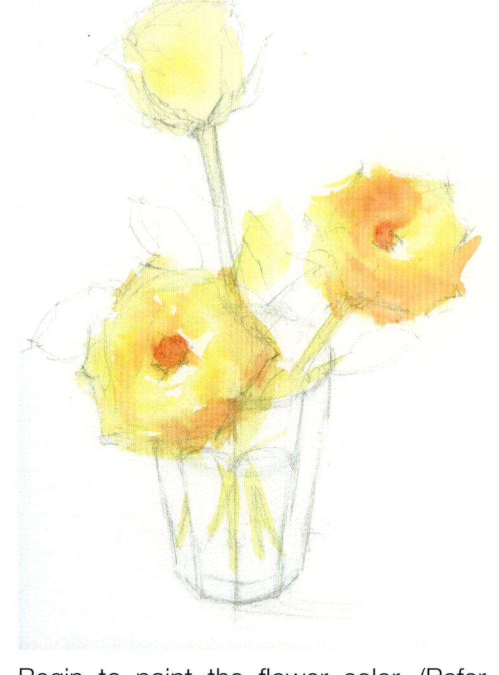

Begin to paint the flower color. (Refer to pages 14–17 for detailed procedures.)

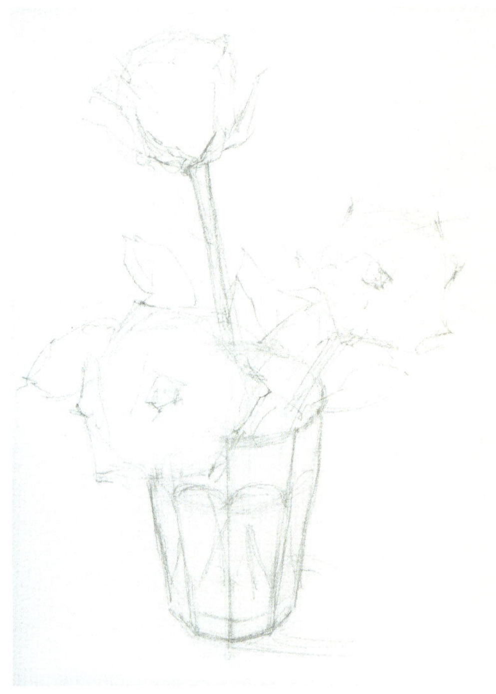

I Tried Out a Red Background

Here, it is not that there is a red wall behind the roses, rather let's imagine that there is a red flowing atmosphere surrounding them.

What's the difference? The difference is that a red wall would only exist behind the roses. In this case, the red air completely fills the space that enfolds the motif. That will make it so the red ambience fills the entire space around the roses and even in front of the cup. (Refer to page 32.)

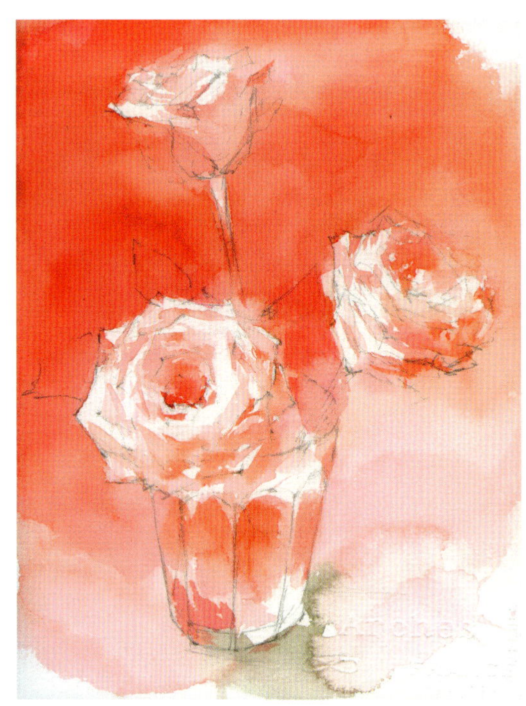

Begin to paint the background. (Refer to pages 20–22 for detailed procedures.)

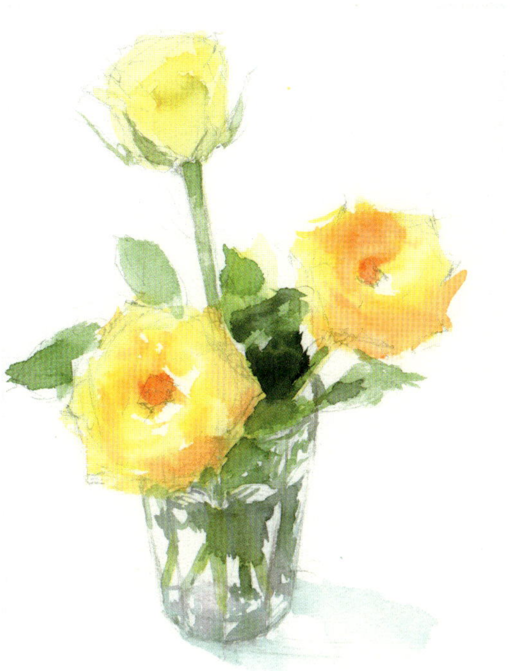

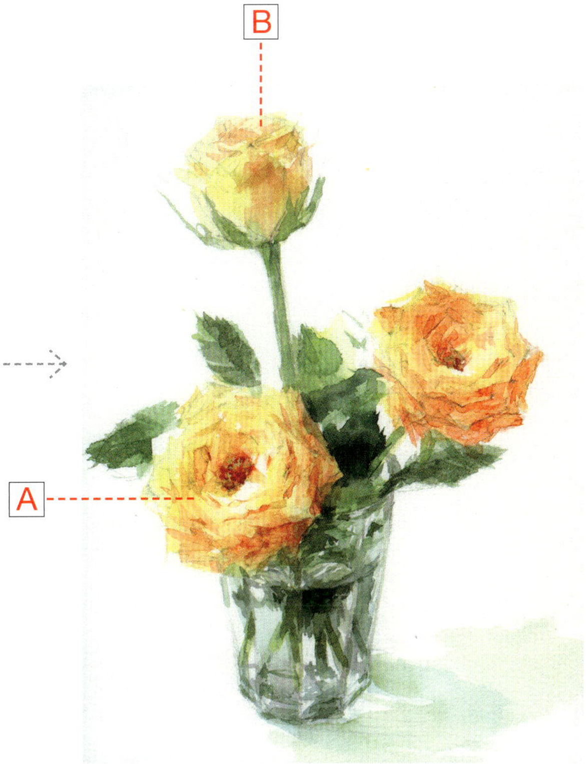

Complete

In contrast to A, I painted B thinner and fainter than seen in real life. What did I try to depict by doing this? The "air," of course.

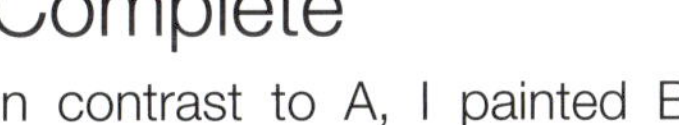

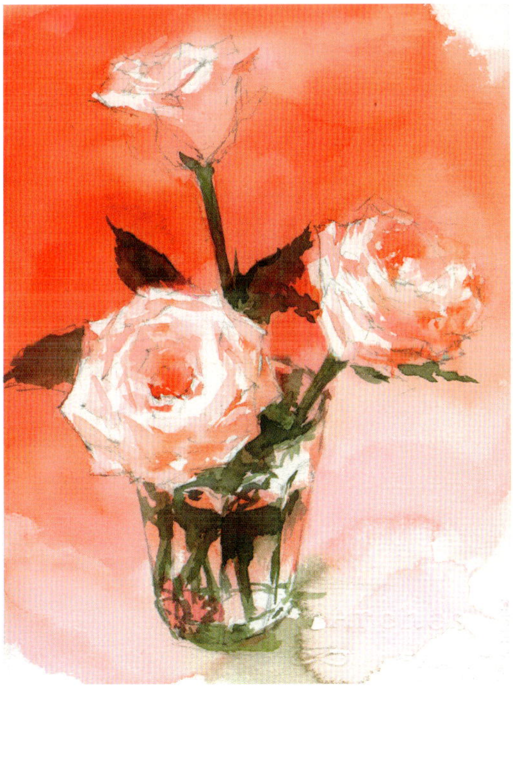

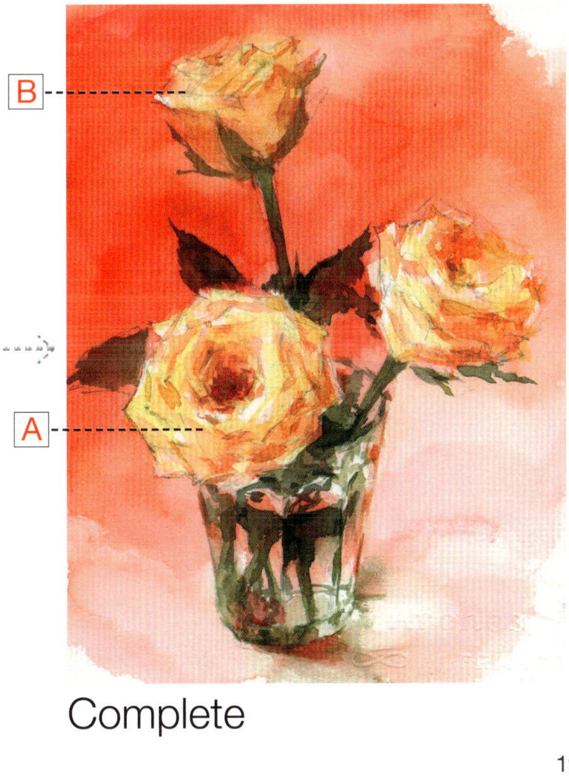

Complete

Roses 2: When to Color Backgrounds First

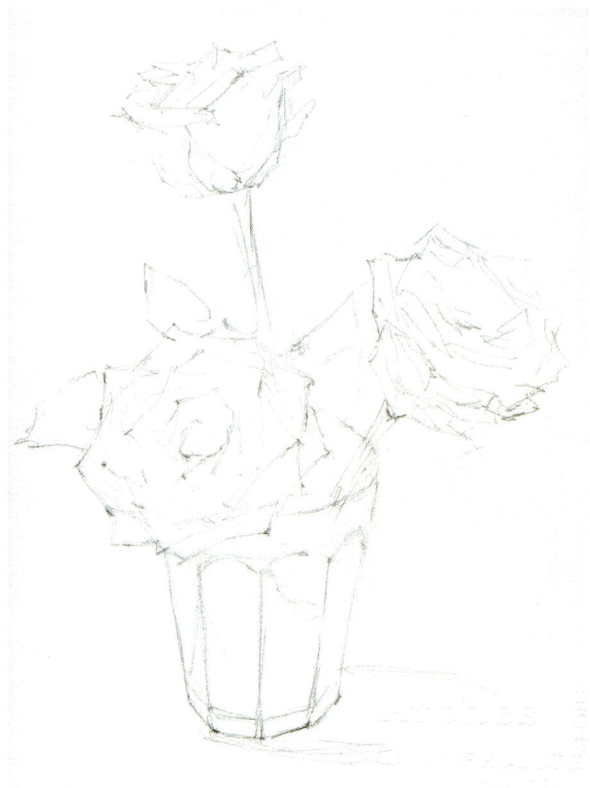

1

Sketching is performed in the same manner as when leaving the background white.

Try to paint using just one color, as if it were a black-and-white photo.

2

When you think: "I want to paint in a different style," or "I want to be adventurous," try bold colors that you wouldn't normally choose! Have the intention of pulling the motif into your own world. It's like, "Welcome to the world of red!"

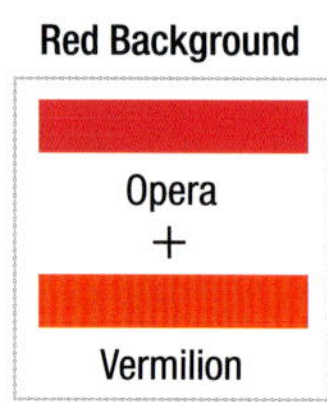

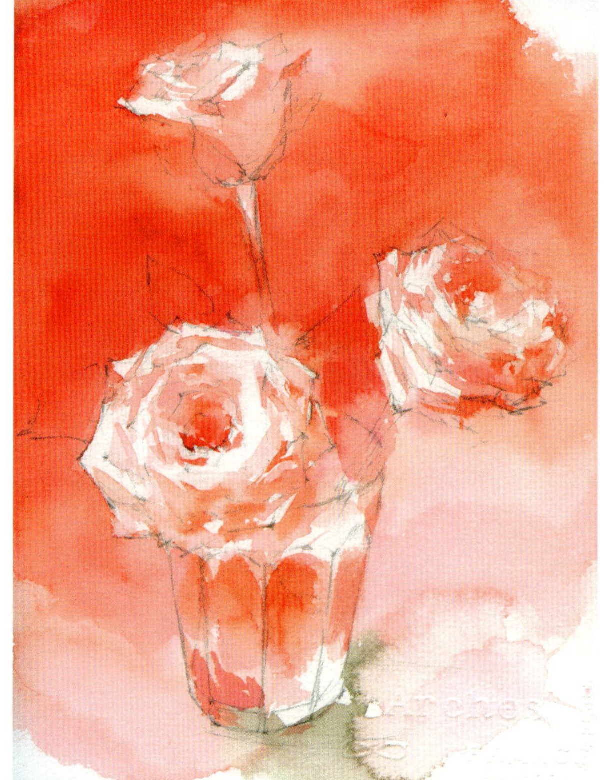

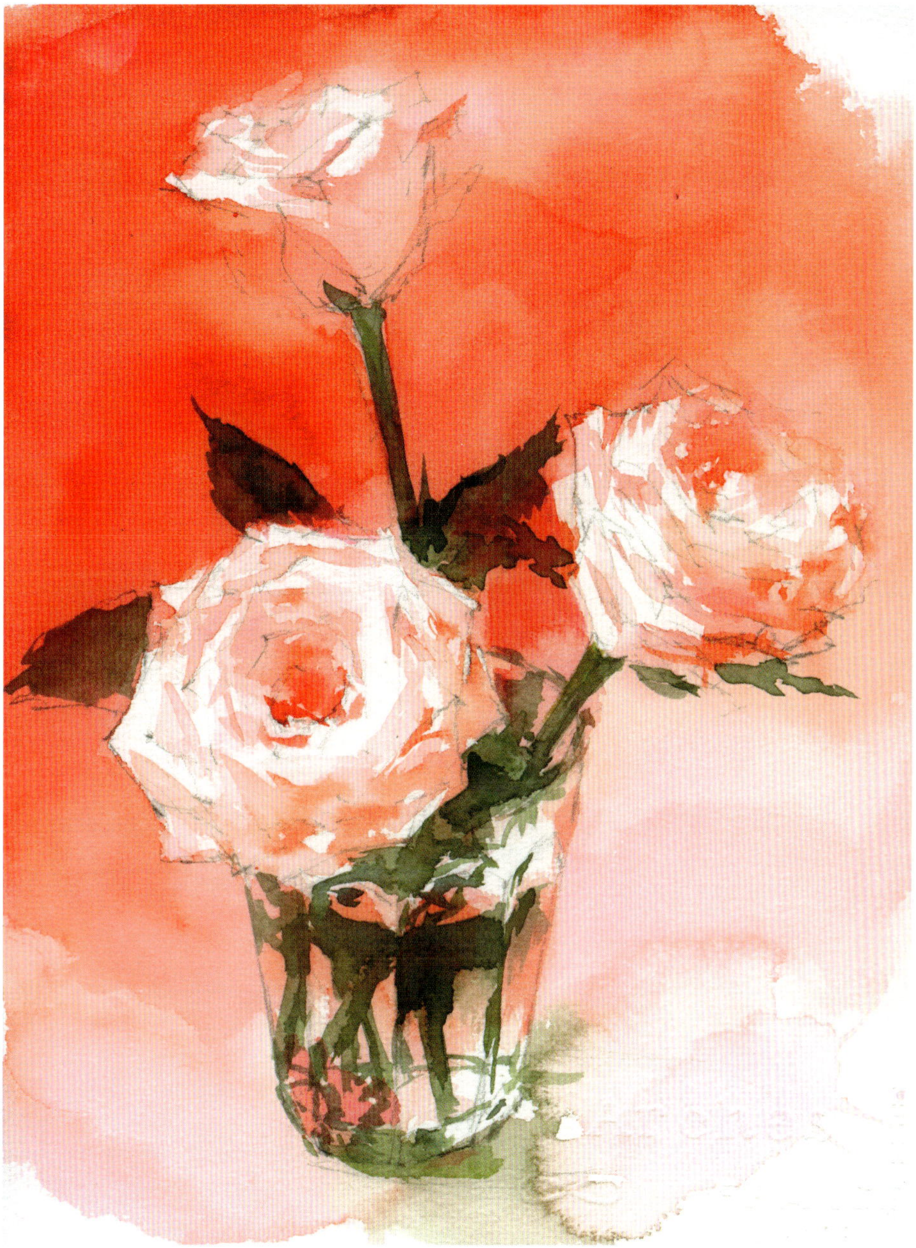

3

Paint the leaves.

Painting the red air first brings a sense of unity to the painting so the background will not stand out.

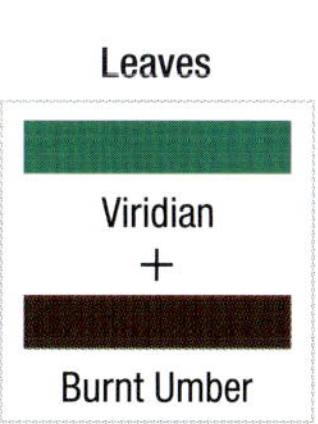

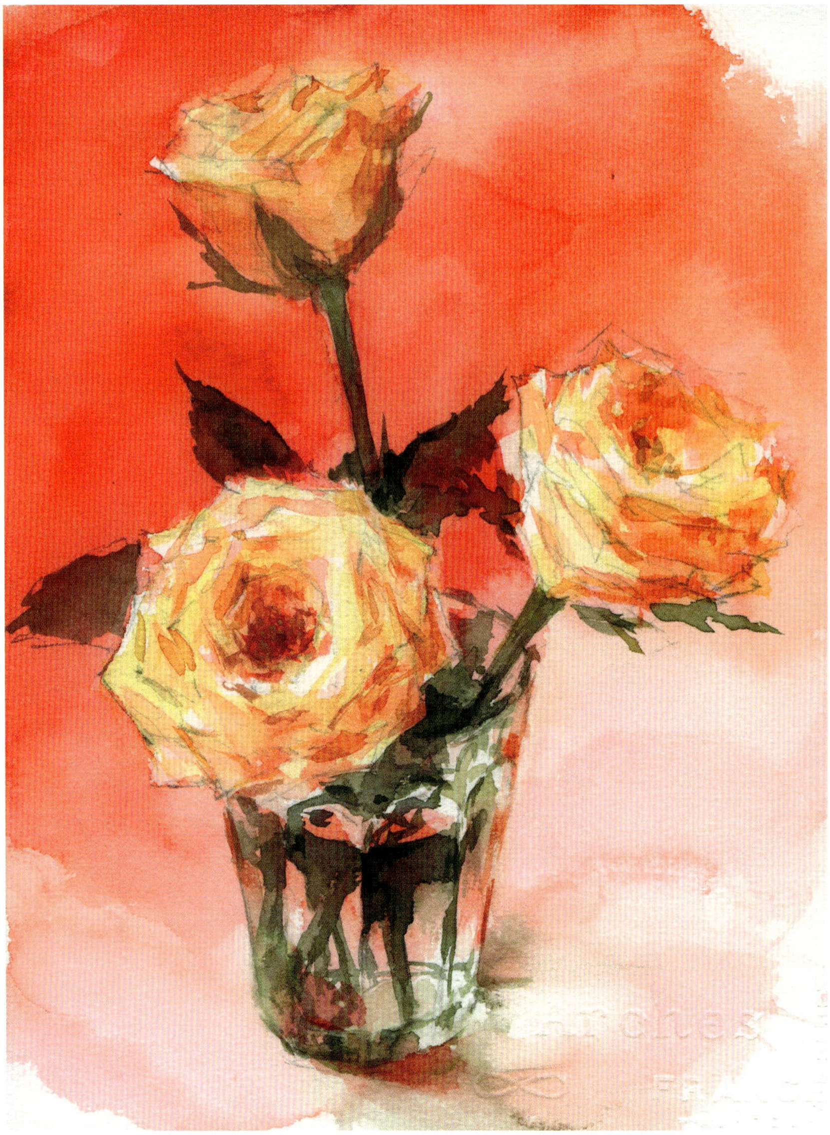

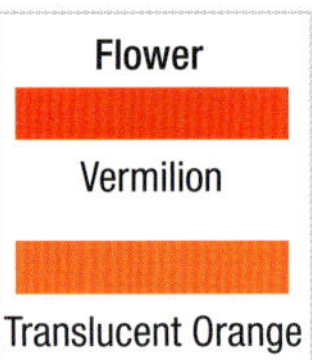

Complete

Leaving the background unpainted and then filling it in with a color as strong as the one seen in the lesson above may, at times, make the painting surprisingly attractive. However, at other times it will spoil the painting. What is important when applying bold colors is to make up your mind first.

Flower
Vermilion
Translucent Orange

Do You Think of the Background as Simply a Rear Wall Color?

I personally think of the background as the color of the air. It is not a colored wall behind the scene. Rather, it is colored air itself. Also, I imagine the air floating all around the motif as if the air were enfolding it.

While setting up motifs, or sketching, think about and imagine the overall color scheme that you intend to use. Despite saying this, I find that my mind keeps changing as I paint and I often end up with a painting that is very different from what I initially intended.

What is a Background?

Though I often hear worried comments like, "I can't decide on a background color," or "my backgrounds always fail," the background is where you show your real intention. It is that precious space where you can express your feelings freely. There are times when objects that are seen behind the motif are drawn, but there are certain examples—like when a motif is placed in the middle of a room—where the background is not the exact color you see. Rather, it is the color as you imagined it.

So, How Should You Decide on a Background Color? ⟶ There are three answers:

1. Similar colors
2. Gray
3. Based on light and shade

1. Similar Colors as a Motif

[Greens, etc., match natural images.]

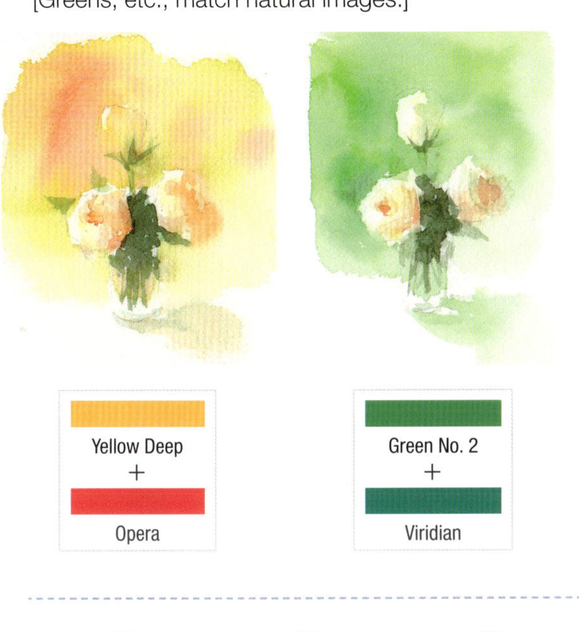

Yellow Deep
+
Opera

Green No. 2
+
Viridian

2. Make Gray by Mixing Two or More Colors

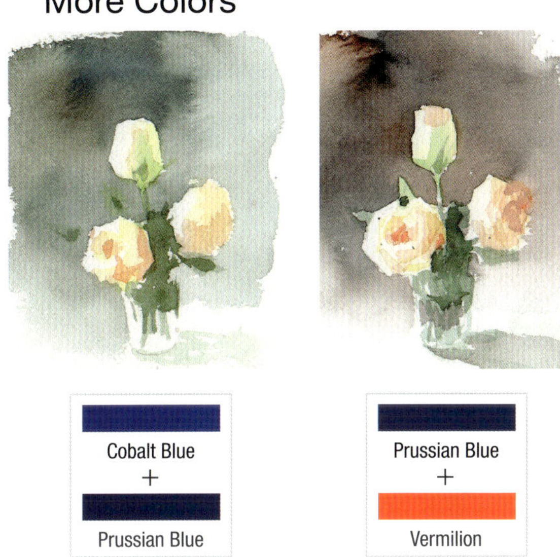

Cobalt Blue
+
Prussian Blue

Prussian Blue
+
Vermilion

The gray colors shown above were made by randomly mixing three to four colors in the palette. We are often told not to mix more than three colors. However, if you apply the mixed color directly to the paper only one time, even a four-color mix will not be turbid. I think that it is okay to mix as many colors as you like as long as you apply the mixed color directly to your paper.

Vermilion
+
Lavender

Opera
+
Terre Verte

Translucent Orange
+
Compose Blue

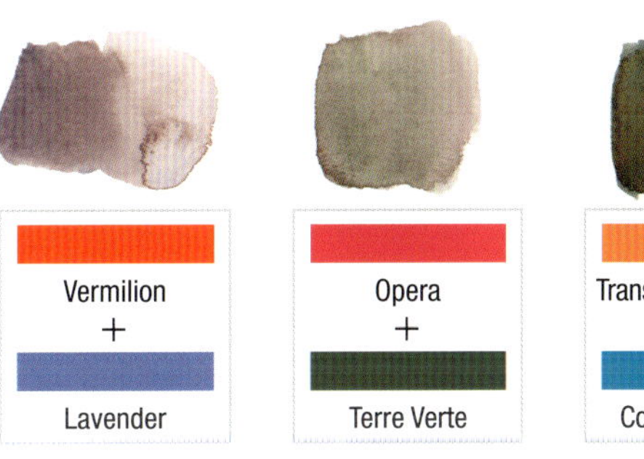

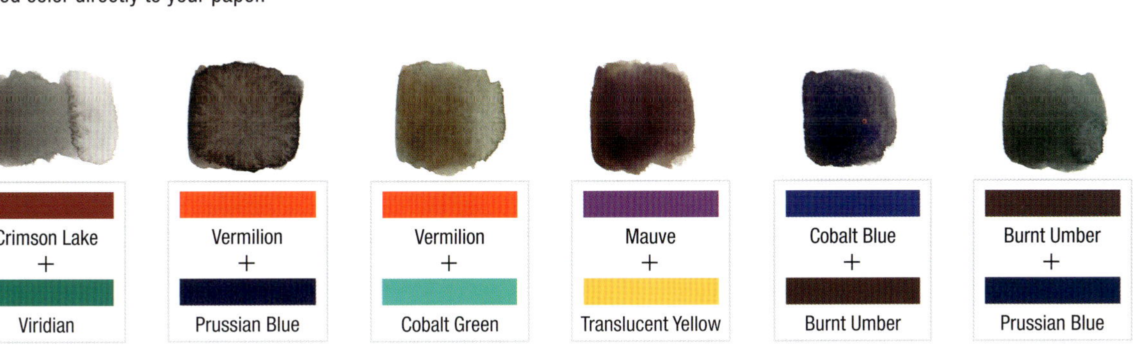

Crimson Lake
+
Viridian

Vermilion
+
Prussian Blue

Vermilion
+
Cobalt Green

Mauve
+
Translucent Yellow

Cobalt Blue
+
Burnt Umber

Burnt Umber
+
Prussian Blue

3. Deciding on Background Colors Based on Light and Shade
Let's Imagine While Looking at a Motif

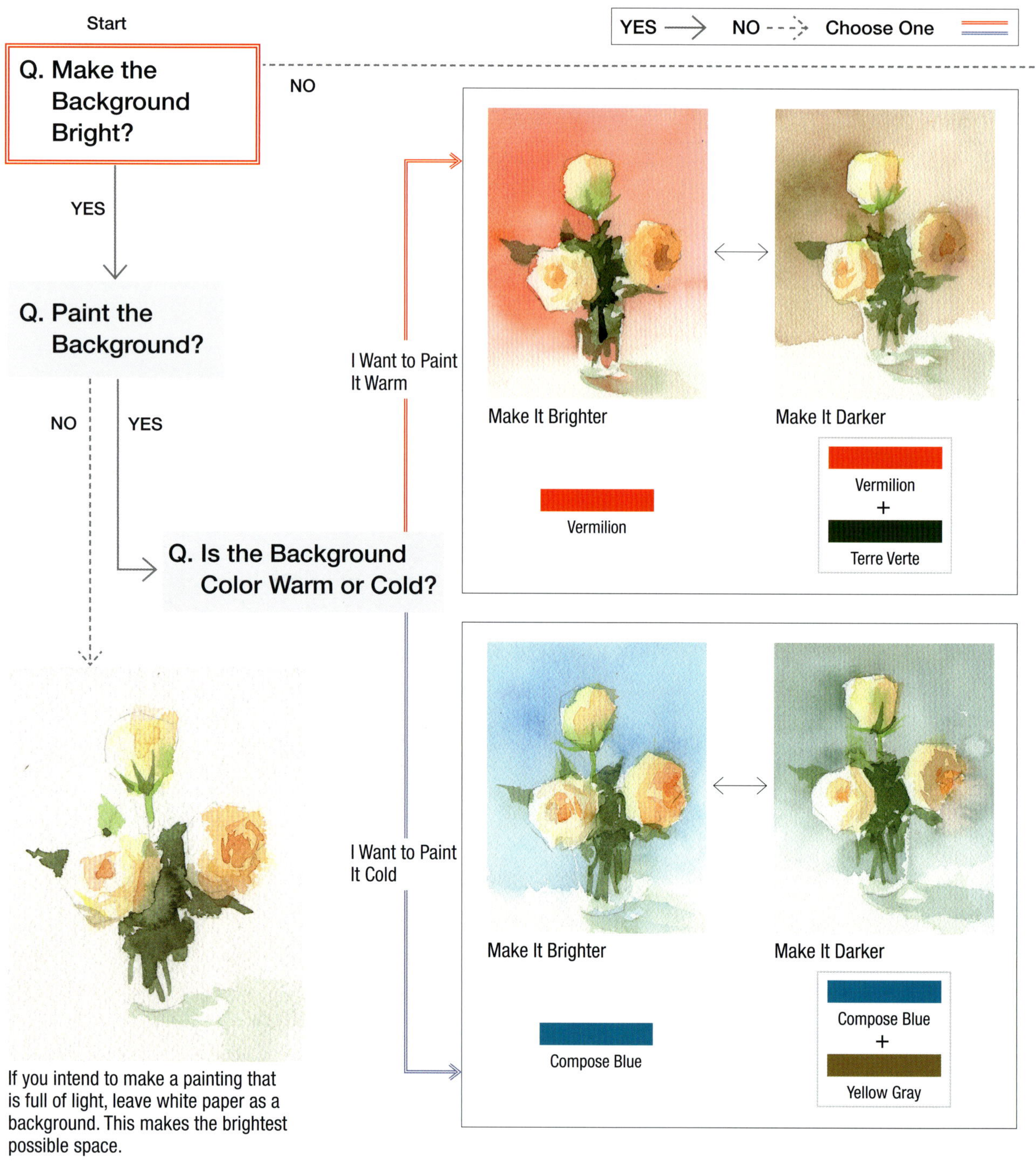

If you intend to make a painting that is full of light, leave white paper as a background. This makes the brightest possible space.

Light	Warm	Bright
		Dark
	Cold	Bright
		Dark
Shade	Warm	Bright
		Dark
	Cold	Bright
		Dark

There are only two choices in the beginning, light and shade. However, in reality, there should be a tone somewhere in between.

The reason why I did not include an in-between tone as one of your choices is that, in many cases, with watercolors, whether you intend to make it bright or dark, the background settles down into a medium tone as you layer on colors, even if you do not wish it so.

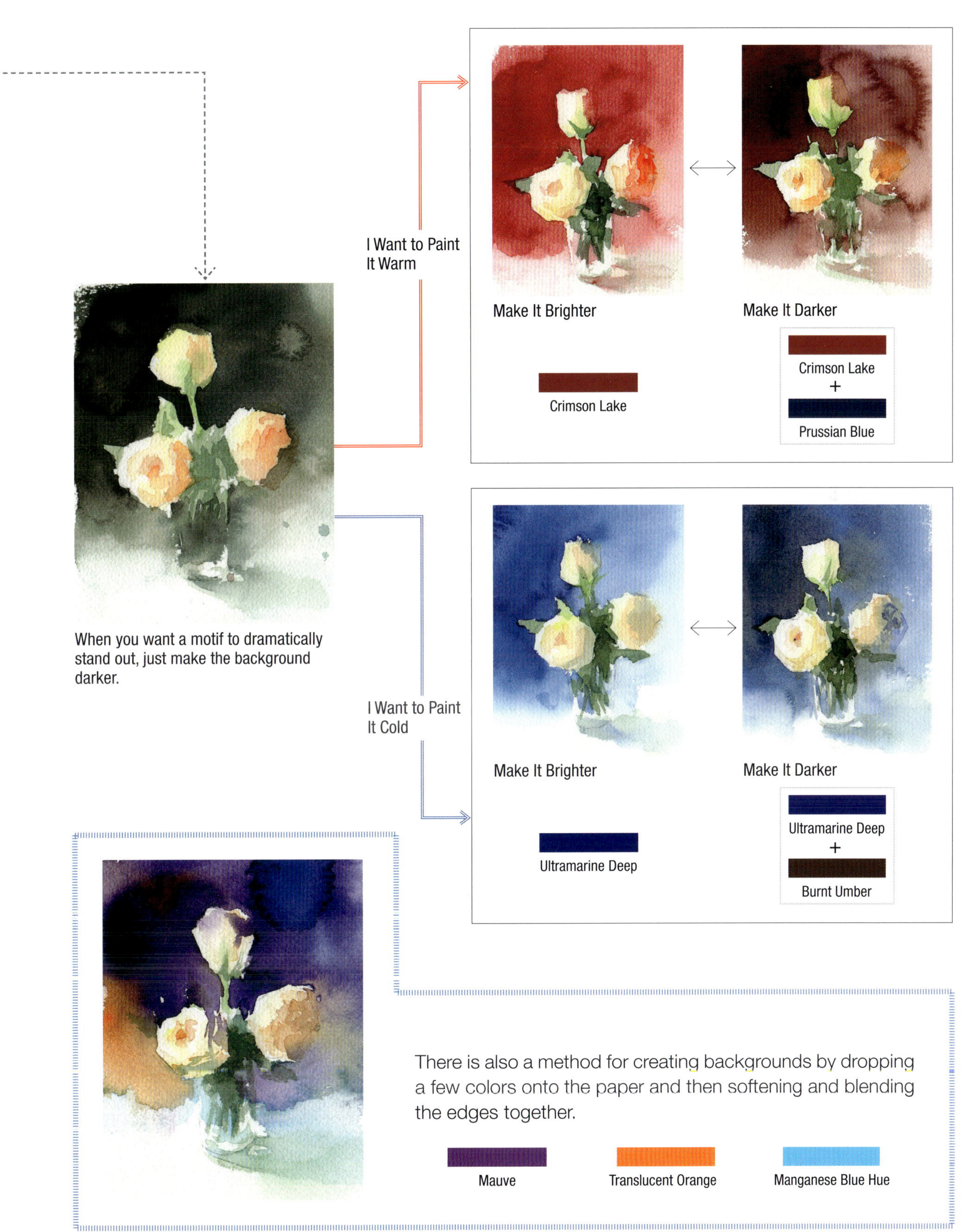

When you want a motif to dramatically stand out, just make the background darker.

There is also a method for creating backgrounds by dropping a few colors onto the paper and then softening and blending the edges together.

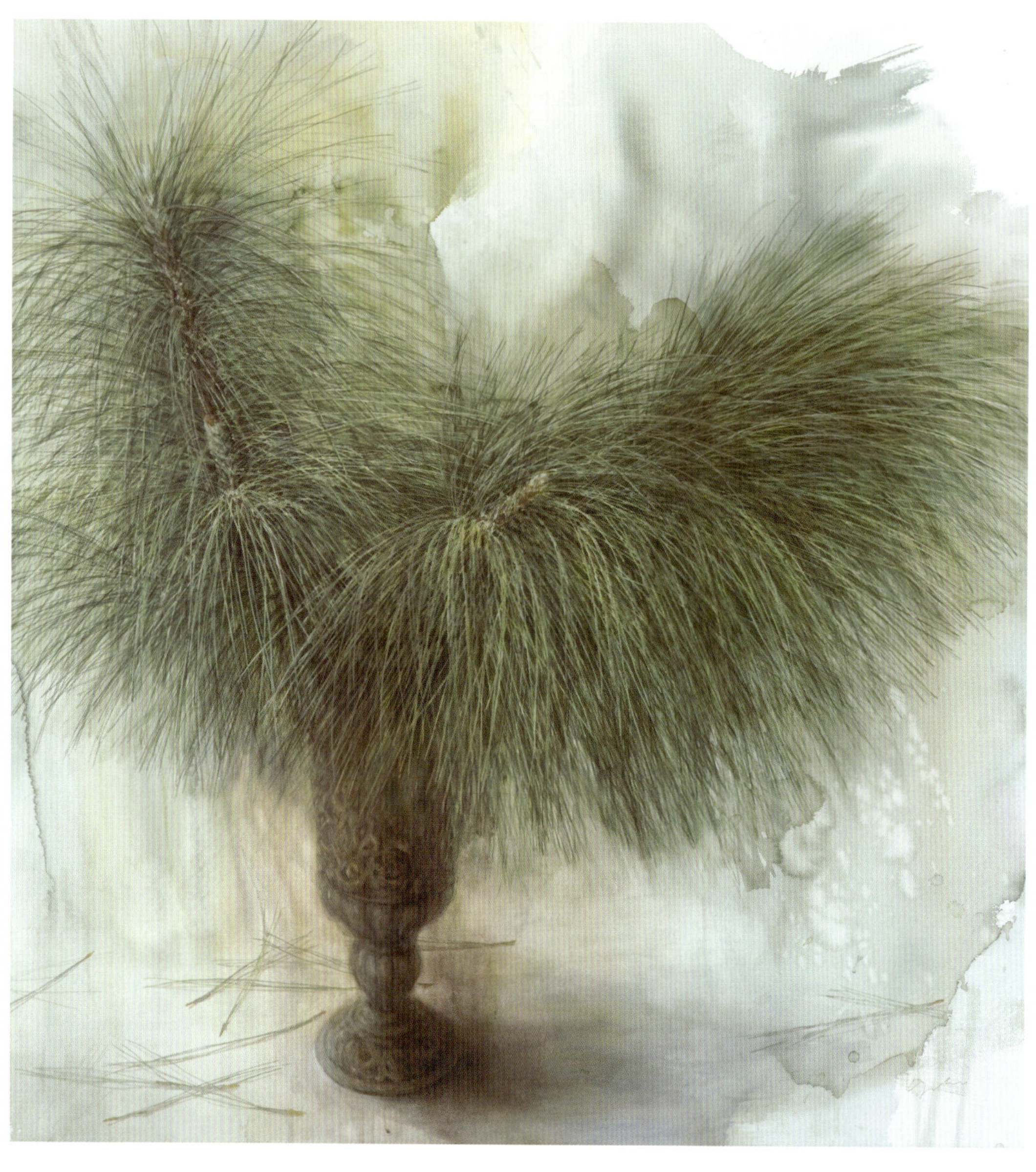

Daiomatsu (Longleaf Pine)
42.5 x 38.25 in (108 x 97 cm)

Paint the background using a color that is similar to pine needles.

Pines are five-needled, three-needled, or two-needled.

This longleaf pine was three-needled. One, two, three, one, two, three—painting the pine needles while in that rhythm allowed me to harmonize with the longleaf pine.

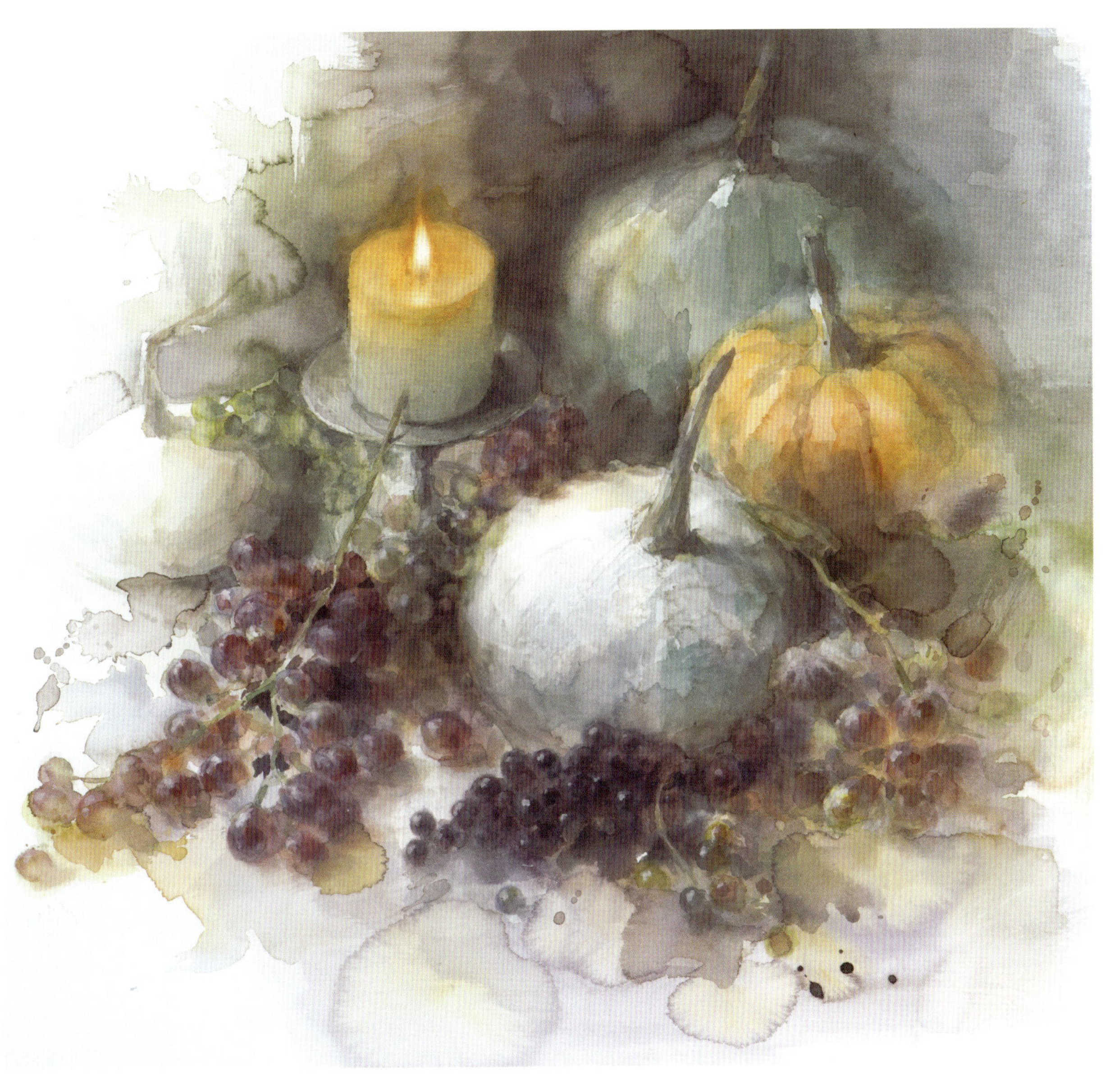

I wanted to paint a motif that is only available in a certain season. Cherry blossoms, hydrangeas, grapes—they are all delicate products of a certain season. I lit a candle to emulate vanitas art.

September
19.75 x 21.25 in (50 x 54 cm)

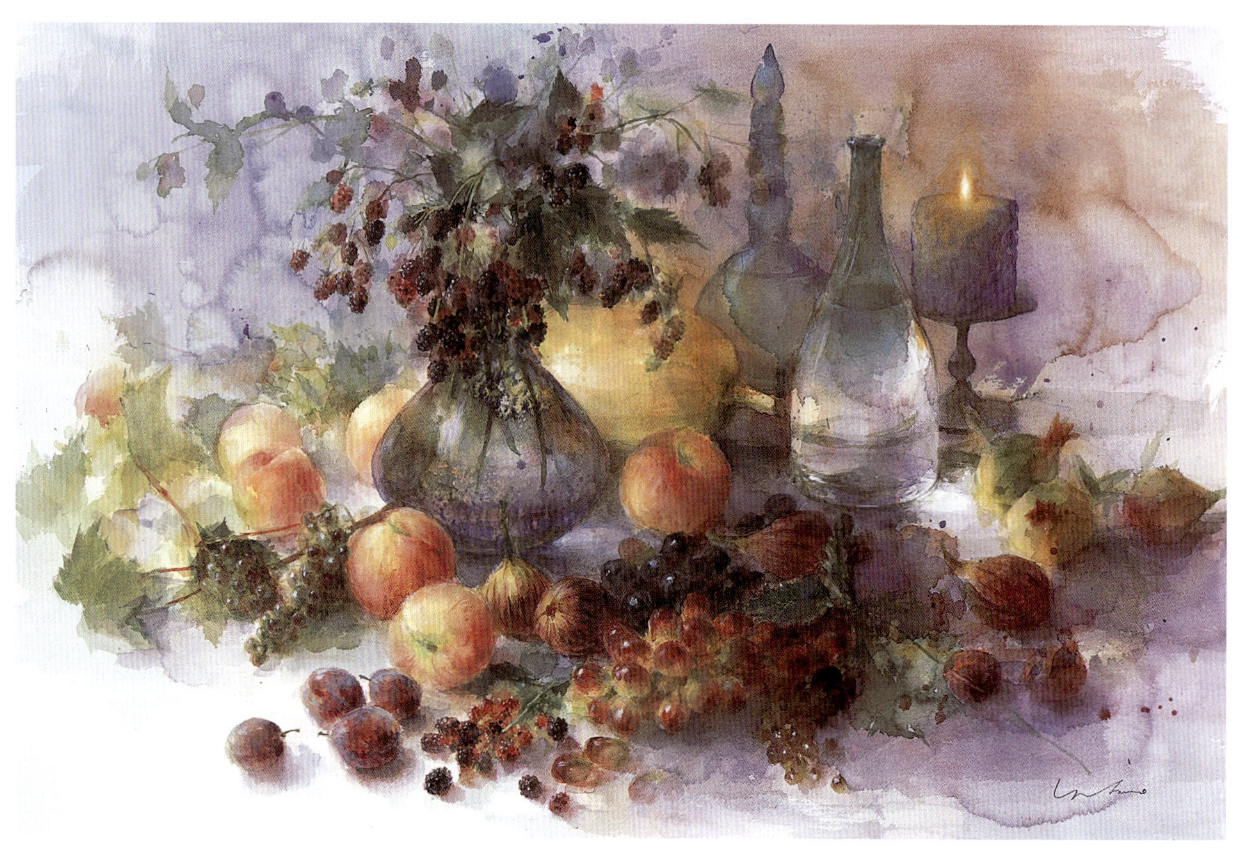

I prefer using stem-on fruit in my work. It can also be used as a discussion starter to debate the types of animals that would have feasted on such fruit.

July
23.5 x 34.75 in (60 x 88 cm)

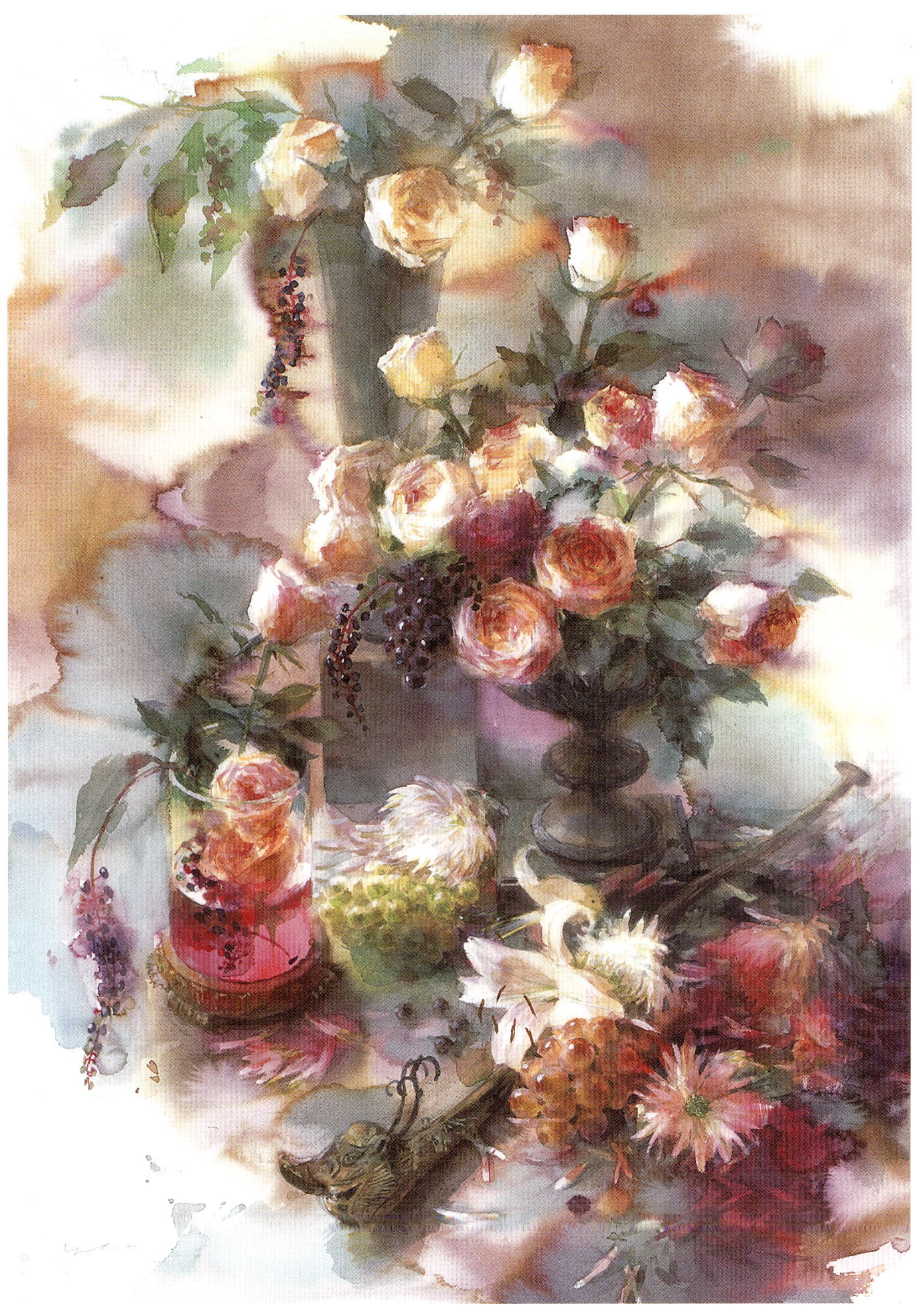

I actually mashed the berries of the pokeweed in this motif and tried them out as a paint. I recalled childhood memories of making colored water using pokeweed berries. I picked some, put them in a dish, and used them to paint. This vibrant pink develops into a color that no watercolor paint can imitate.

Asobit Sukarete Nemuru (Playing Until Tired and Then Falling Asleep)
37 x 25.5 in (94 x 65 cm)

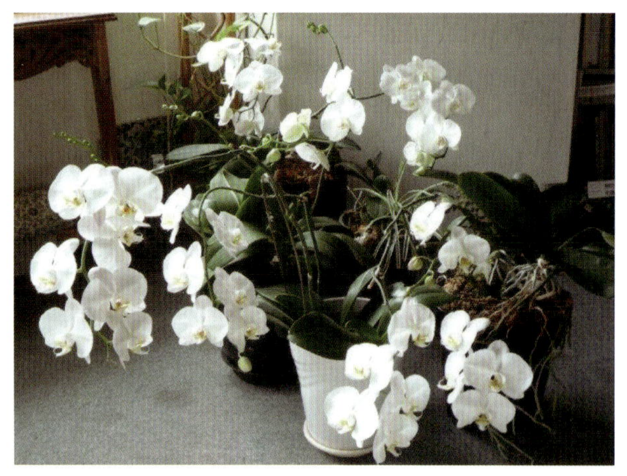

The background was painted using bleeding and soft edges. As if dancing a waltz, these orchids bloomed carefree in my studio.

I expressed how the orchids danced by bleeding colors together. It was fun to see how, as the colors changed, it appeared as though the music changed.

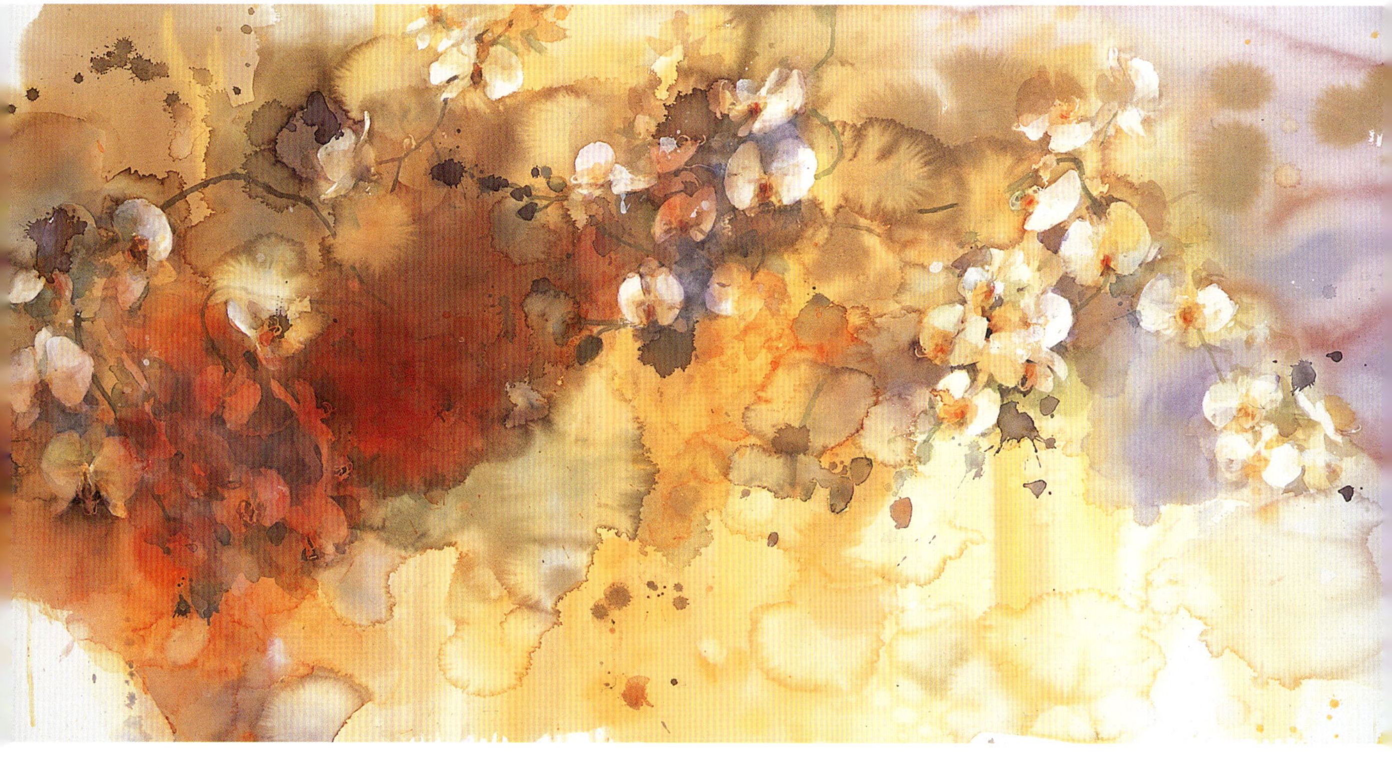

RONDO (1)
29.5 x 57 in (75 x 145 cm)

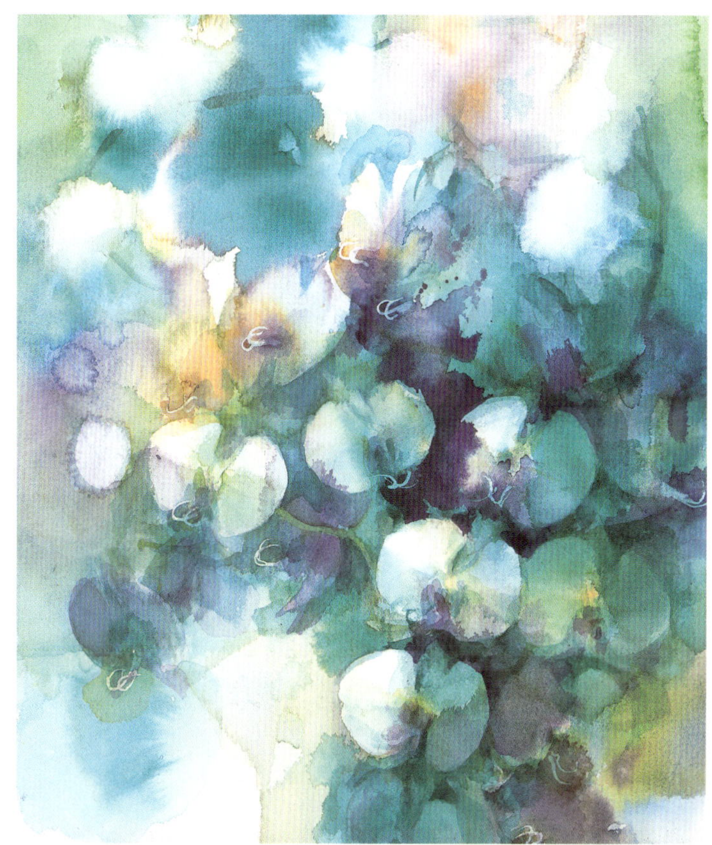

RONDO (2)
17.75 x 14.75 in (45 x 37.5 cm)

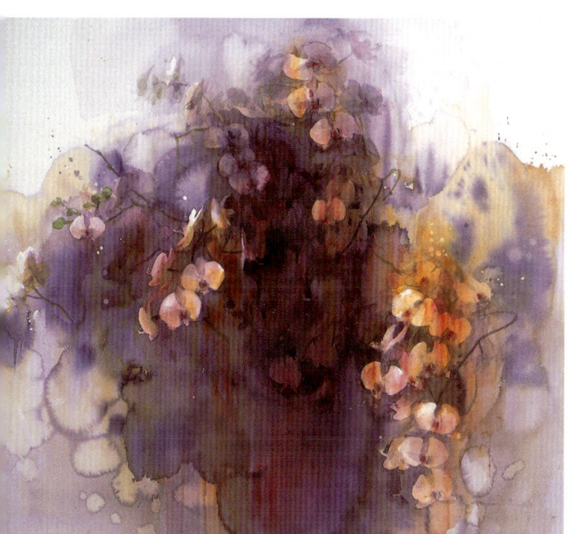

RONDO (3)
38.5 x 46.5 in (98 x 118 cm)

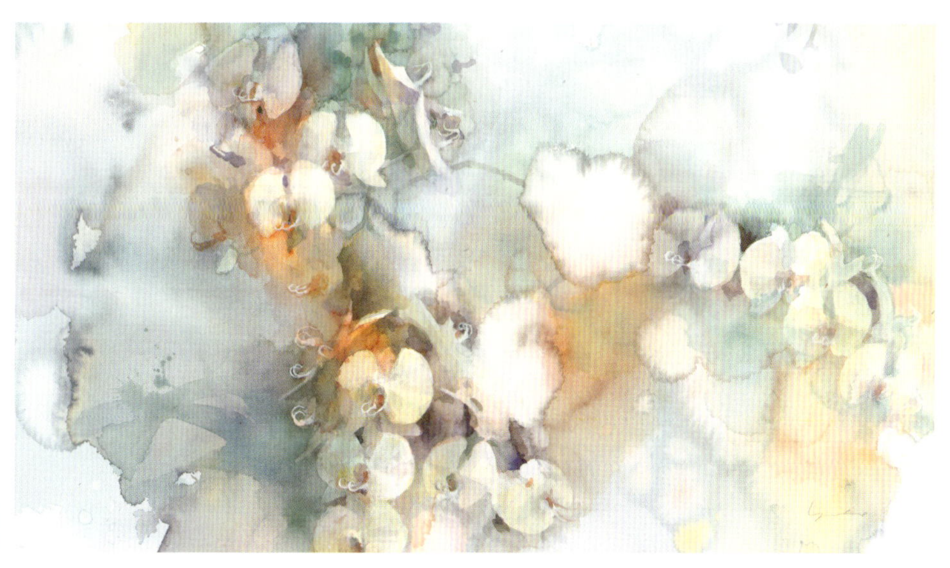

RONDO (4)
15.75 x 25.25 in (40 x 64 cm)

Tips for Laying Colors on Landscapes

I took the plunge and tried using pink for the background but the motif did not blend in well with it.

I initially used dark blue to paint the background but it did not settle correctly.

Is there a solution to these types of problems?

I think that the background color is "the color of air."

Please look at the three landscape photos below. These photos do not have any color processing.

The color of the sky blends perfectly with the shading of the building.

The background color is the color of air, as it were. Since it is the air, the painted surface is full of it. Isn't it fascinating to think that it's the color of air? You can color the air any way you please. That is the art of painting.

Drawing some conclusions we can say that laying the background color involves foreground motif shading as well. That is the solution.

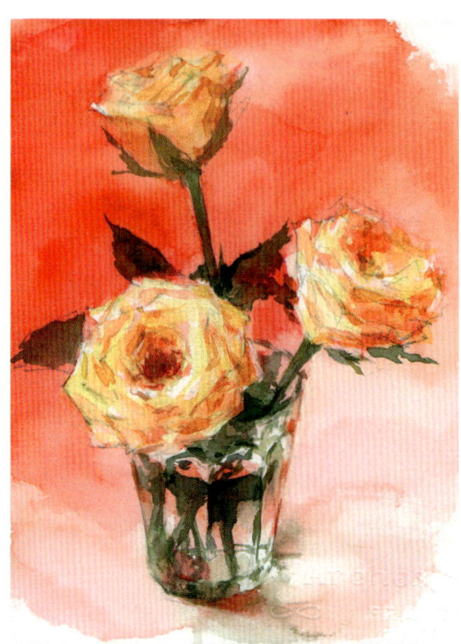

Using background colors to shade flowers.

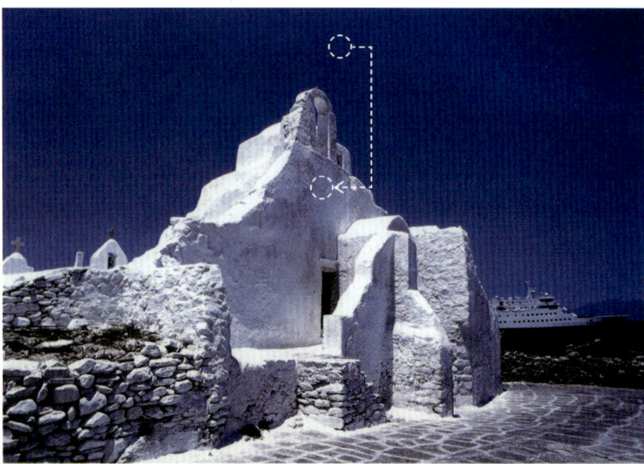

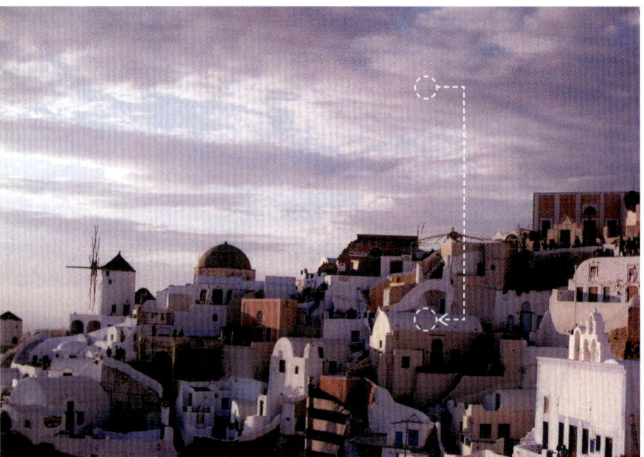

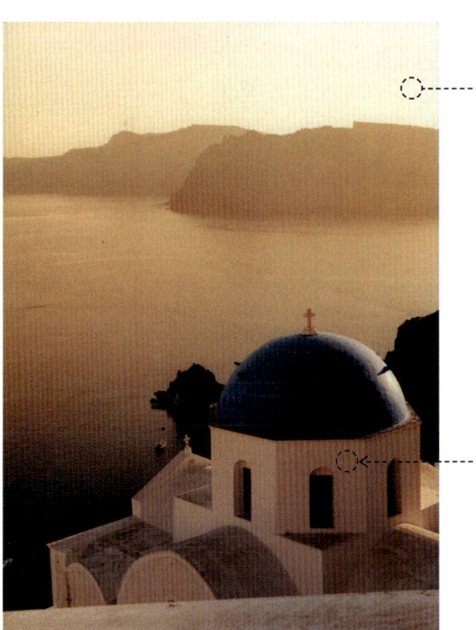

Chapter 3

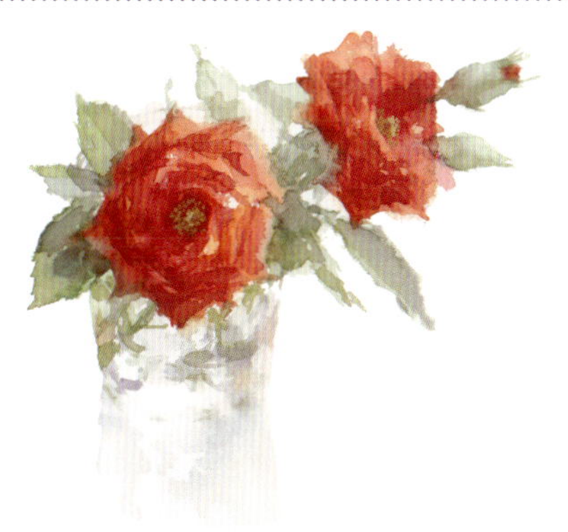

Lessons on Shapes and Colors

Cup and Saucer and a Pot: Gold on Porcelain and How to Overlap

Cup and Saucer

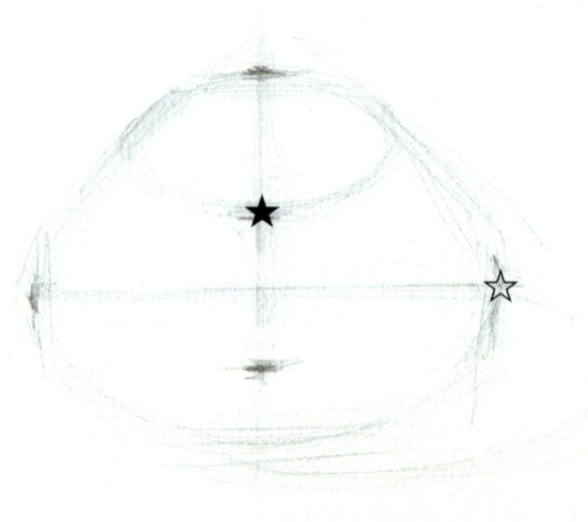

1

Draw a rough shape as if the cup and saucer were wrapped in a piece of cloth. Shading is also part of the motif, so include it from the beginning. If you try to insert the shading later, the composition might degenerate.

2

Gauge the approximate position where the saucer protrudes outward the most (marked as ☆). Gauge the position of the foremost edge of the cup (marked as ★).

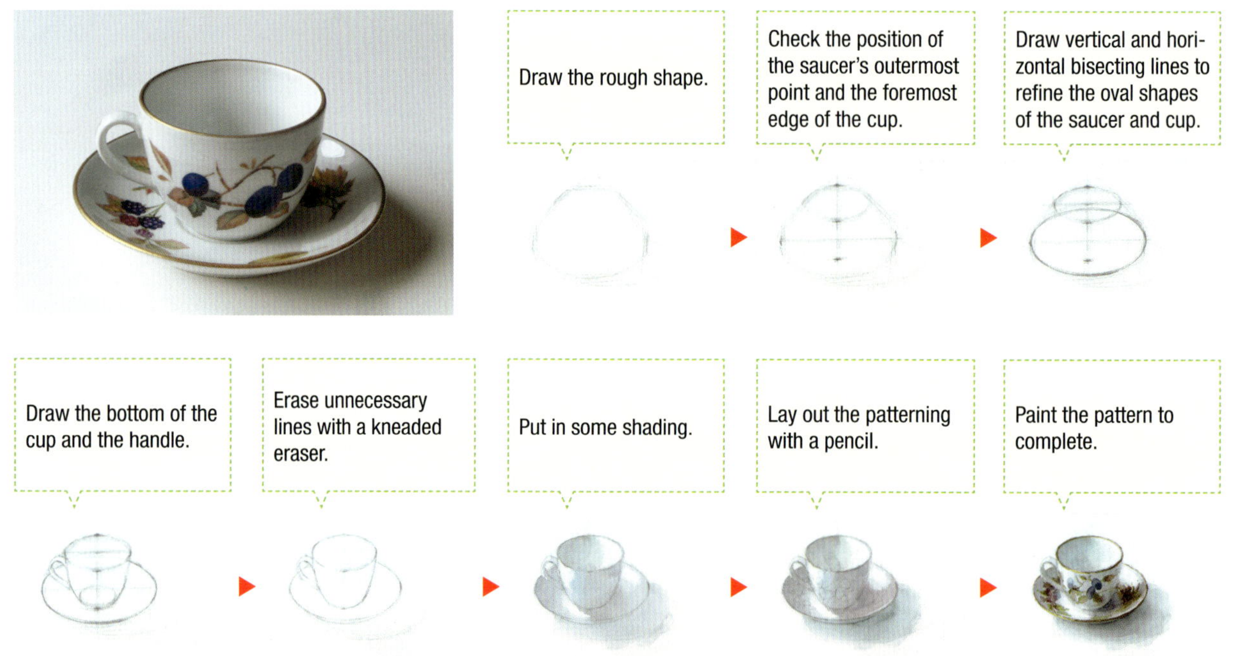

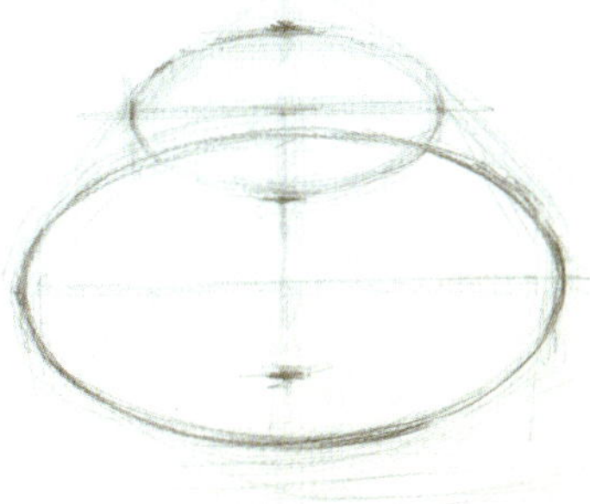

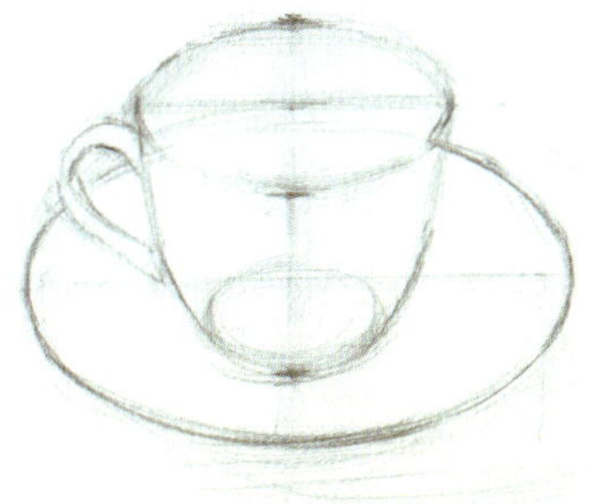

3

In order to obtain the oval shape of both the saucer and the mouth of the cup, draw vertical and horizontal bisecting lines.

4

Draw the shape for the bottom of cup and then attach the handle.

Bad example

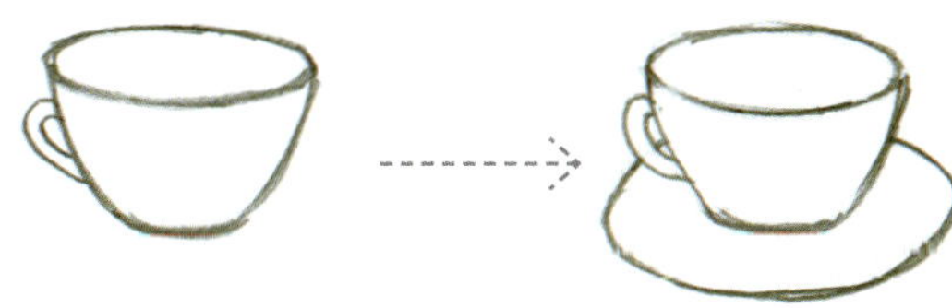

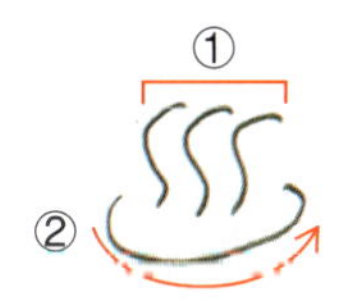

Some people draw a plate encircling a cup or a piece of fruit that has already been drawn. When you do this, the composition will look like the mark shown on the left. (This is the geographical mark for "hot spring" in Japan.)

Good example

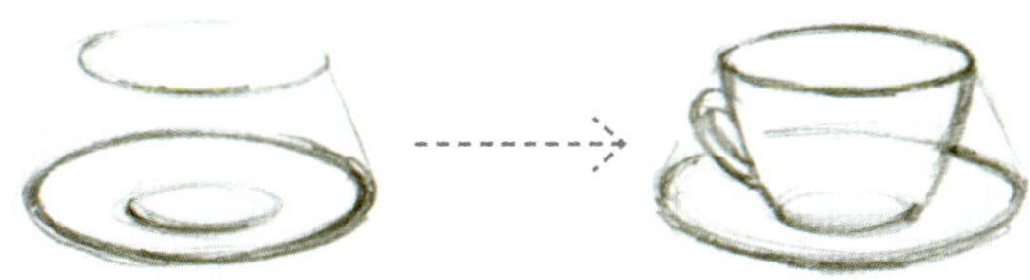

After roughly sketching the proportions, begin by drawing the plate. Do this not only with a coffee cup but also when bread or fruit is on a plate. Remember to draw the objects according to the order in which they were placed on the plate.

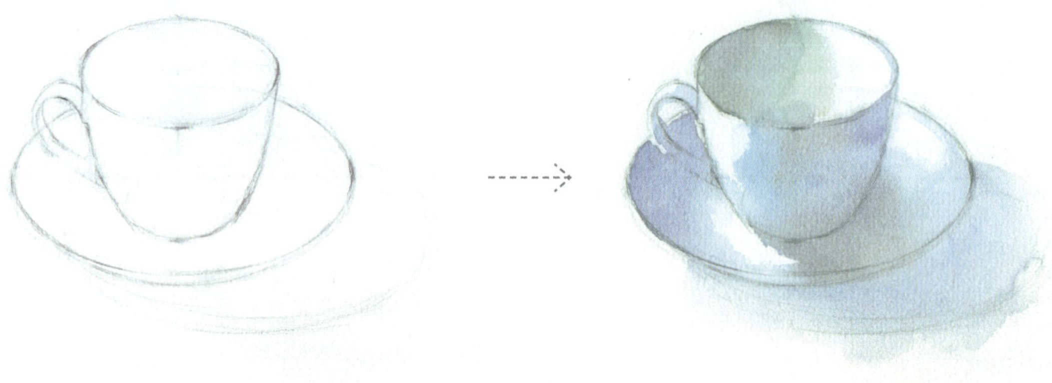

5

To bring out the whiteness of the porcelain, add shading in green, purple, and blue. The outside and inside of the cup reflect light differently so the coloring will be different.

| Cerulean Blue | Green No. 1 | Ultramarine Deep | Lavender |

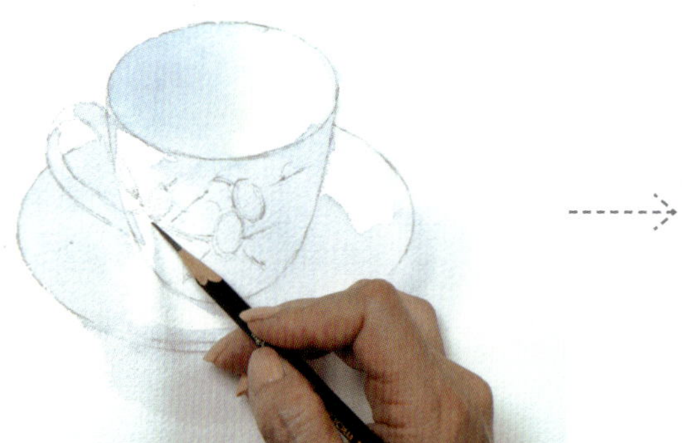

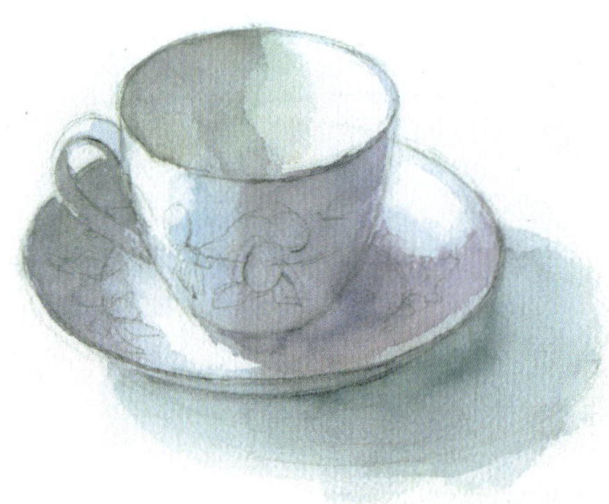

6

Continue to add shading and then allow the paint to dry. After it has dried, add the patterning with a pencil by following the rounded contours of the cup and saucer.

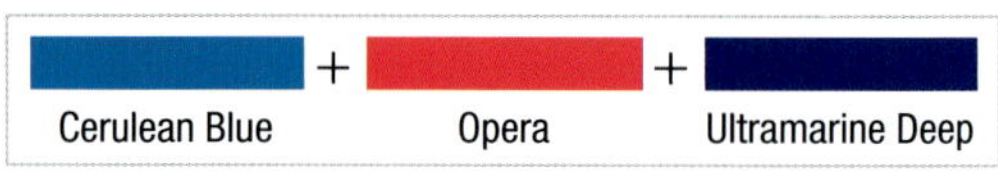

| Cerulean Blue | + | Opera | + | Ultramarine Deep |

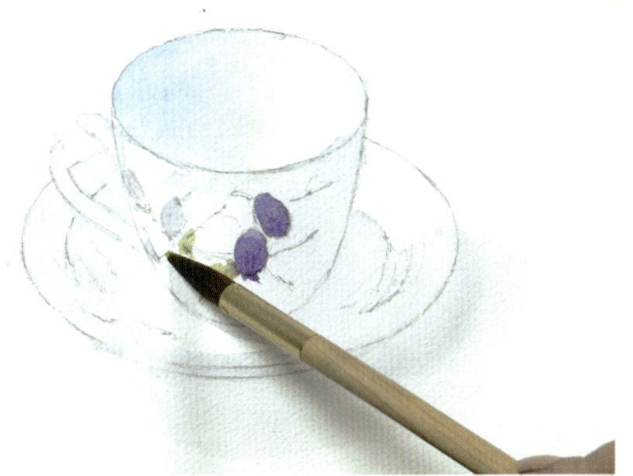

7

Color the pattern lightly where it is brightly lit and color it deeply where shaded.

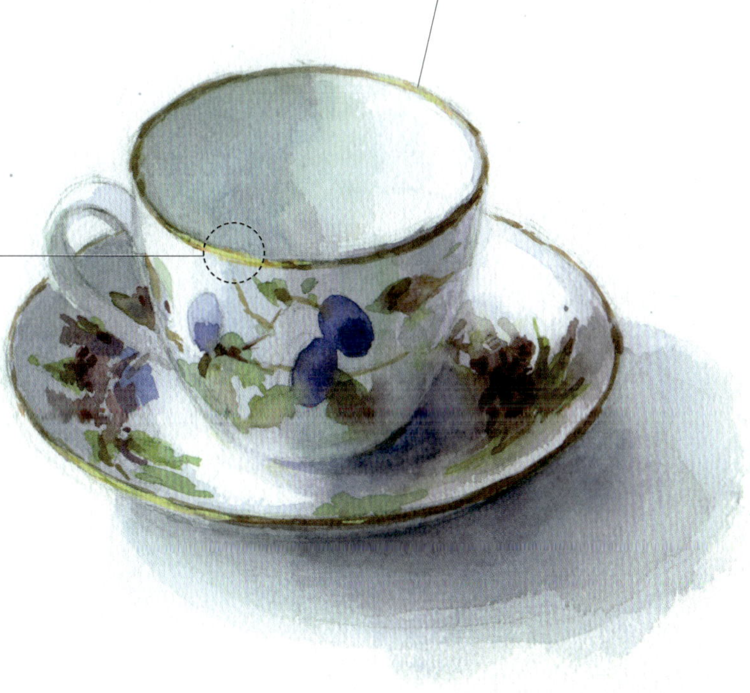

Brown on the golden rim

Burnt Sienna
+
Yellow Deep

Brown on the golden rim

White gouache
+
Yellow Deep

Complete

Pot

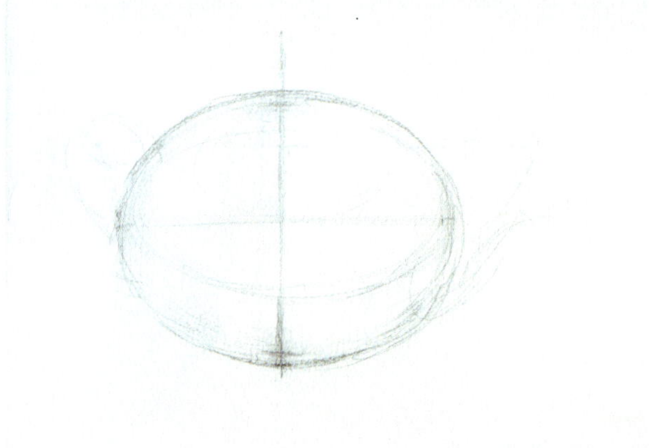

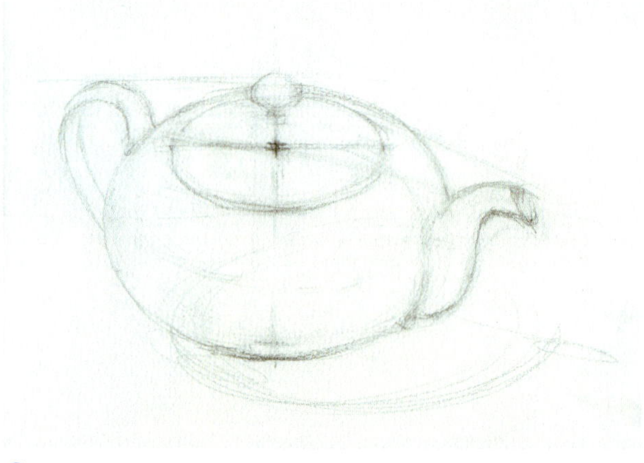

1

Draw the center line and then the rough shape of the pot.

2

The lid's knob is at the center. The mouth of the spout and the bottom of the handle are straight through the centered line.

Japanese teapots (not shown) have their handles and spouts at 90 degree angles. When you observe a teapot from directly above and from the side, you should be able to find the conventional shape that meets its functionality.

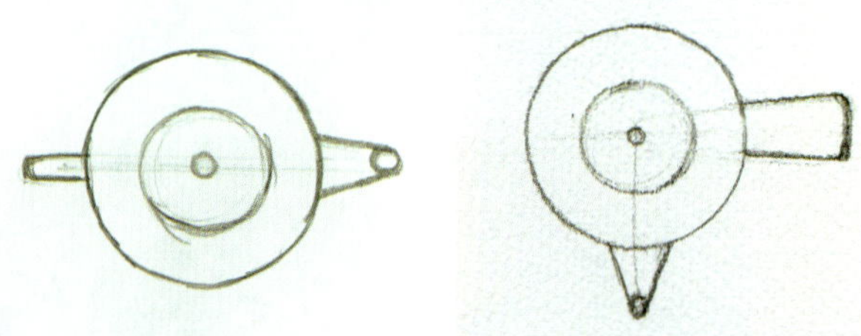

Handles are not randomly attached to pottery and teapots. Observe carefully by looking at these drawings from above and from the side.

What's important is that the shape was made with the center as its axis. When you sketch, you must decide where the center of the teapot is before you start, otherwise its shape will be distorted.

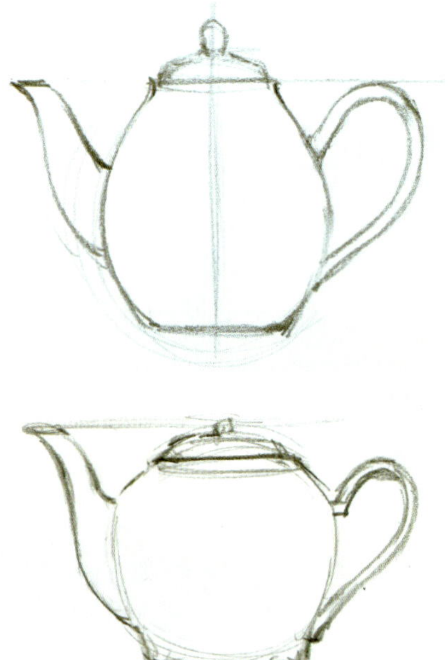

Even though the height is the same, the pots are different.

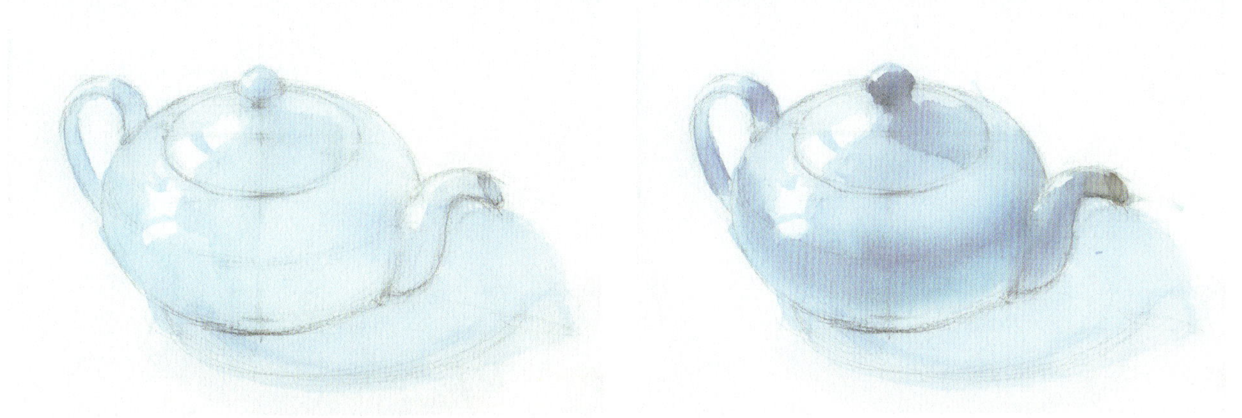

3

Use a lot of water and paint the pot blue. Then lay down a different shade of blue while the surface is still wet. Doing so brings a three-dimensional feel in just one underpainting.

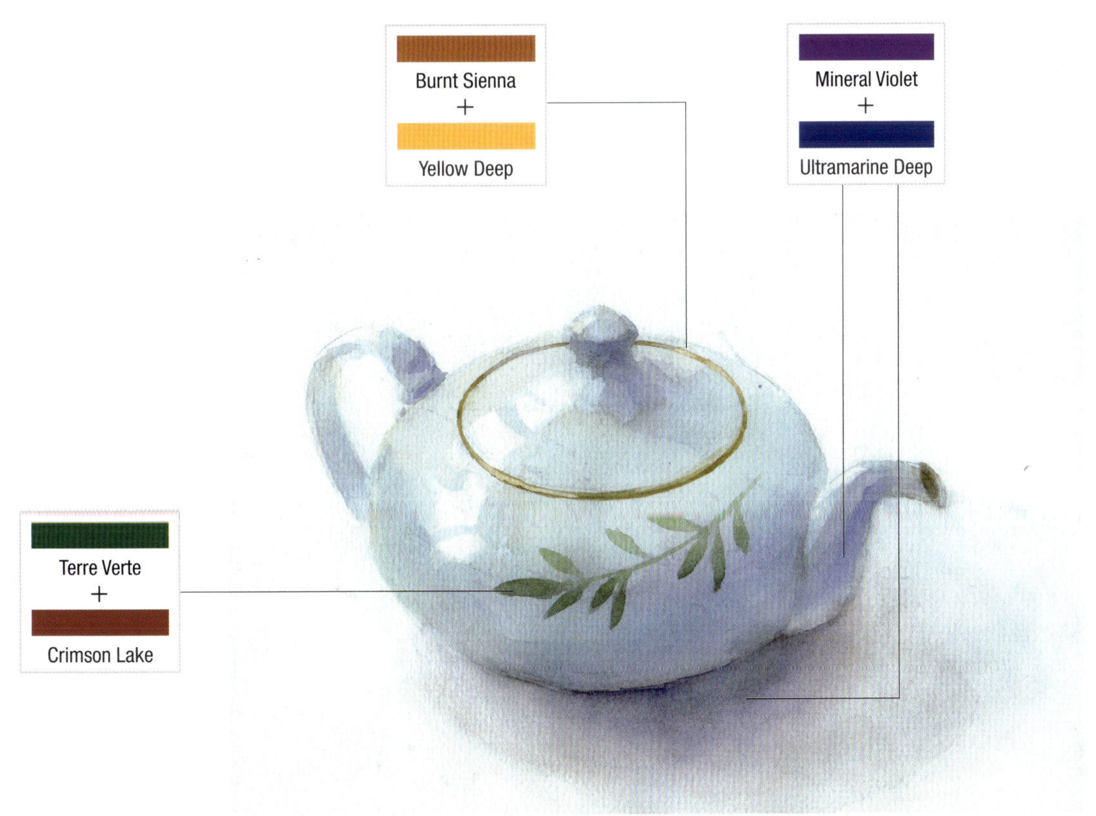

Complete

Cherry Blossoms and a Plate: Drawing a Plate Using Salt

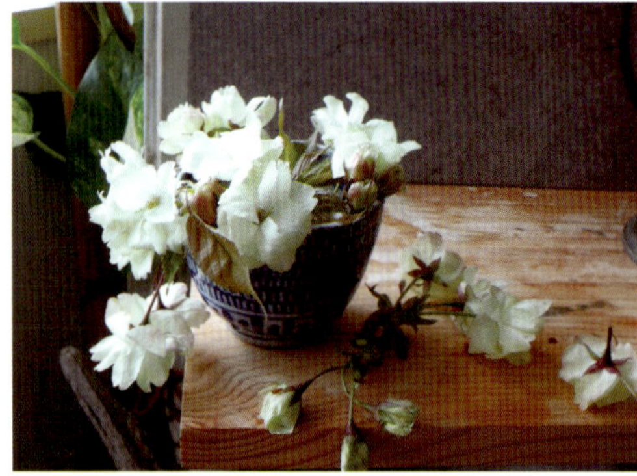

Arrange cherry blossoms in a small porcelain bowl and paint. Use salt to depict the white base and blue patterns on the porcelain.

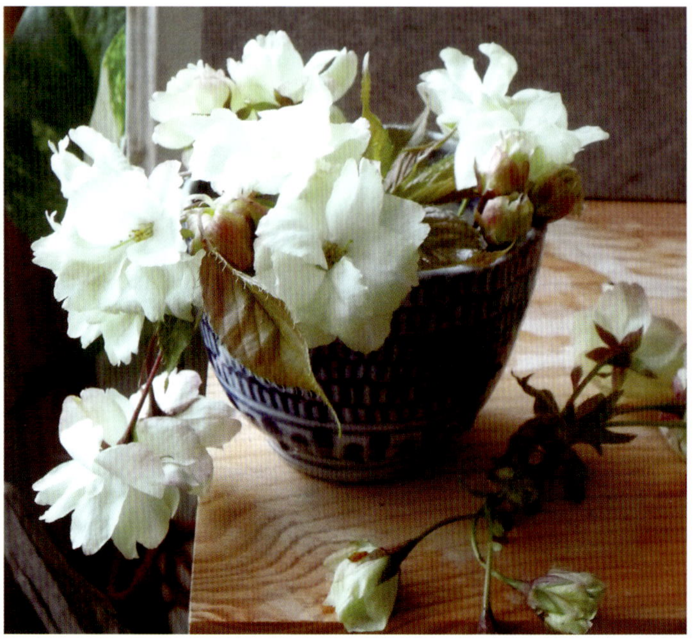

Preparation: Salt

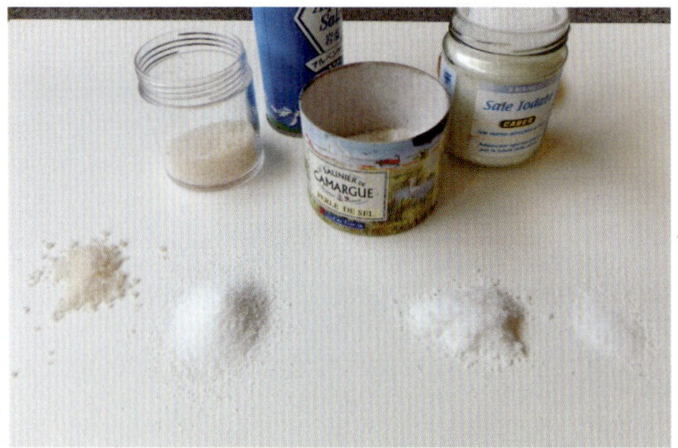

The size of the salt grain varies depending on its type. The effect of each type of salt will be different.

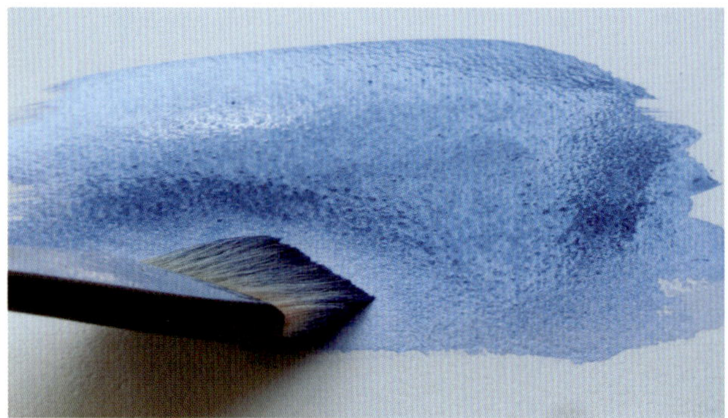

Apply paint. At this point, the paint is thinly puddled on the surface of the paper. It should be neither too wet nor too dry.

Changes in Pottery Paintings When Salt is Applied

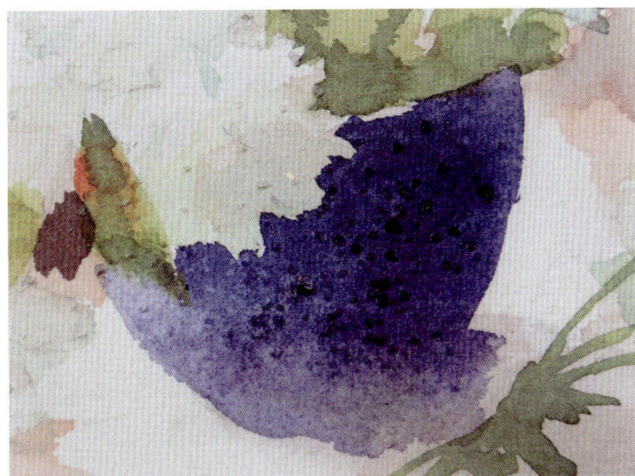

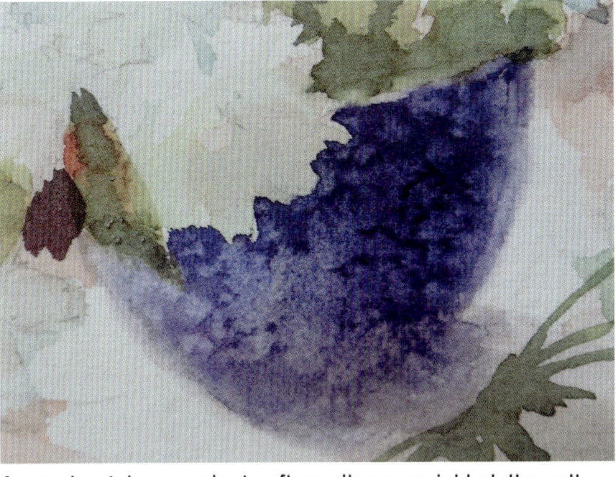

The photo above shows what happened immediately after applying salt. Slightly large salt grains were used.

Approximately one minute after salt was sprinkled, the salt starts to melt and turns a whitish color.

Approximate amount of water:
salt does not begin to melt after one minute → too little water
salt floats on the surface after two minutes → too much water

Salt Grains

Large

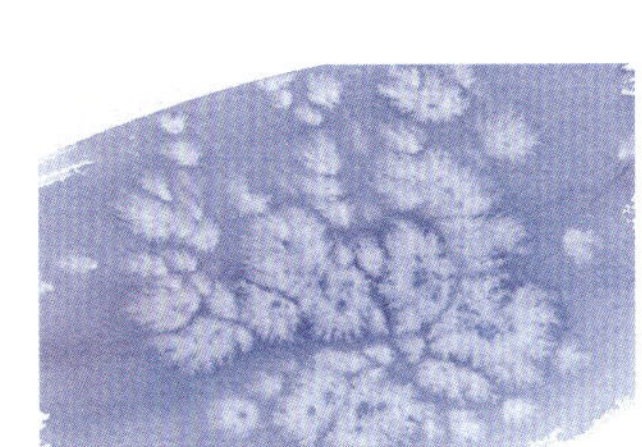

Brush off the salt after the surface has completely dried.

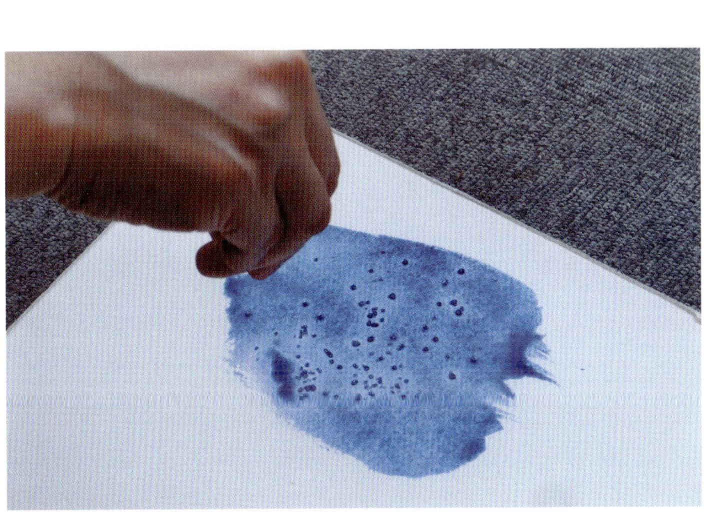

Sprinkle the salt while the surface is still wet.

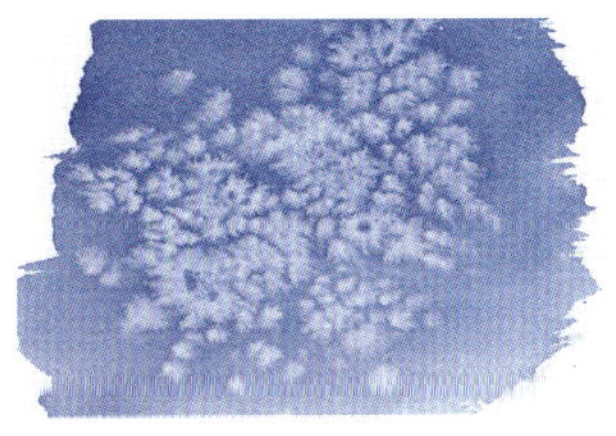

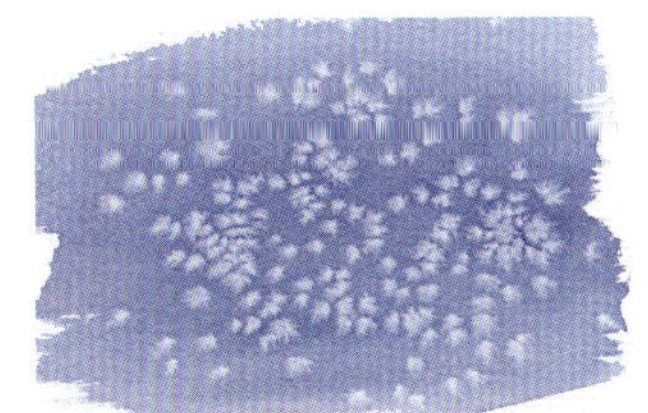

Small

Small salt grains create small patterns. The larger the grain gets, the louder the pattern.

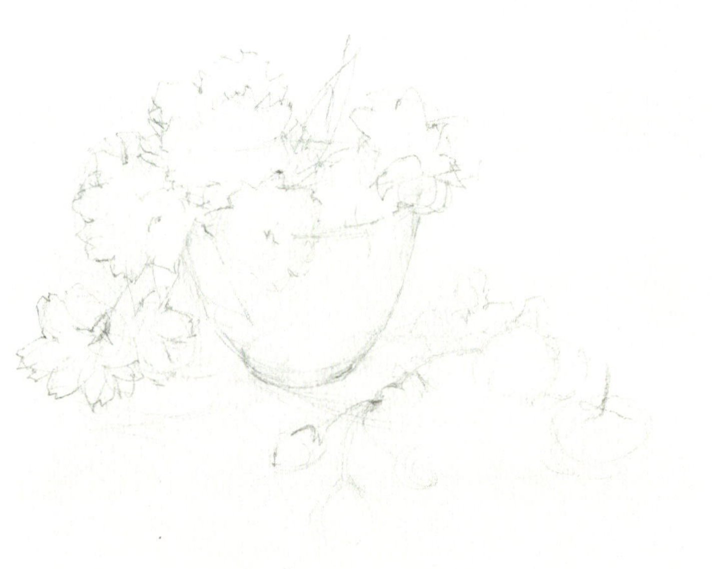

1

I draw the shape of the white petals relatively carefully with the intention of making the background darker.

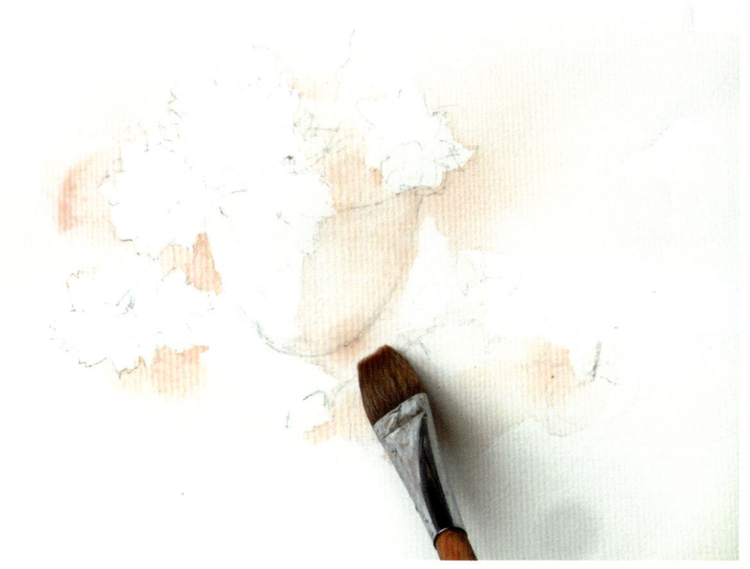

2

Leave bright portions unpainted and paint the rest using plenty of water.

3

Add colors while the surface is wet.

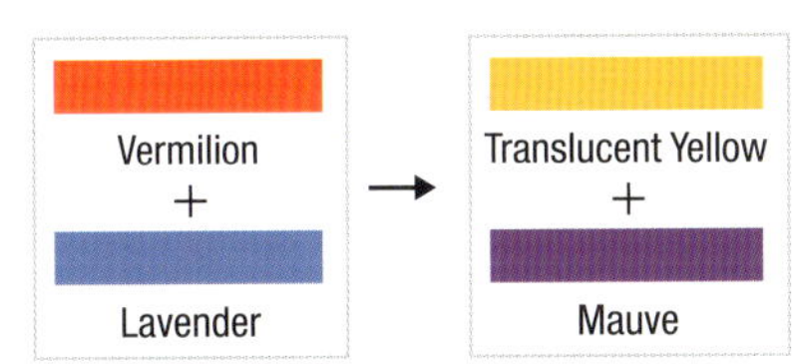

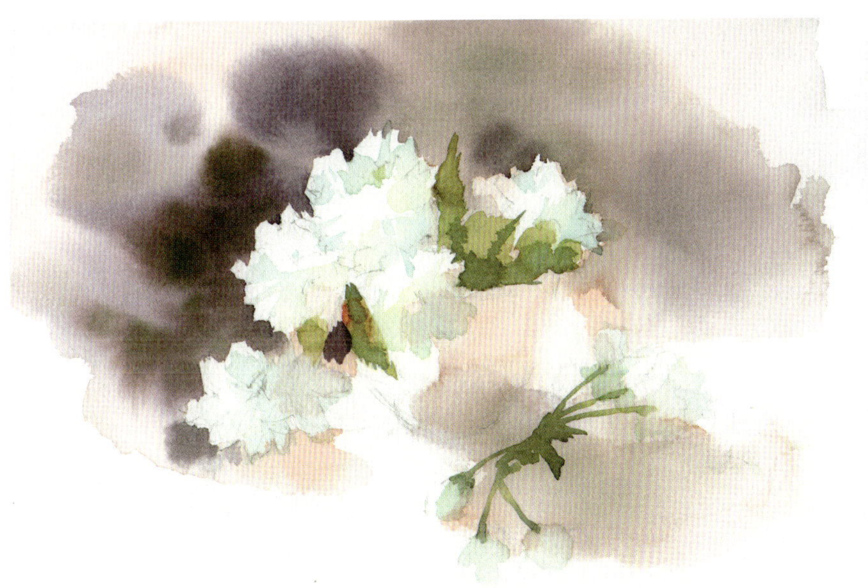

4

The background behind the bright side of each flower was made darker in order to make the flowers pop out.

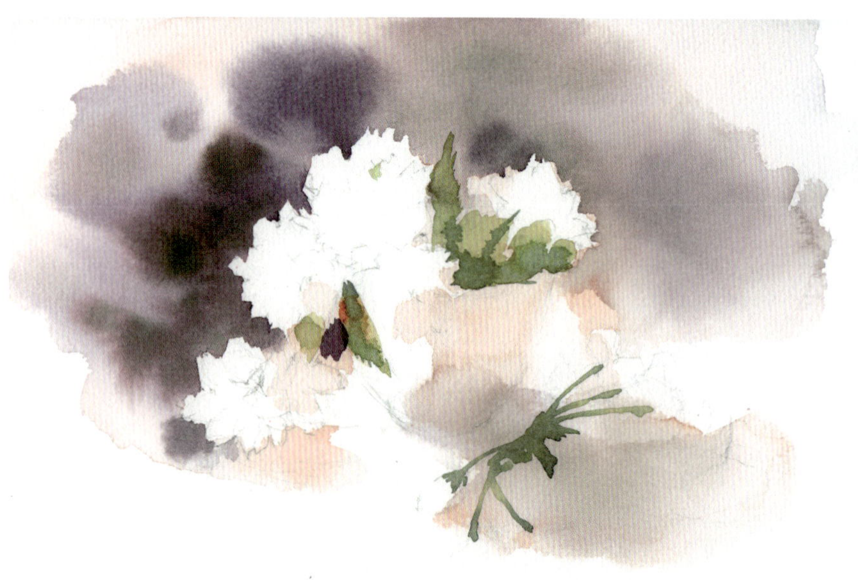

5

Paint the leaves.

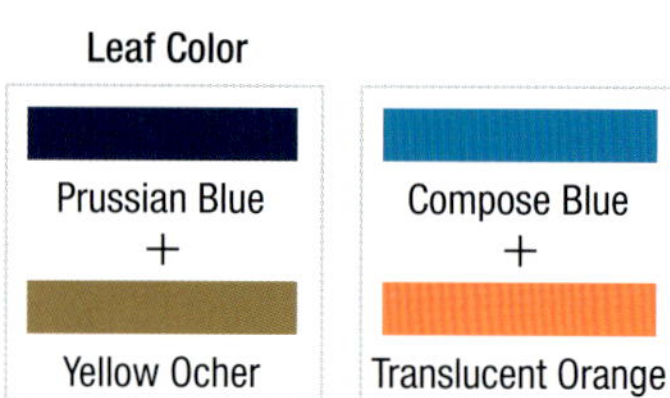

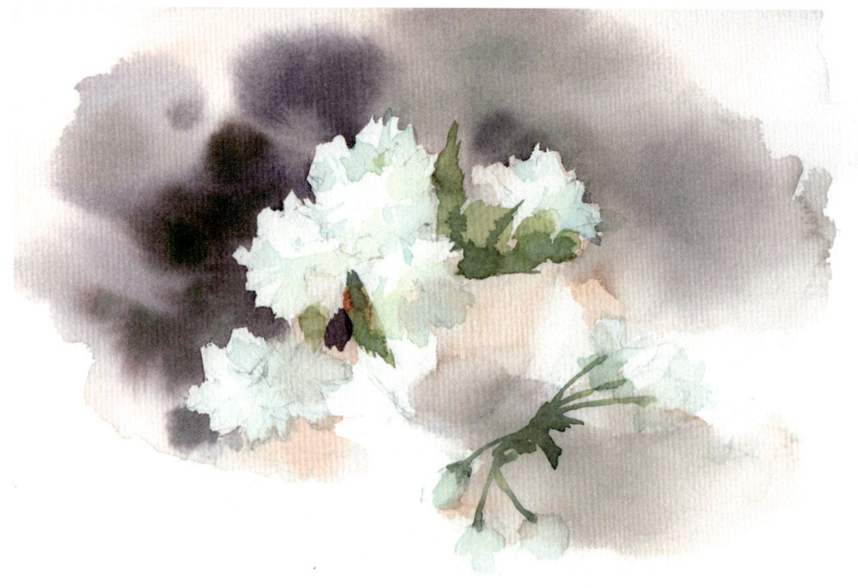

6

Add shading colors.

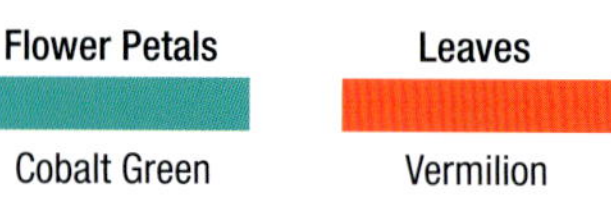

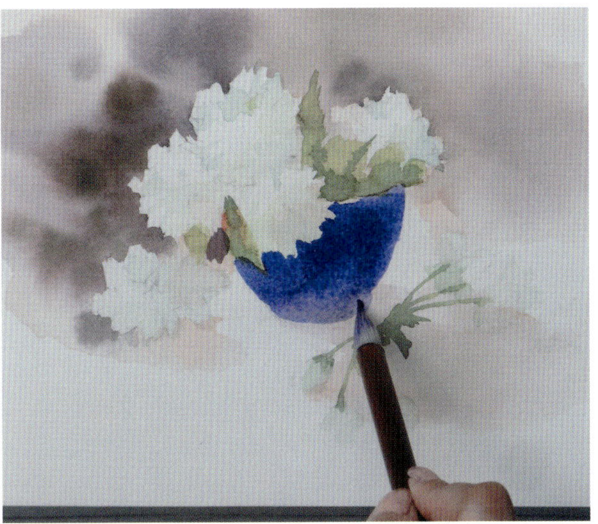
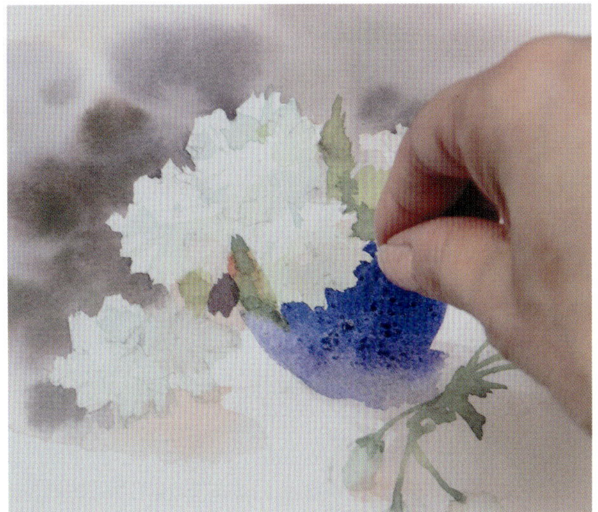

7

Paint the porcelain and then sprinkle salt to make a pattern. Be sure to sprinkle the salt before the surface dries out. If the amount of water is sufficient, the salt should become slightly white after 40 seconds.

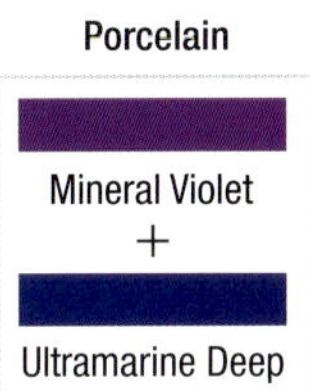

Porcelain

Mineral Violet
+
Ultramarine Deep

Stems and Stamen

Crimson Lake

Shading on Flower Petals

Rose Madder
+
Yellow Deep

Highlights on Flower Petals

Chinese White

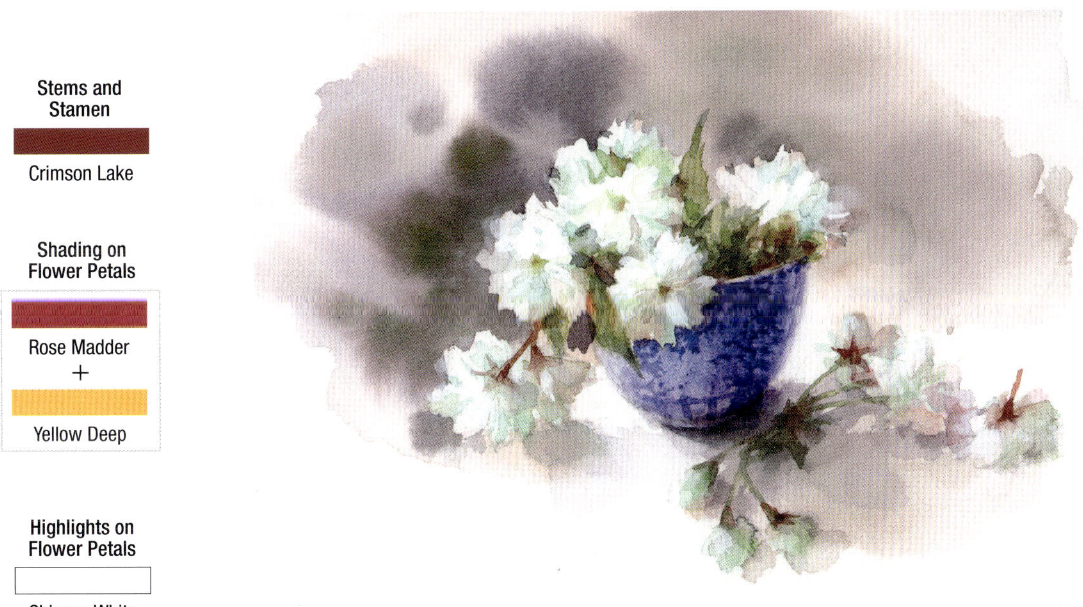

Complete

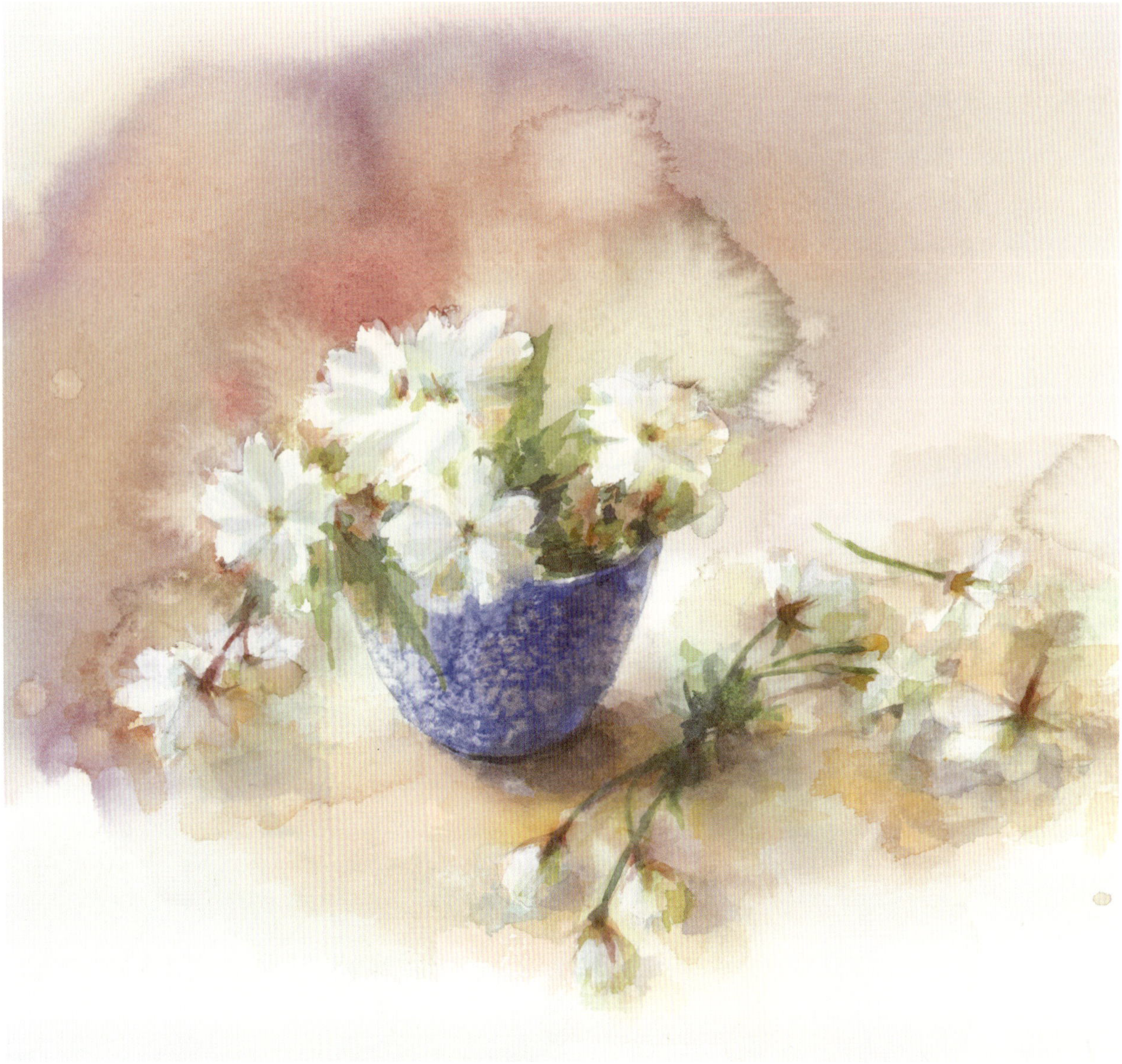

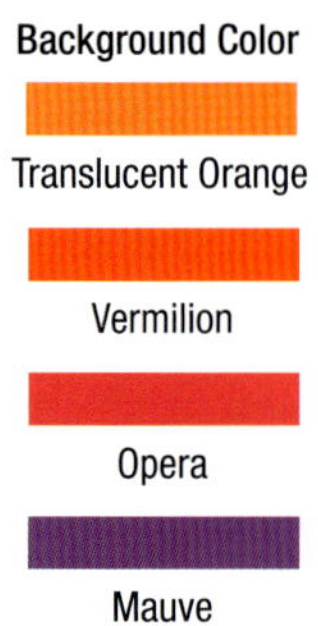

I tried painting the same motif with a different background color. I usually paint three paintings simultaneously. Using this method, I compare them as I go.

Yuku Haru (The Departing Spring)
13 x 13 in (33 x 33 cm)

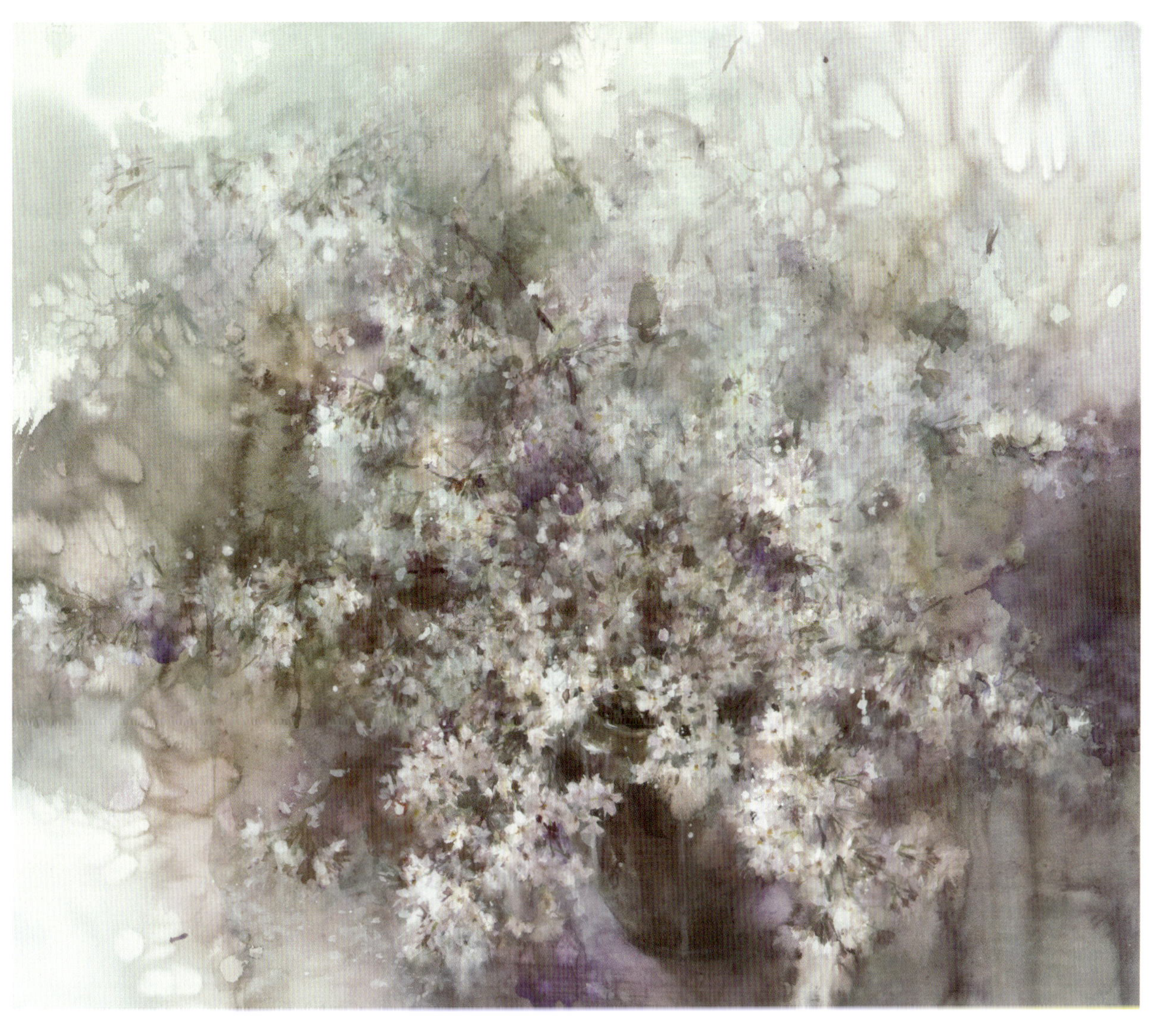

In spring of the year of the Great Western Japanese Earthquake I must have seen many cherry trees blossoming, but I do not recall them at all. However, this year I could view them calmly and at my leisure.

Shizukana Haru (A Quiet Spring)
35 x 39.75 in (89 x 101 cm)

Squid: Drawing Them Using Salt

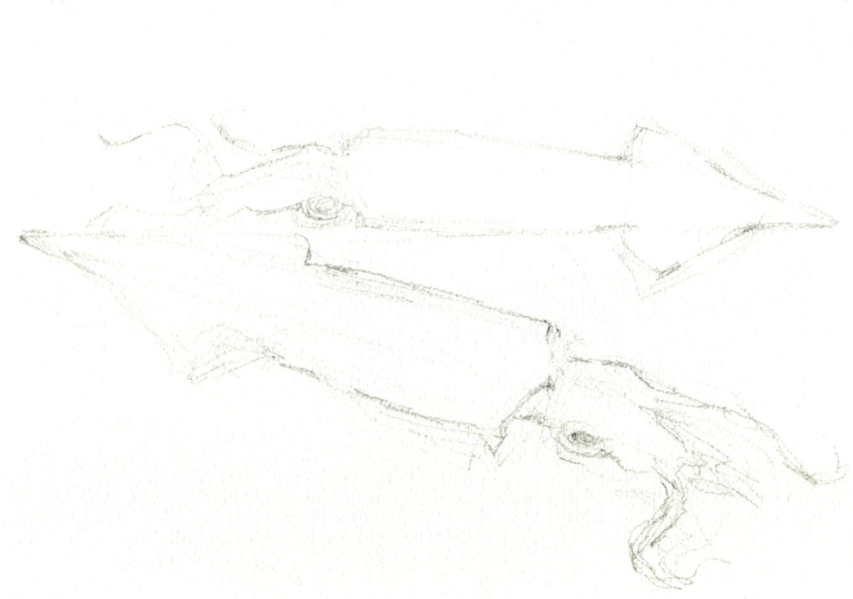

1

Arrange the squid so as to portray movement.

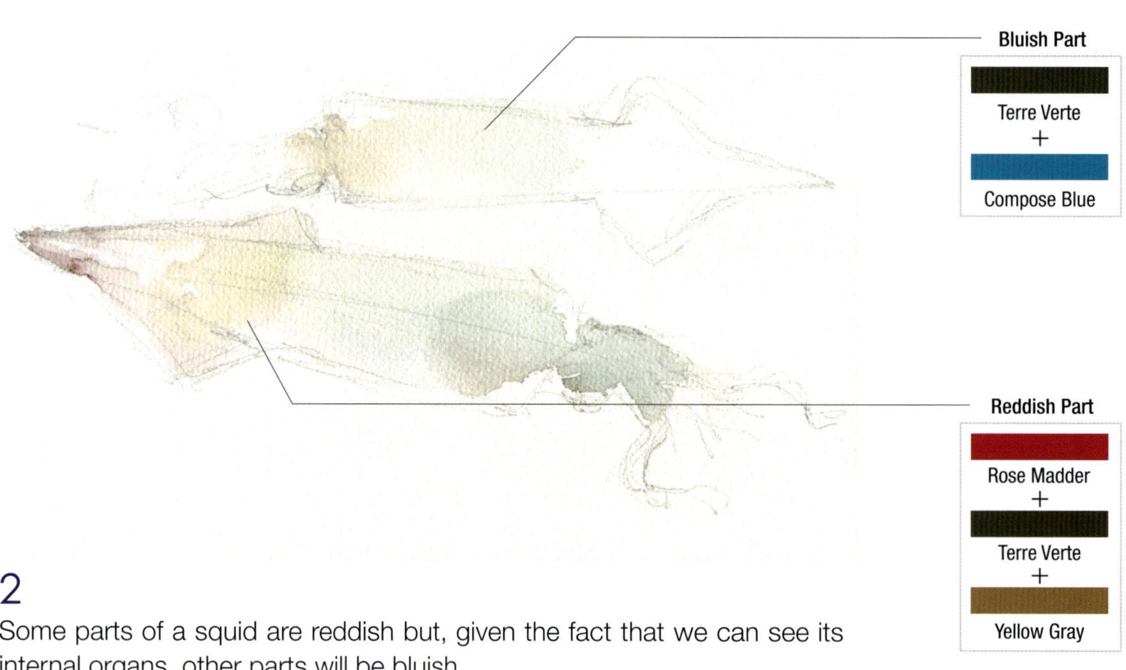

2

Some parts of a squid are reddish but, given the fact that we can see its internal organs, other parts will be bluish.

3

Sprinkle salt before the paint dries.

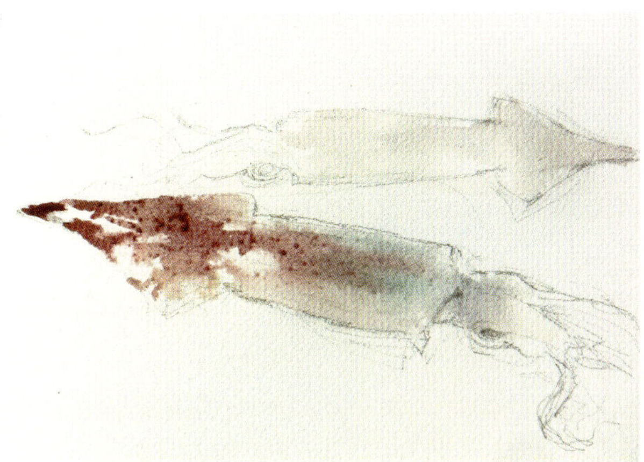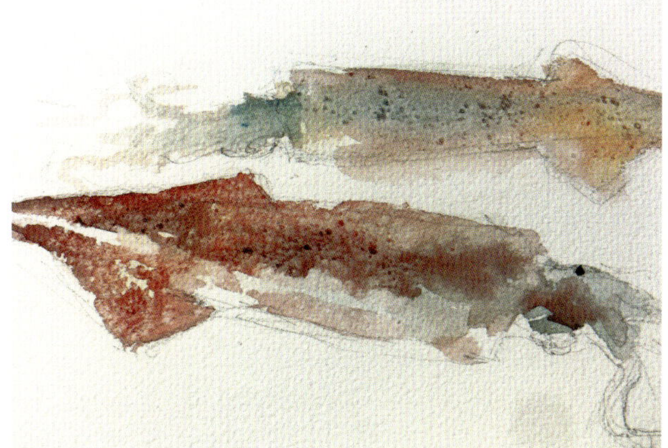

The effect of salt application will vary depending on the type of salt and paper.
Make sure to brush off any salt grains that remain on the surface.

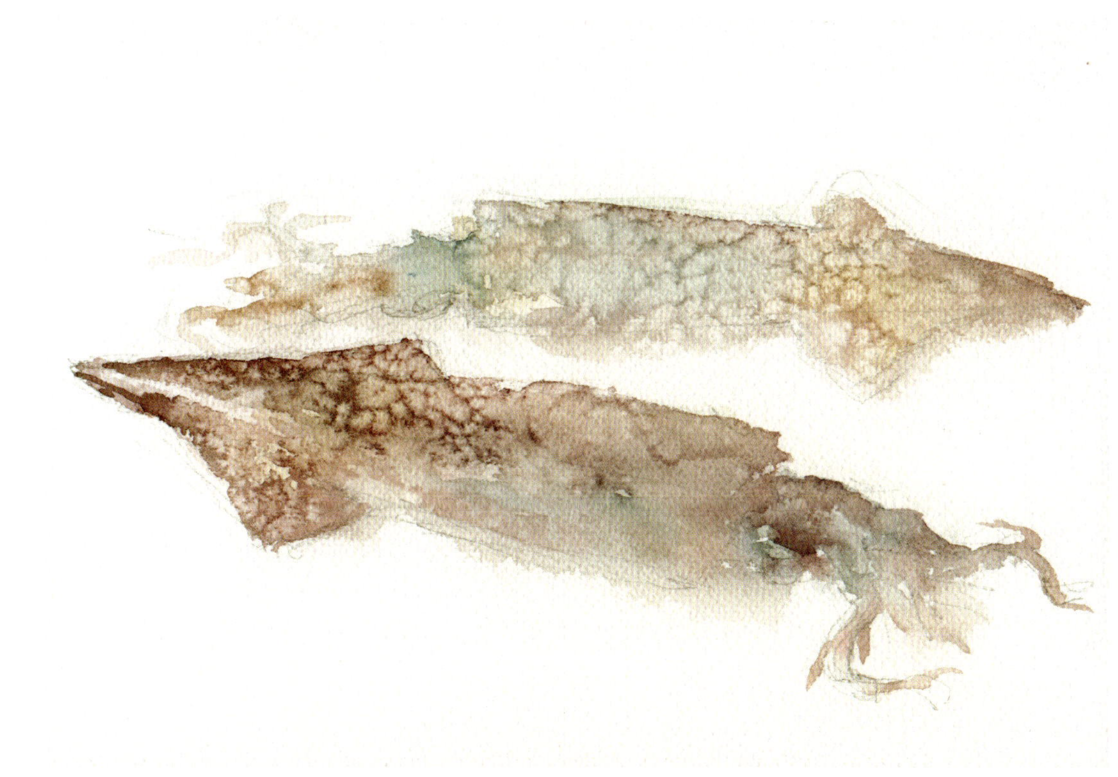

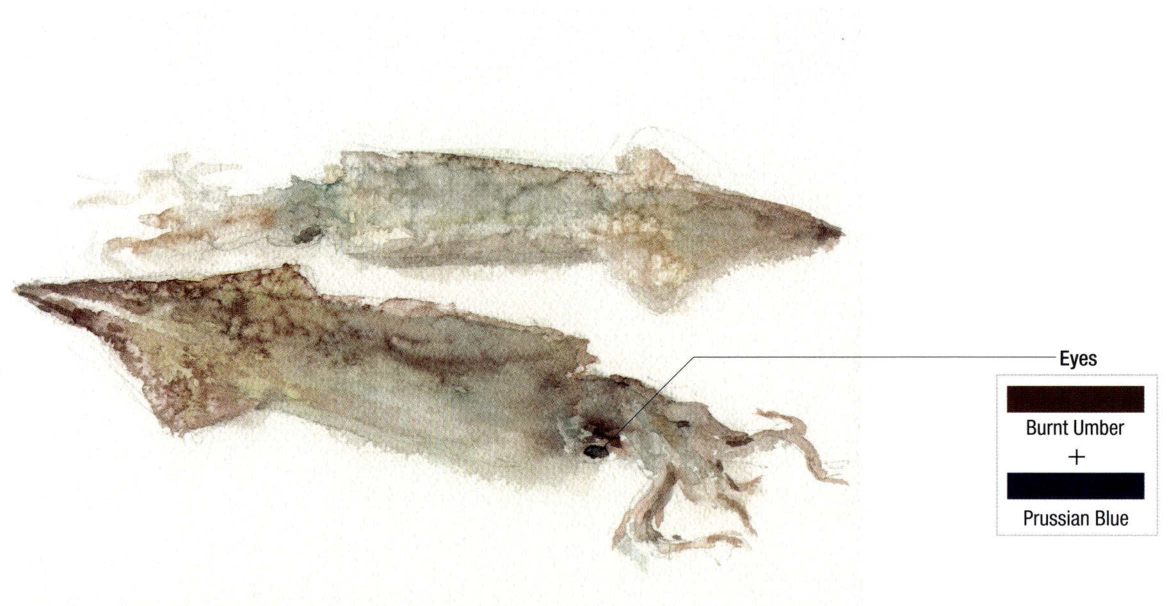

4

Paint in the eyes.

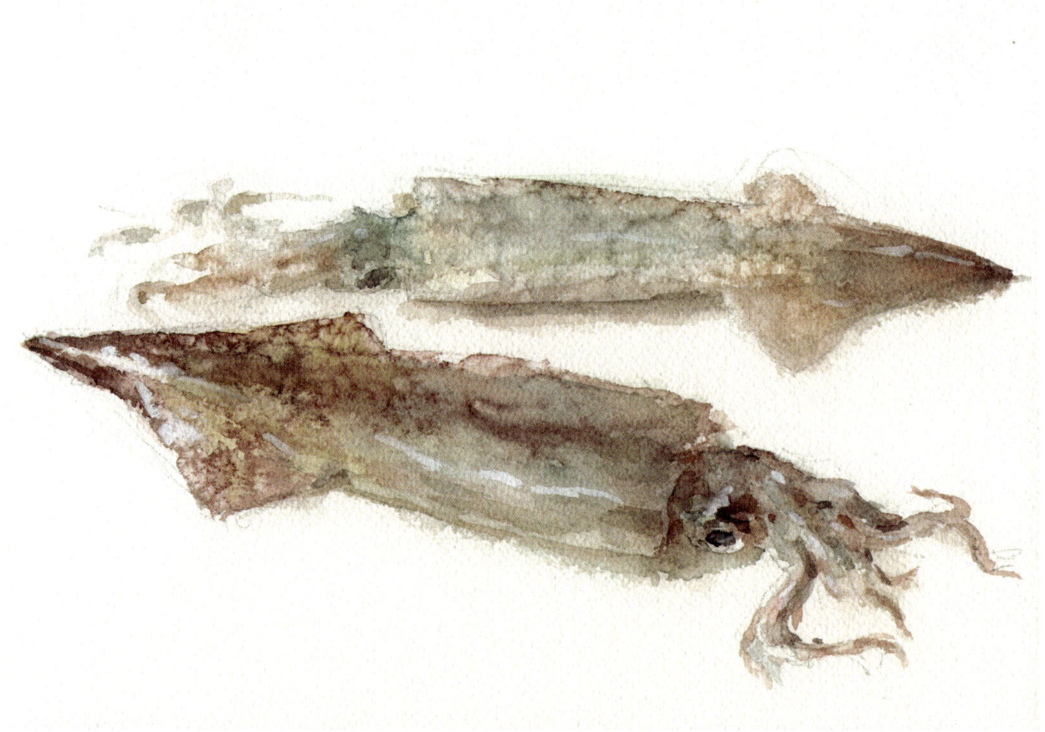

Complete

Bring out a wet look by applying white gouache.

Fish: The Shape and Color of Blueback Fish

One great merit of watercolors is quickness. They are suitable for painting fresh fish in just one go.

First, though, you should really observe the fish.

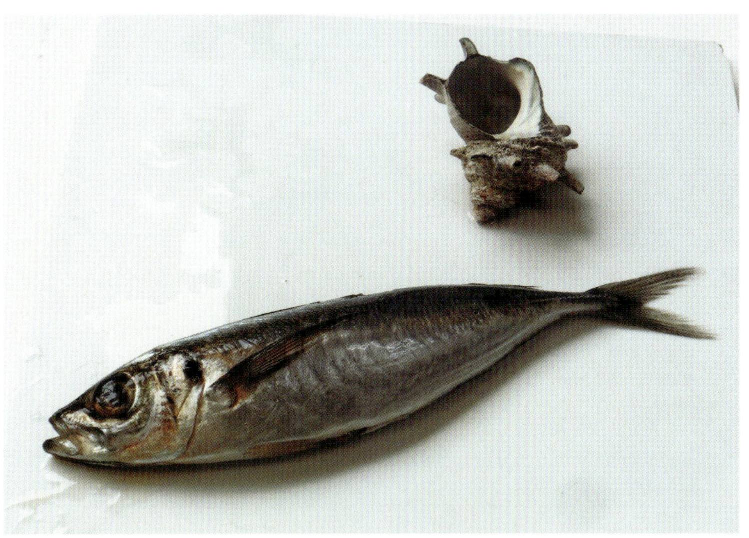

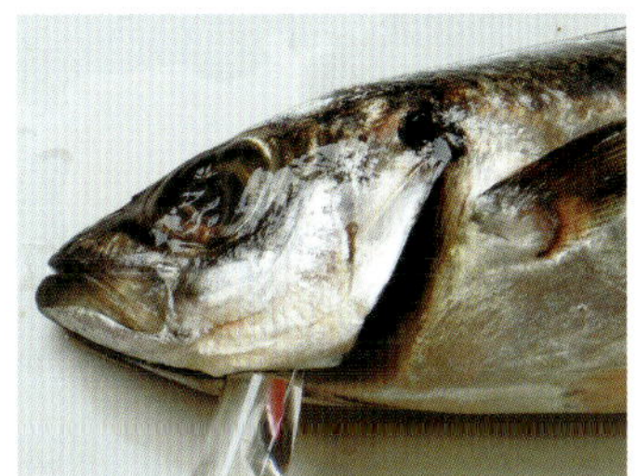

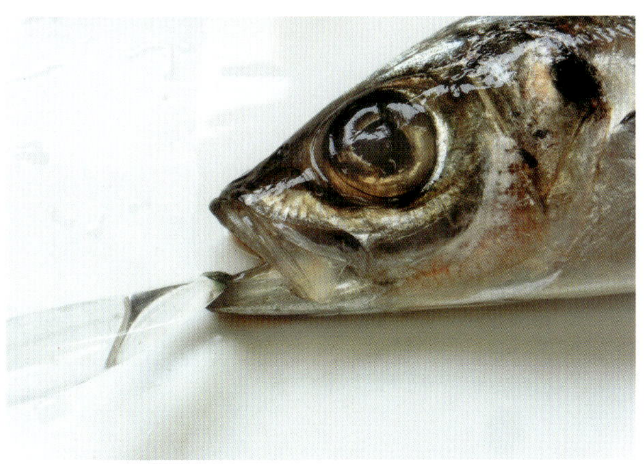

Observe the upper jaw or lower jaw to determine which one sticks out more and how far the gills come down.

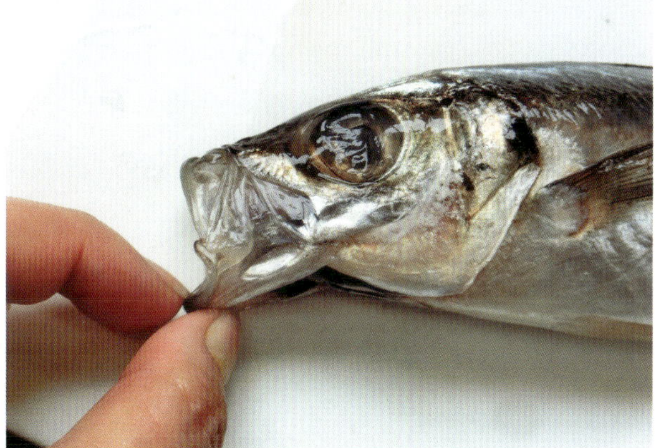

Wow! The mouth can open this wide.

Let's expand the pectoral and dorsal fins and look at them. How beautiful!

The rules of nature apply to everything, even seashells. Draw them while trying to find which rule of nature applies to them.

Spiral shells always have an axis with a spiral structure. After capturing the contours of the seashell, draw it as if you were wrapping curved lines around that axis.

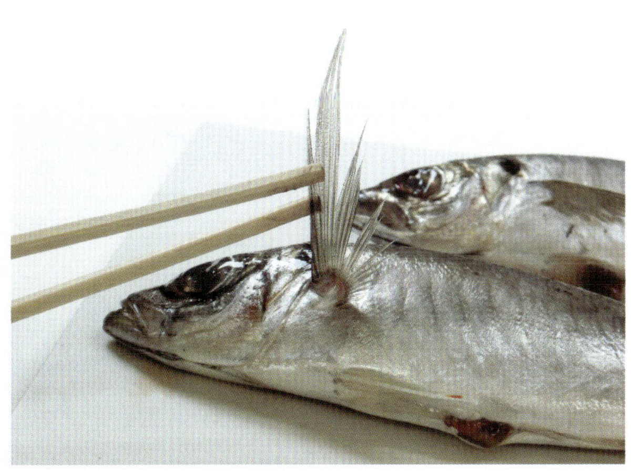

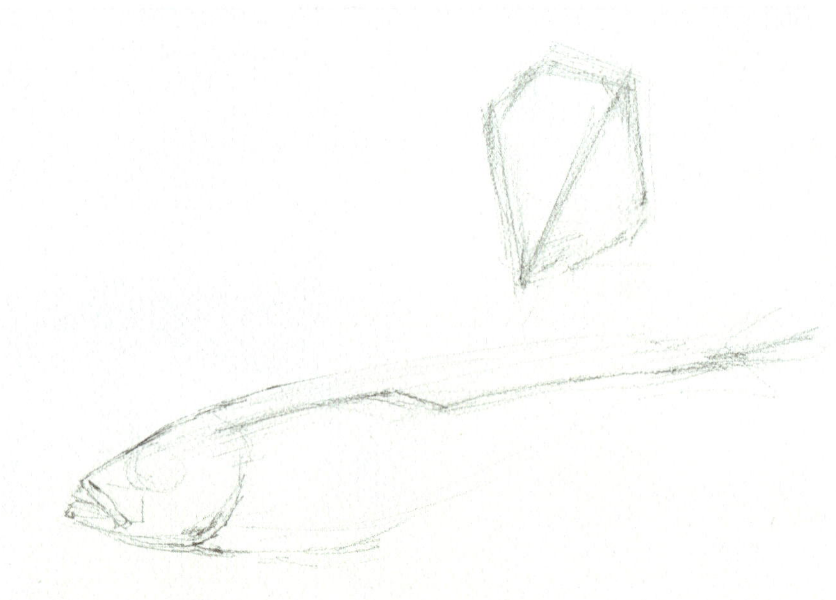

1

After carefully observing the shape of the jaw and the gills, draw in the scute (i.e., the part with the hard scales).

For turban shells, draw the center axis and roughly sketch the rest using straight lines.

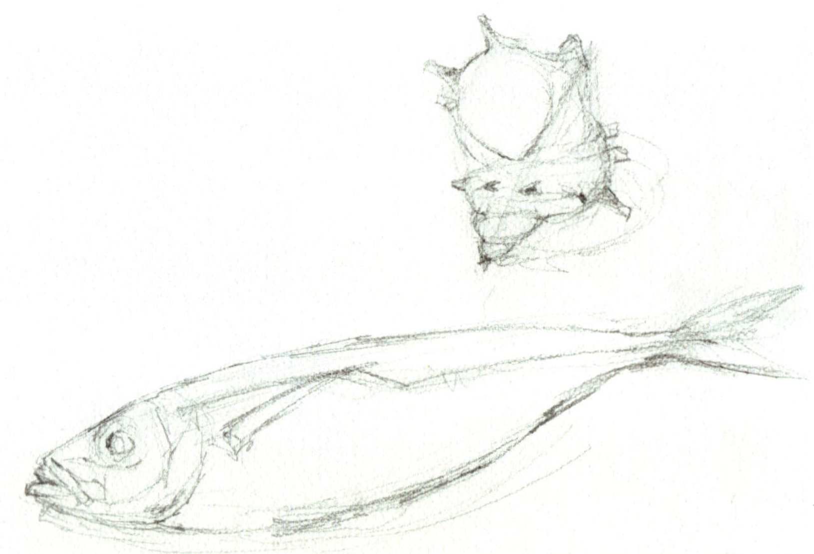

The red dotted line indicates the scute.

2

Using the scute as a measuring stick, draw in a dorsal line and a ventral line.

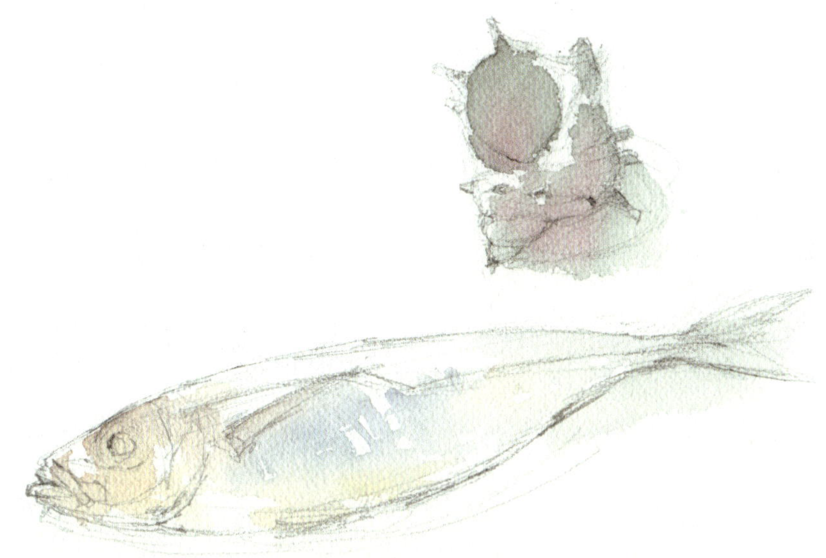

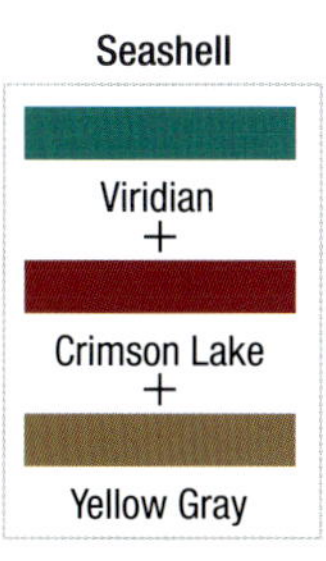

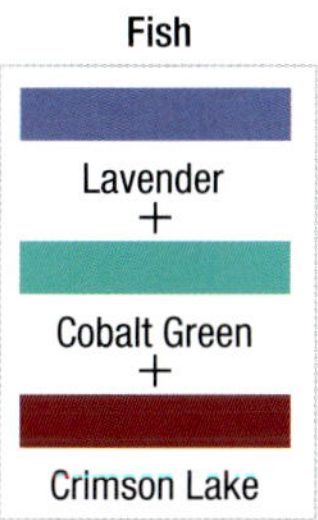

3

People who paint blueback fish tend to use only blue or navy blue when, in reality, various colors can actually be seen.

As for the silver-colored stomach and back, please be sure to blend the colors without hesitating. Don't stop to think, "Hey, I can see such-and-such a color."

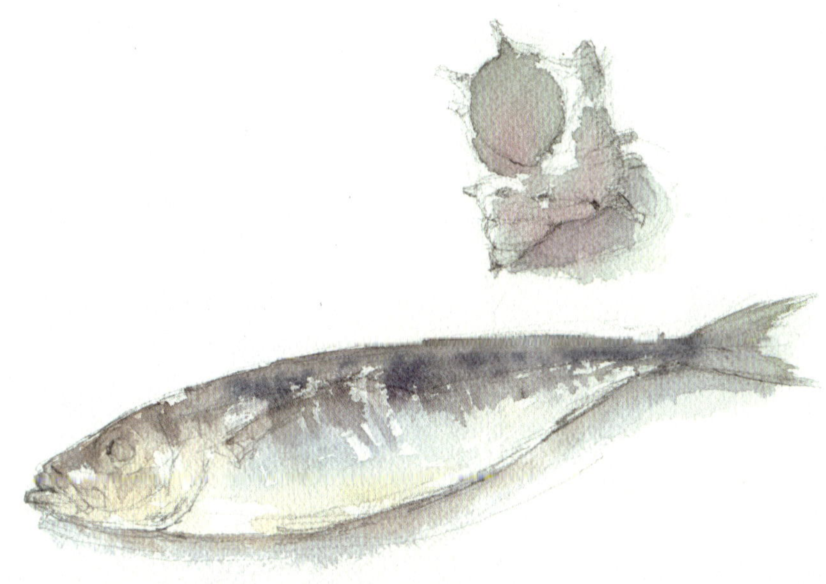

4

Before the paint applied in step 3 dries out, lay down the color of the back.

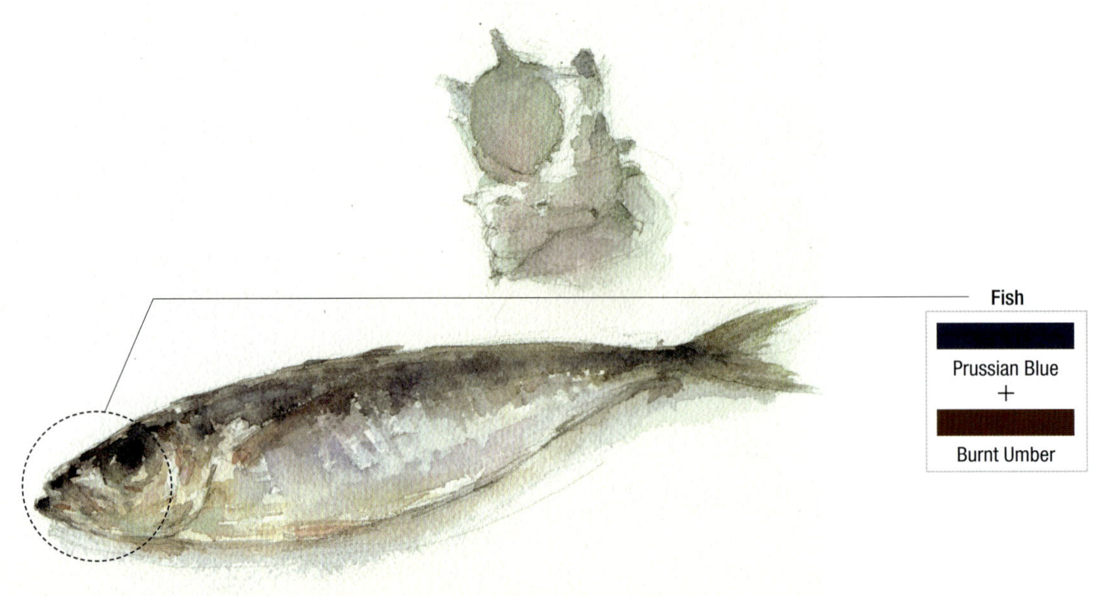

5

As long as you look carefully at the head and tail while painting, you can be playful with the middle portion of the fish and overdo the colors that you see in the fish a little bit.

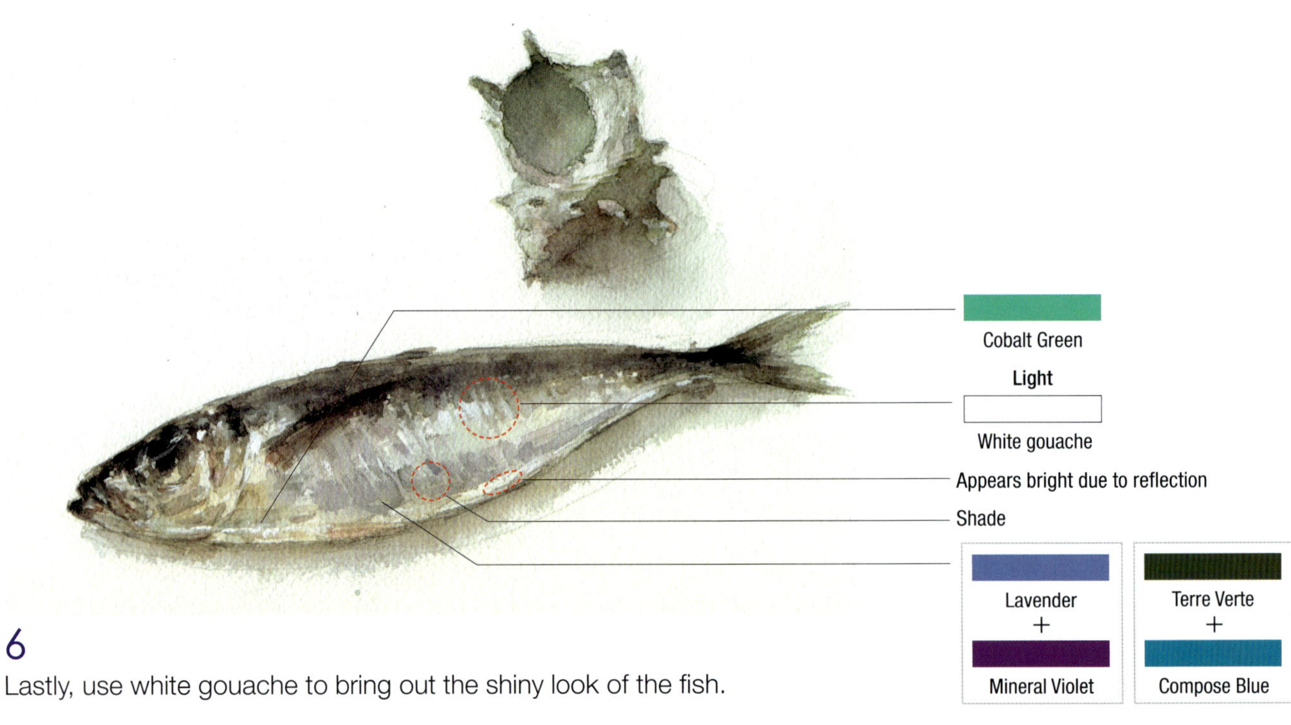

6

Lastly, use white gouache to bring out the shiny look of the fish.

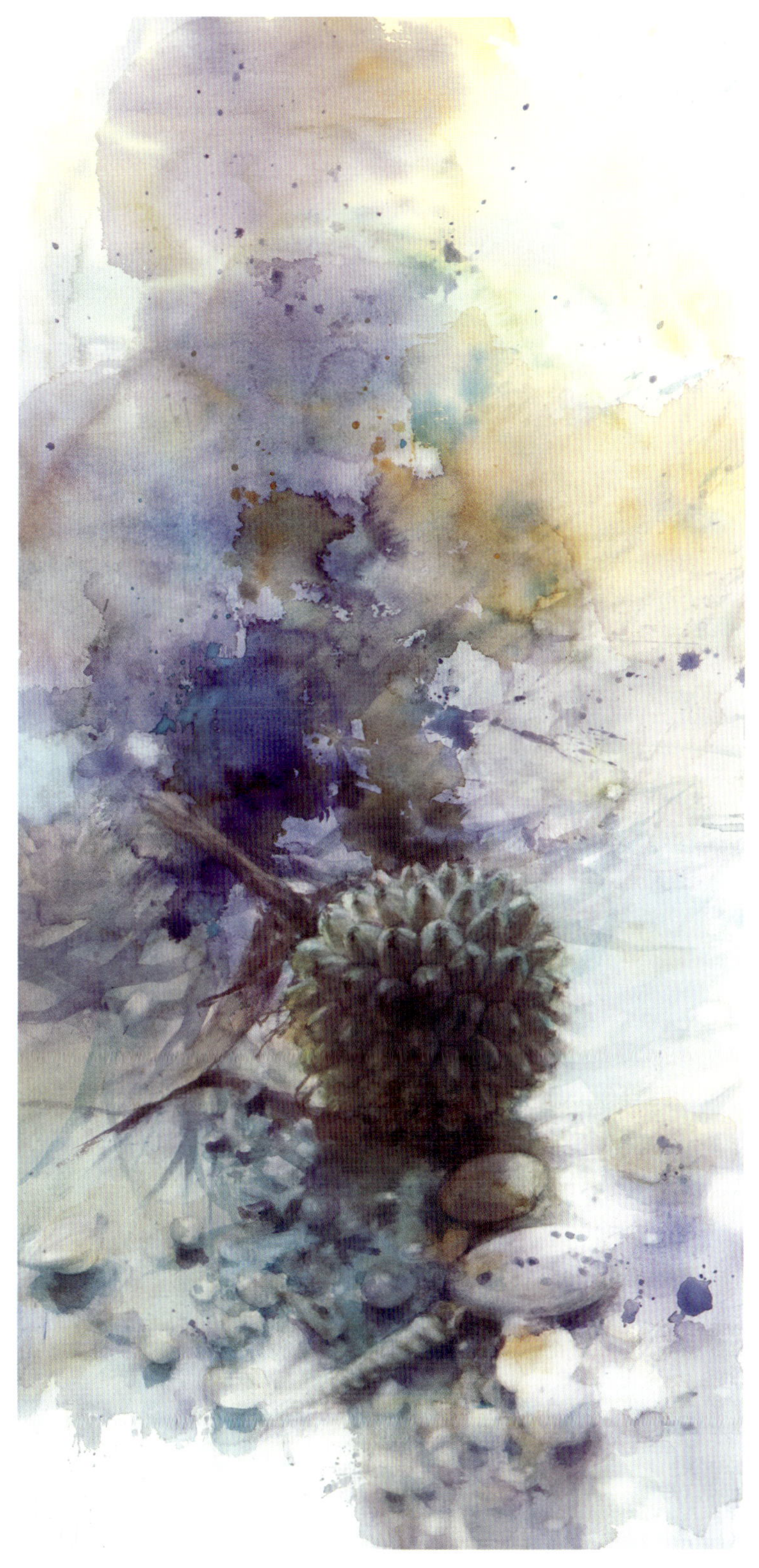

A pandanus fruit, which I have only seen in Tanaka
Isson paintings, is right before my eyes. It came all
the way from the shore of some far-off sea and now
here it is—right in front me.

Adan (A Pandanus Fruit)
43.25 x 20.5 in (110 x 52 cm)

Various Metals: Silver, Copper, and the Reflections Found in Them

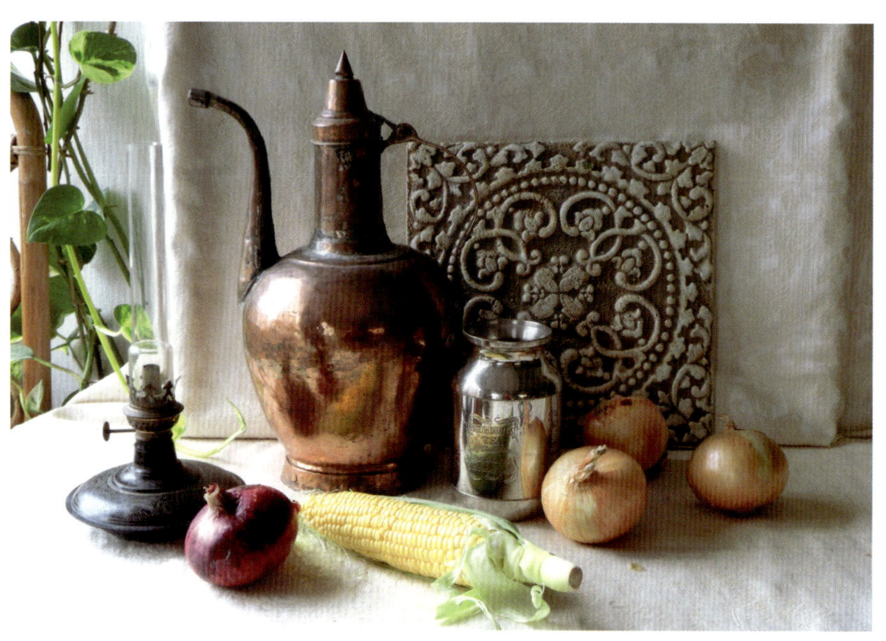

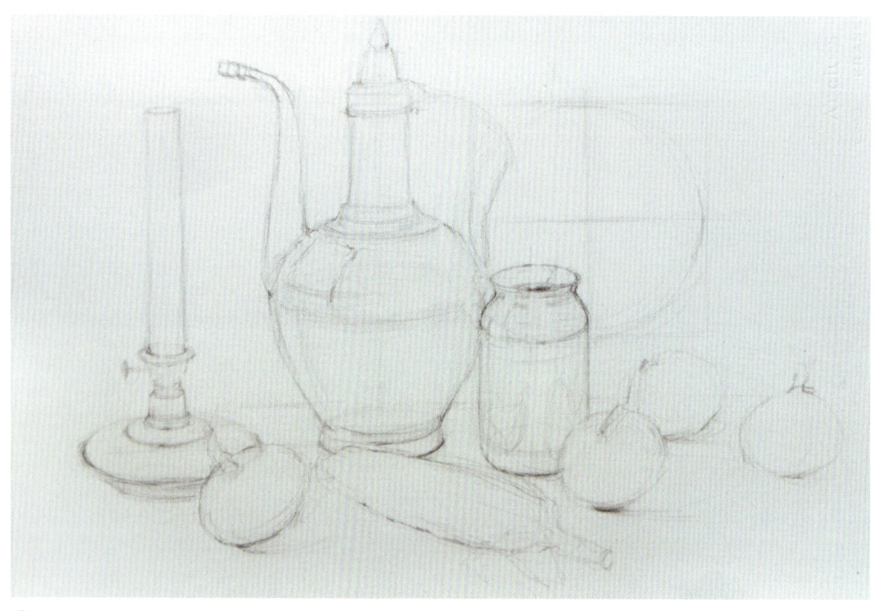

1

I sketched this using a 2B graphite pencil. For the pots, lamps, etc., capture their shapes by drawing a center line first.

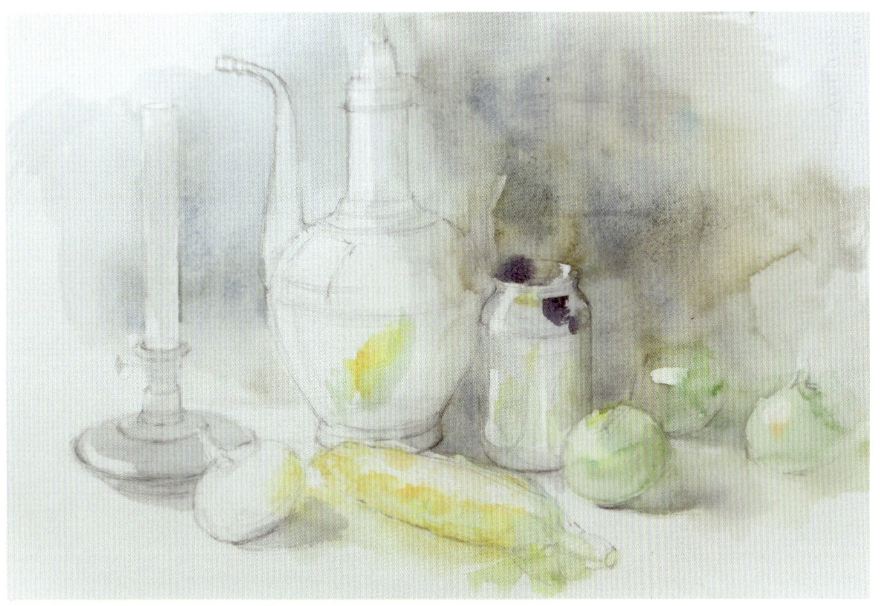

2

After laying down some yellow for the corn, as well as some yellowish green for inside the onions, paint the rear wall. For the shadows that can't be clearly seen (i.e., the copperware handle, the rearmost onion, etc.) be sure to paint them while blending them into the background.

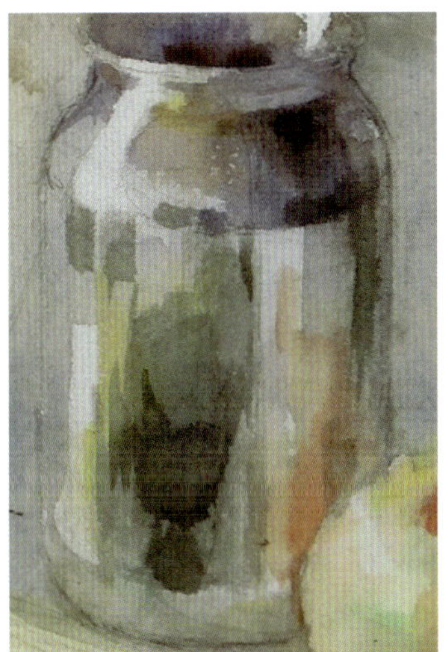

| Note |

Use a flat brush here. Since the shadow is reflecting on the smooth metal surface, paint it by moving the brush up and down.

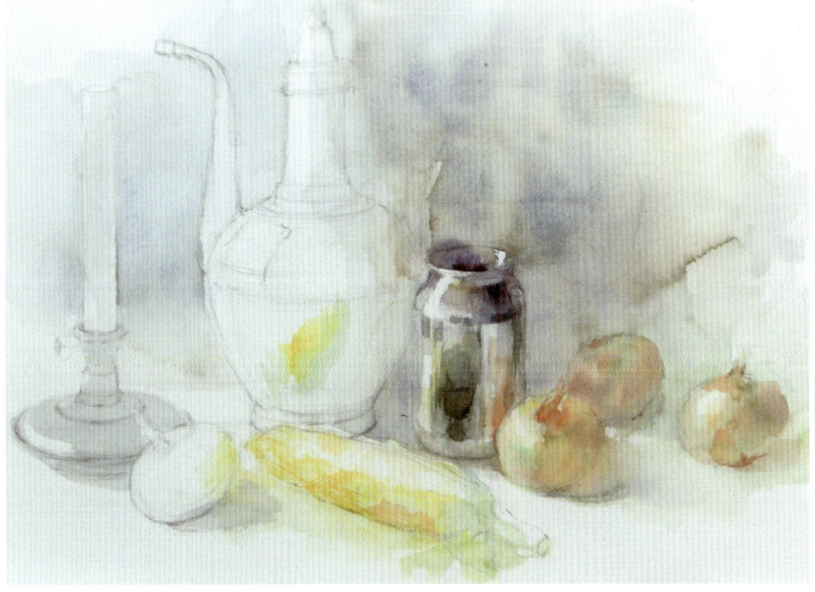

3

Lay down the color for the onion skin and, at the same time, paint the reflection of the corn and onions on the copperware.

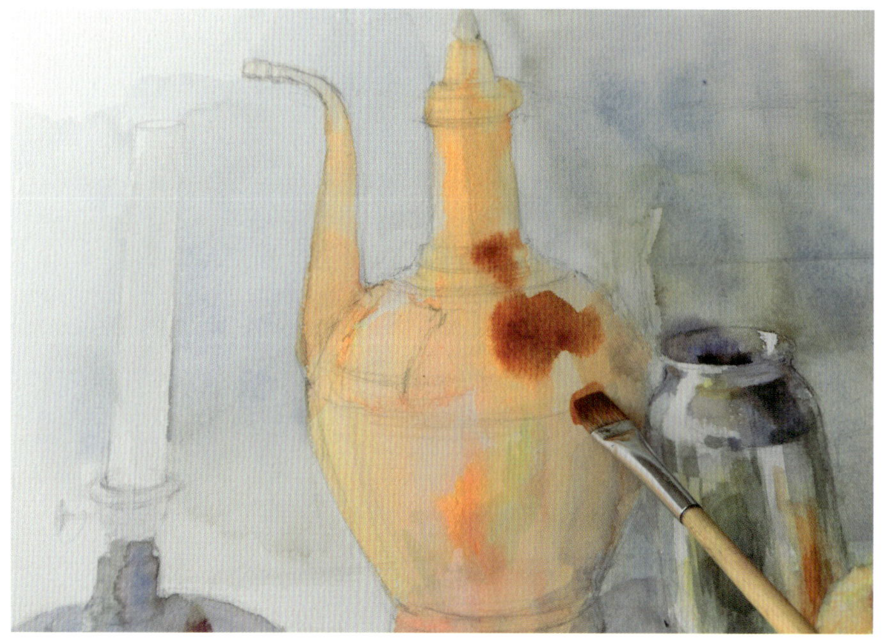

4

First lay down some translucent orange for the copperware and then, before it dries, blend in the darker parts. Similarly to the silverware, there is a
reflection of the inside of the studio.

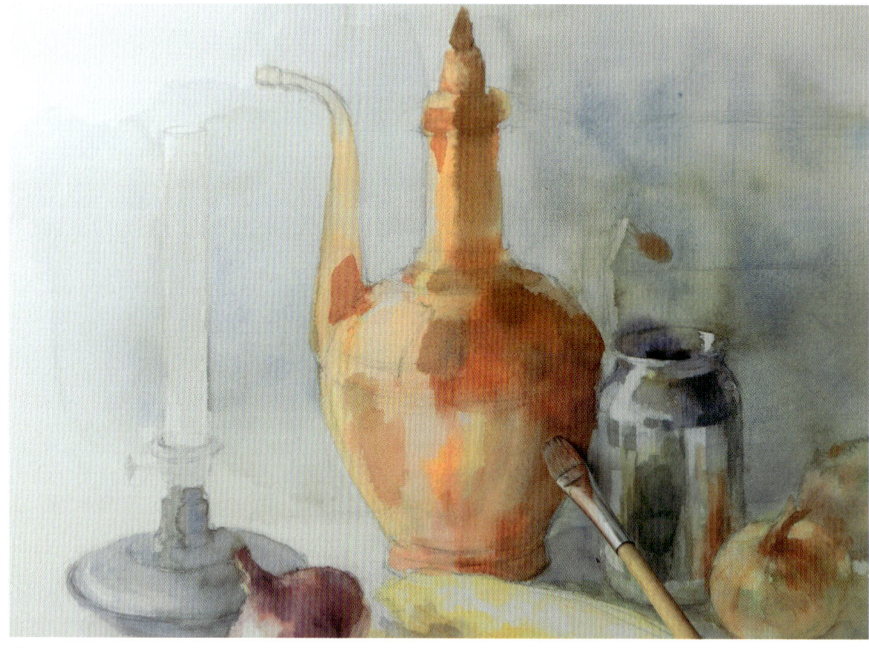

5

Make variations of brown by mixing orange with green or blue. If you have
fixed ideas like, "shadows are brown," and then paint only following those
ideas, your paintings will lack depth and appear monotone.

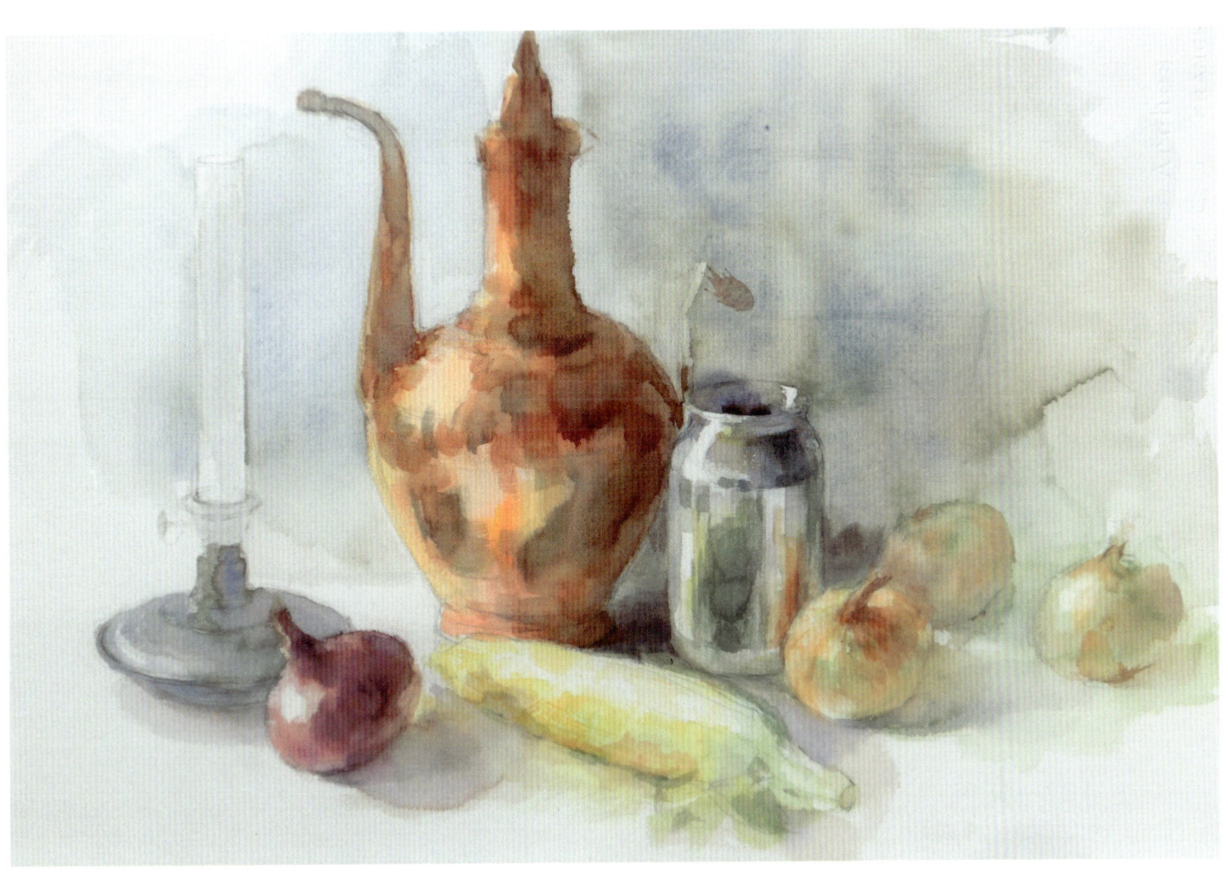

6

Simple gray and brown colored porcelain looks monotonous at first glance, but that is exactly where the fun in making a colorful painting is hidden. Vibrant flowers and fruit can be painted with the aid of certain coloring. However, gray and brown are created by mixing or layering colors and this shows not just the effect of the paint, but also your ability and your individuality.

Reflections and Copperware Expressions

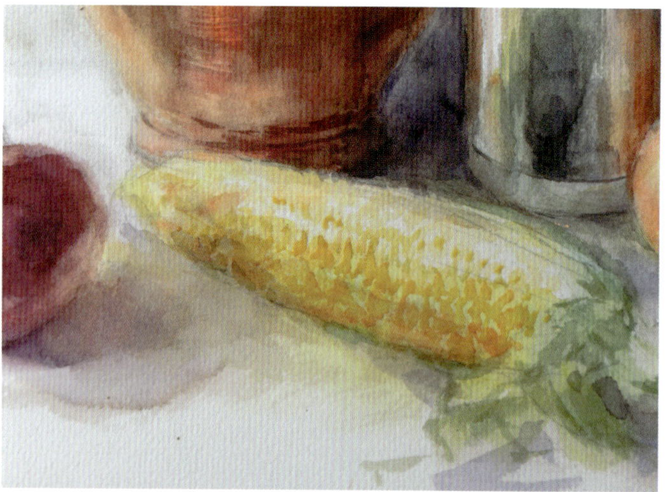

Do not paint reflections excessively. I used a flat brush for the entire process. (For lessons on how to properly capture corn, refer to page 62.)

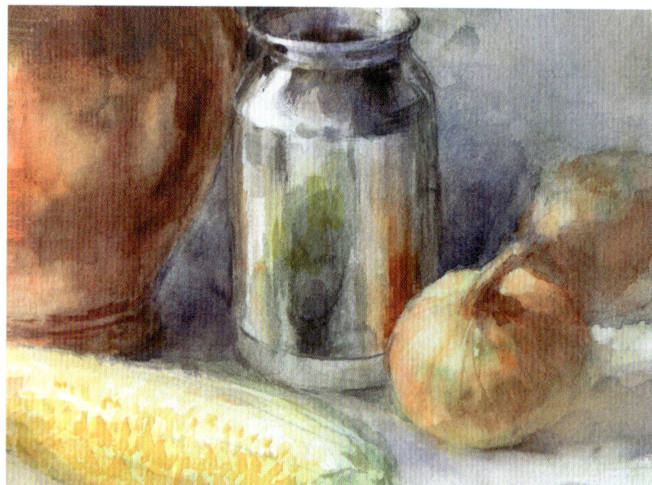

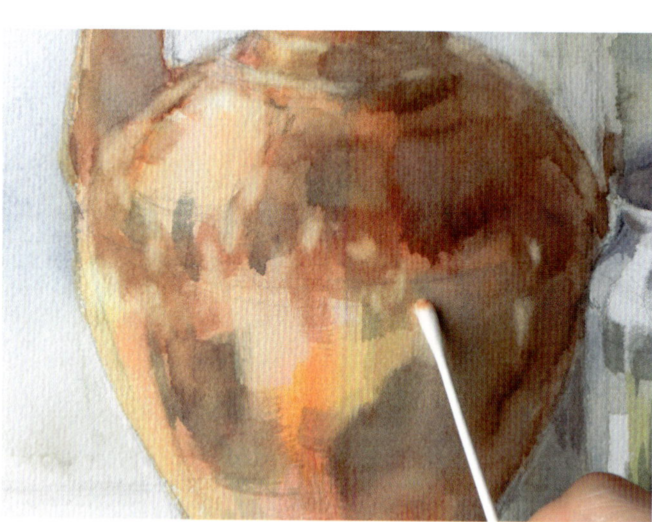

I wanted to depict the copper's handcrafted unevenness, not a smooth surface, so I dipped a cotton swab in water and then wiped paint off with it.

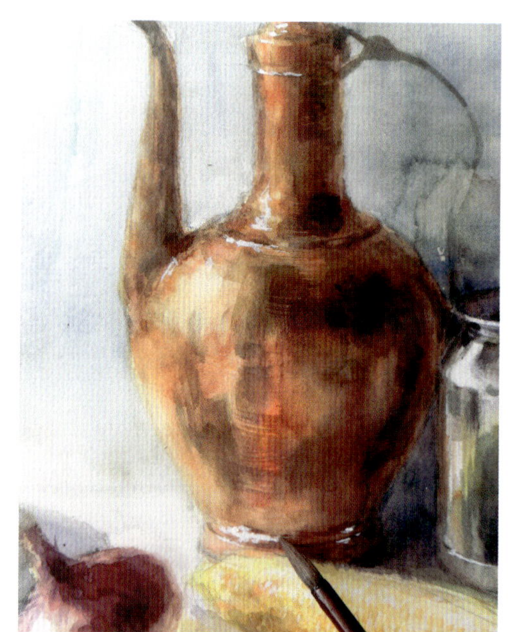

I laid white gouache for highlights.

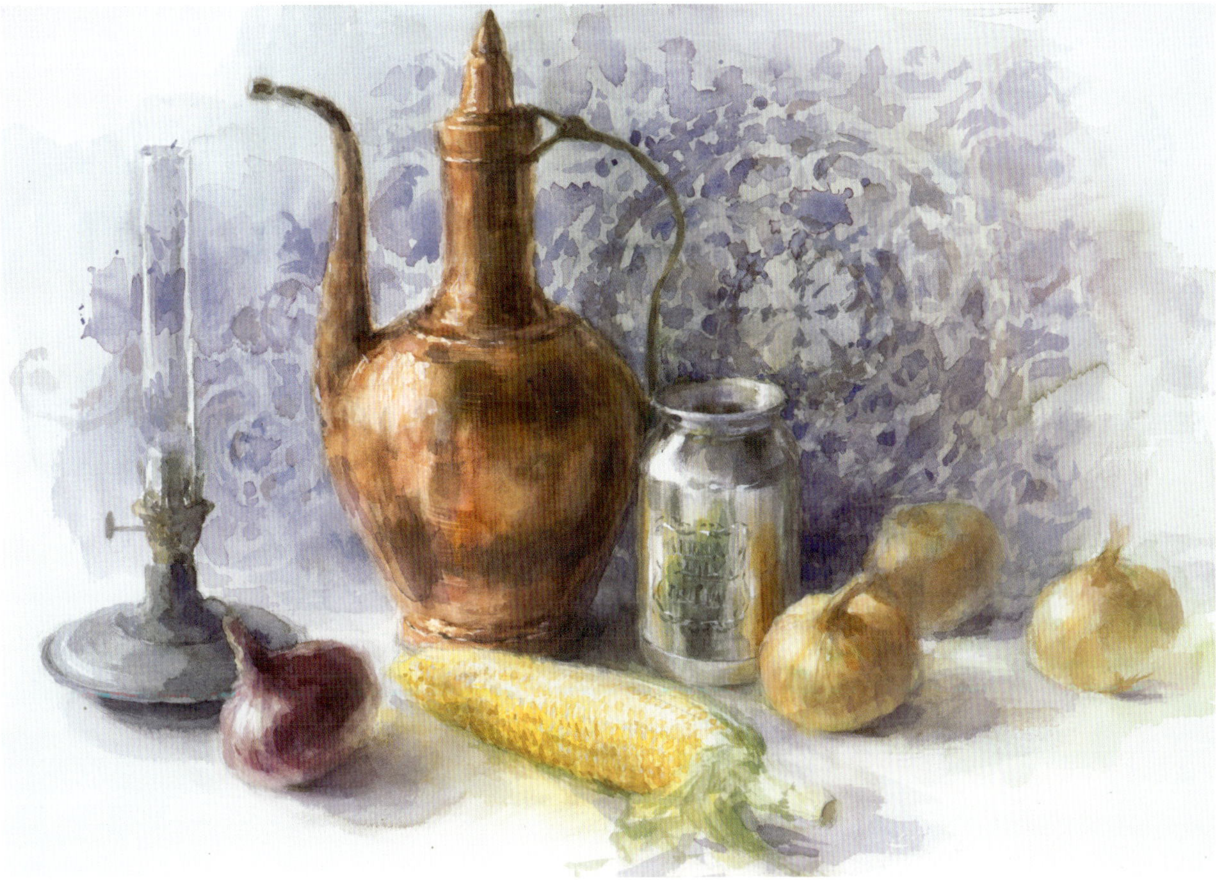

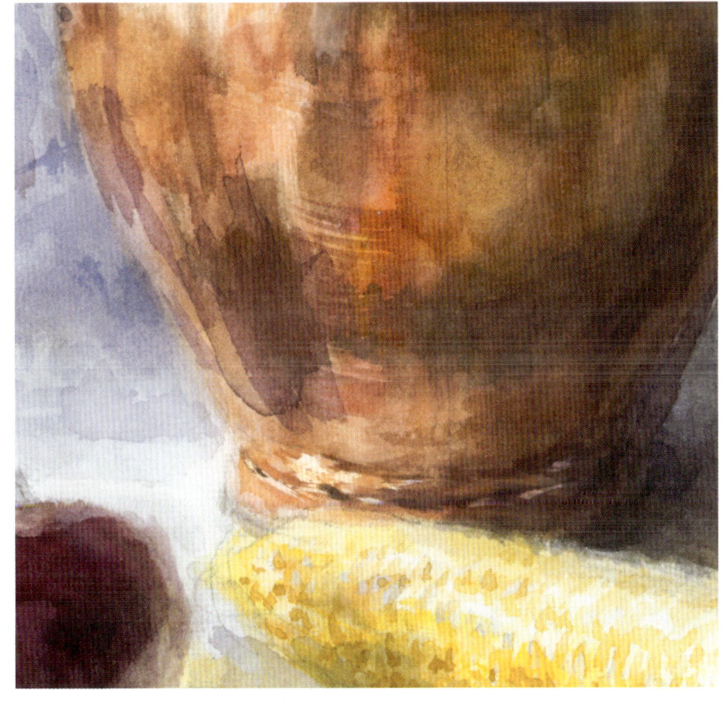

Complete

15.25 x 21.25 in (38.5 x 54 cm)

Apply translucent orange over the highlighting using a flat brush. Be careful not to let the white underneath bleed through.

Methods for Leaving Spaces White

- Leaving Spaces White
- Dermatograph 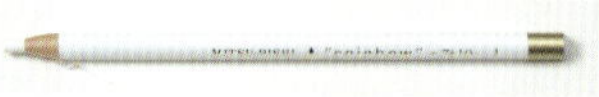
- Candlesticks 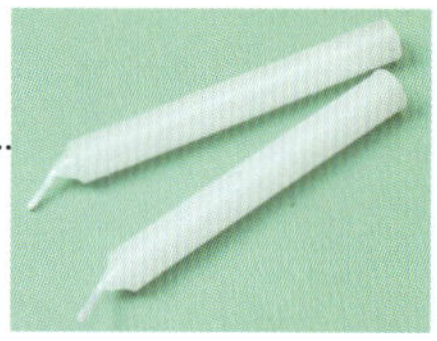
- Masking Ink

Liquid Type

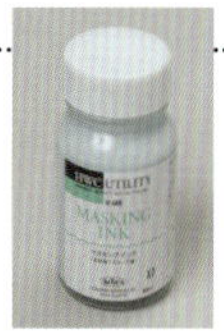

Dispensing
Bottle Type

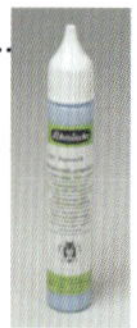

Painting by Leaving Spaces White: Corn

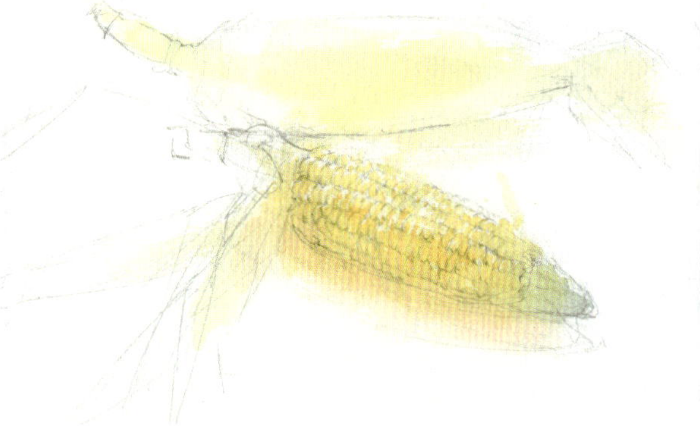

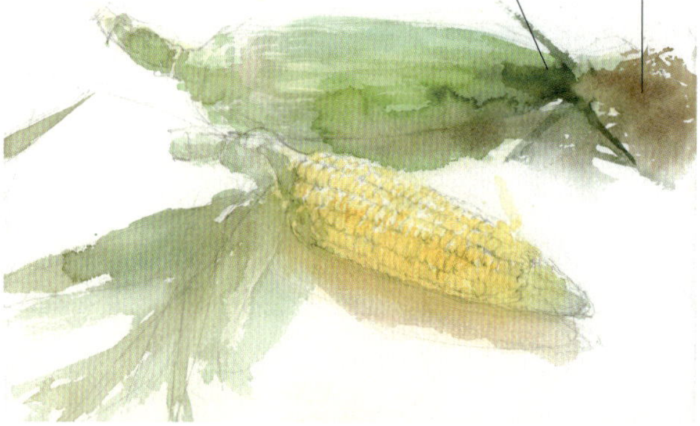

Darker Part

Cobalt Blue
+
Yellow Gray

Lighter Part

Yellow Gray
+
Burnt Umber

1

Soften the sketched lines using a kneaded eraser, then lay down some yellow. Carefully leave white spaces on the paper.

Yellow Lemon
+
Yellow Deep

2

Corn silk is connected to each individual kernel. Thus, there should be the same amount of kernels as corn silk strands.

Viridian
+
Yellow Gray

Yellow Deep
+
Vermilion

Complete

Make the deepness of the yellow pop.

When there are two long objects in a single composition, placing them in two different directions and not parallel with each other will help bring out movement.

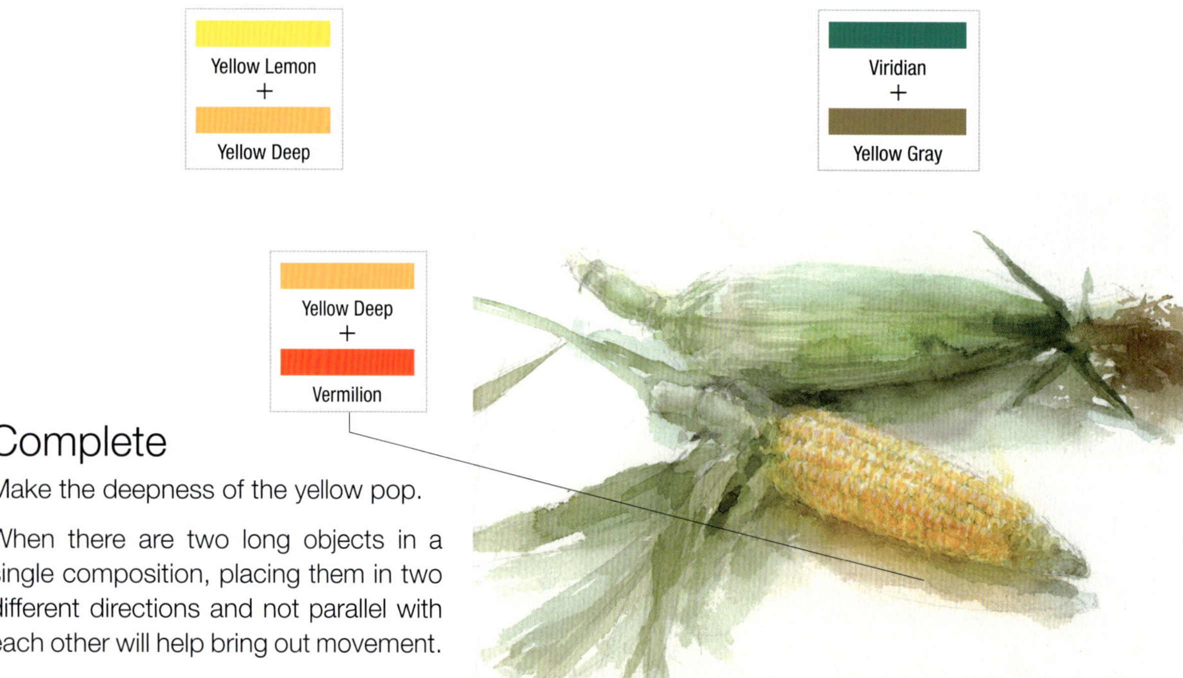

* Dermatograph is used in the same manner.

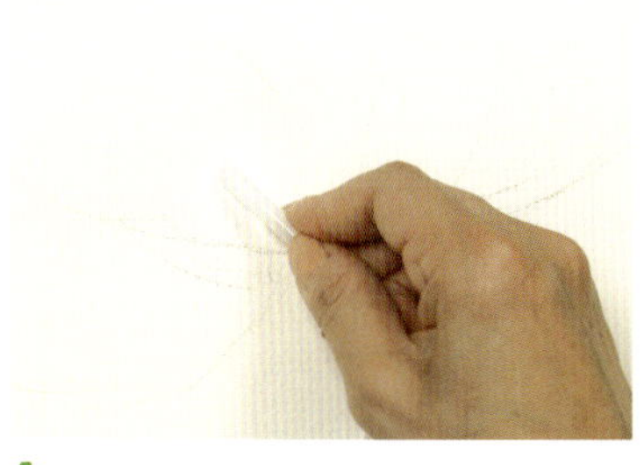

1

Before applying any color, draw the core portion of the cabbage with a candlestick. This portion will be white.

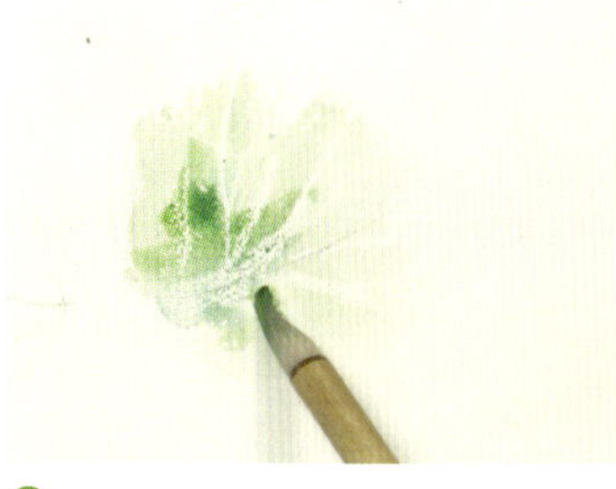

2

Underpaint the cabbage. The core portion of the cabbage, which was covered with candle wax, should remain white because the candle wax will repel the paint.

3

Given that candle wax repels paint, do not use it anywhere except where you expect to make it absolutely white.

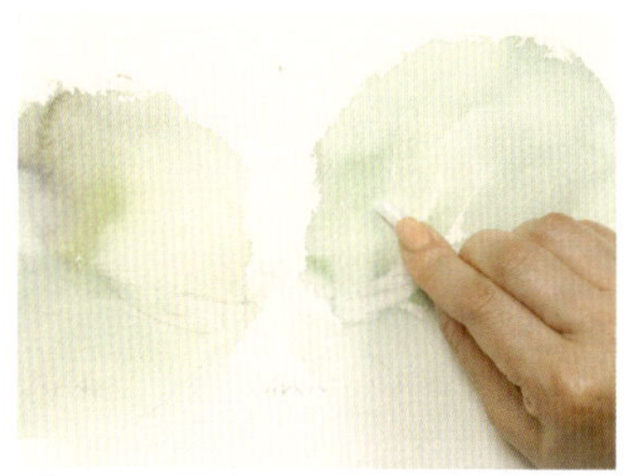

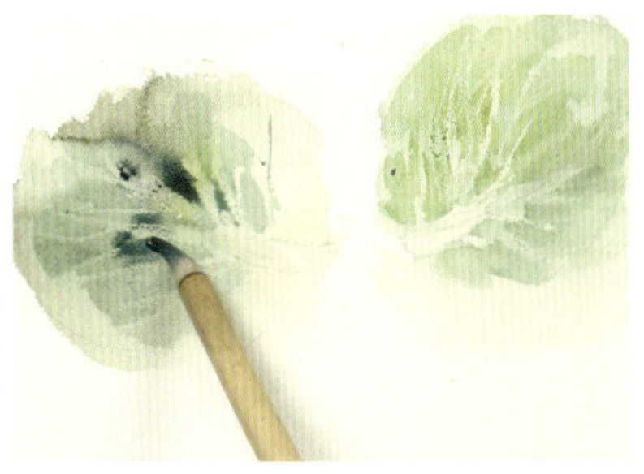

4

Once the underpainting has dried, rub a candlestick over the portions you want to preserve with wax. Then paint over the wax. This allows the underpainting color to remain.

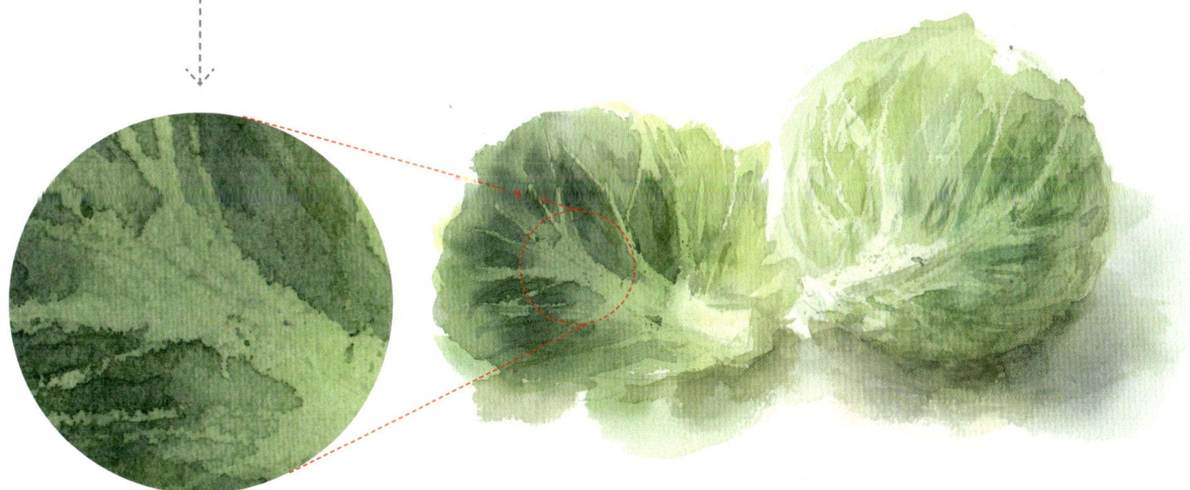

Complete

Using Dispensing Bottle Type Masking Ink: Glass

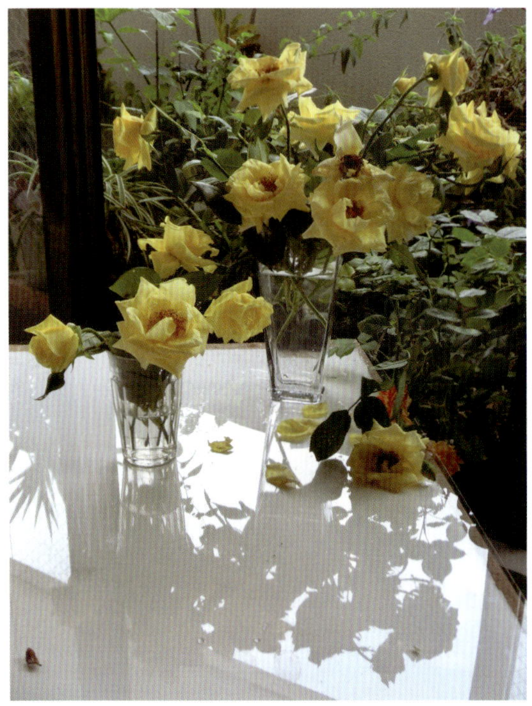

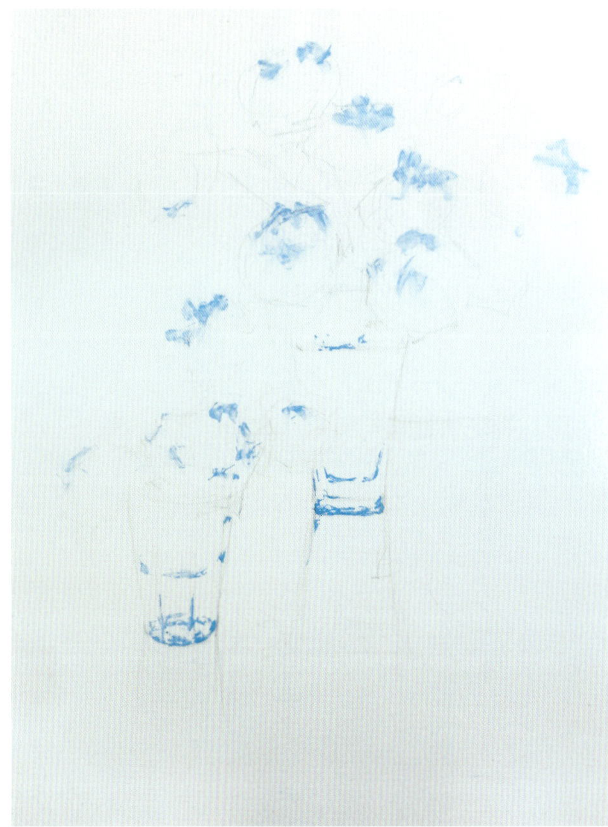

Apply masking ink where light hits the cut glass and flowers.

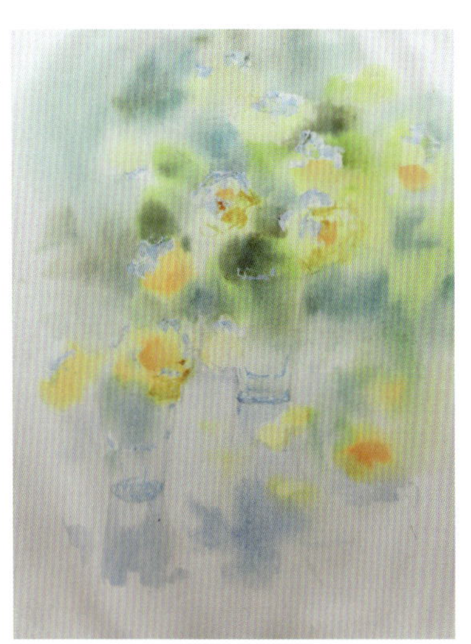

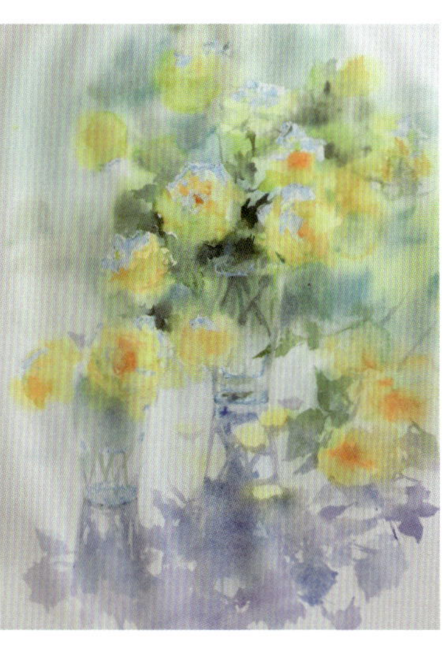

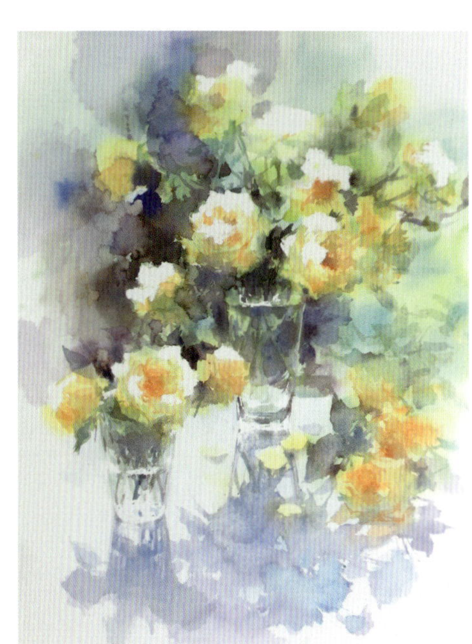

Once you roughly add shading to the underpainting, you can peel the masking off. After removing the masking, add even darker colors to complete.

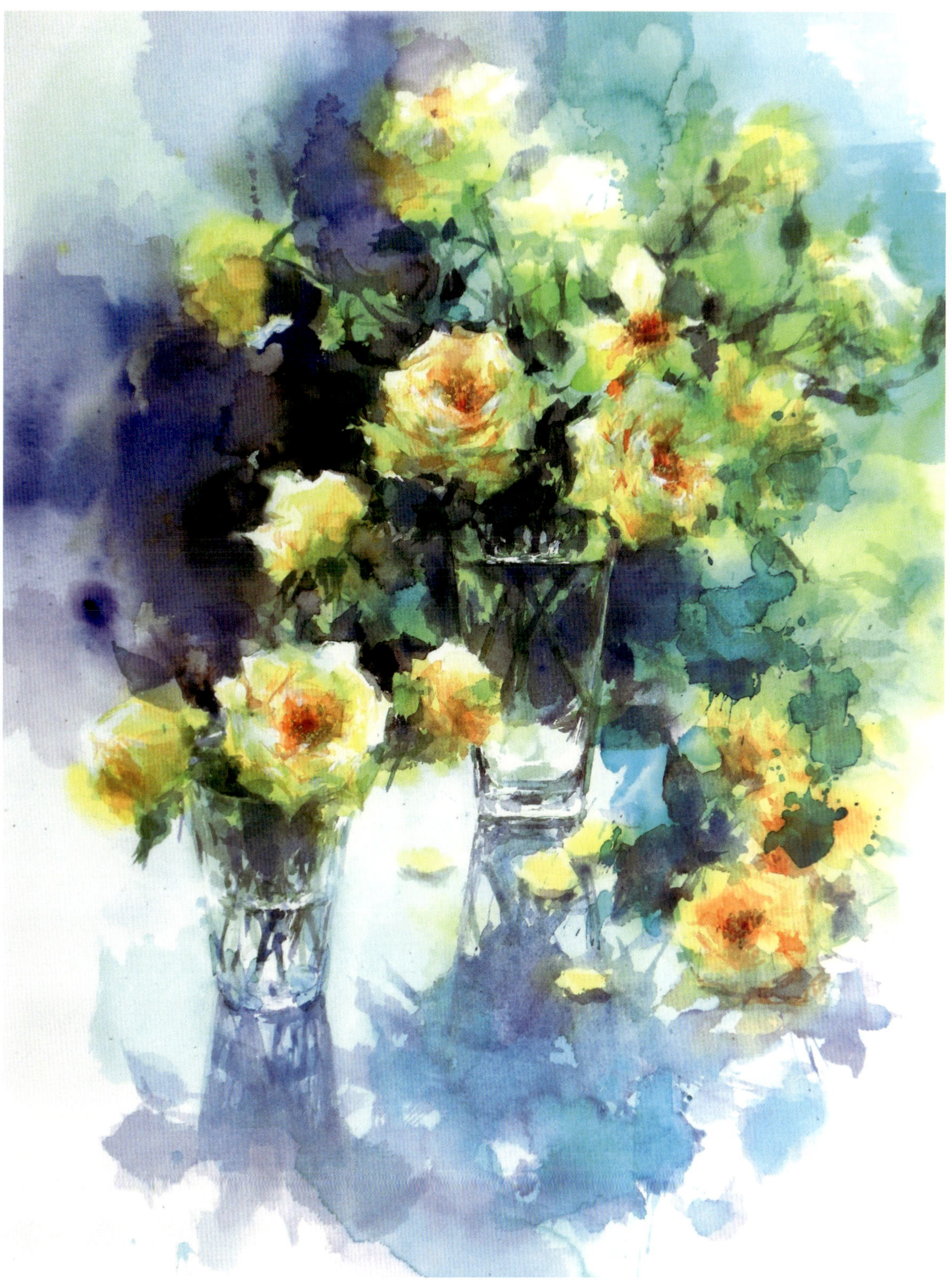

You want to paint roses, but you also want to paint today's blue sky. Well, then, lay a sheet of glass below your motif so that the sky will be reflected. Within the motif, clouds drift along and birds fly by.

Kumo ga Nagarete Iku (Clouds Drift Away)
29.25 x 21.75 in (74 x 55 cm)

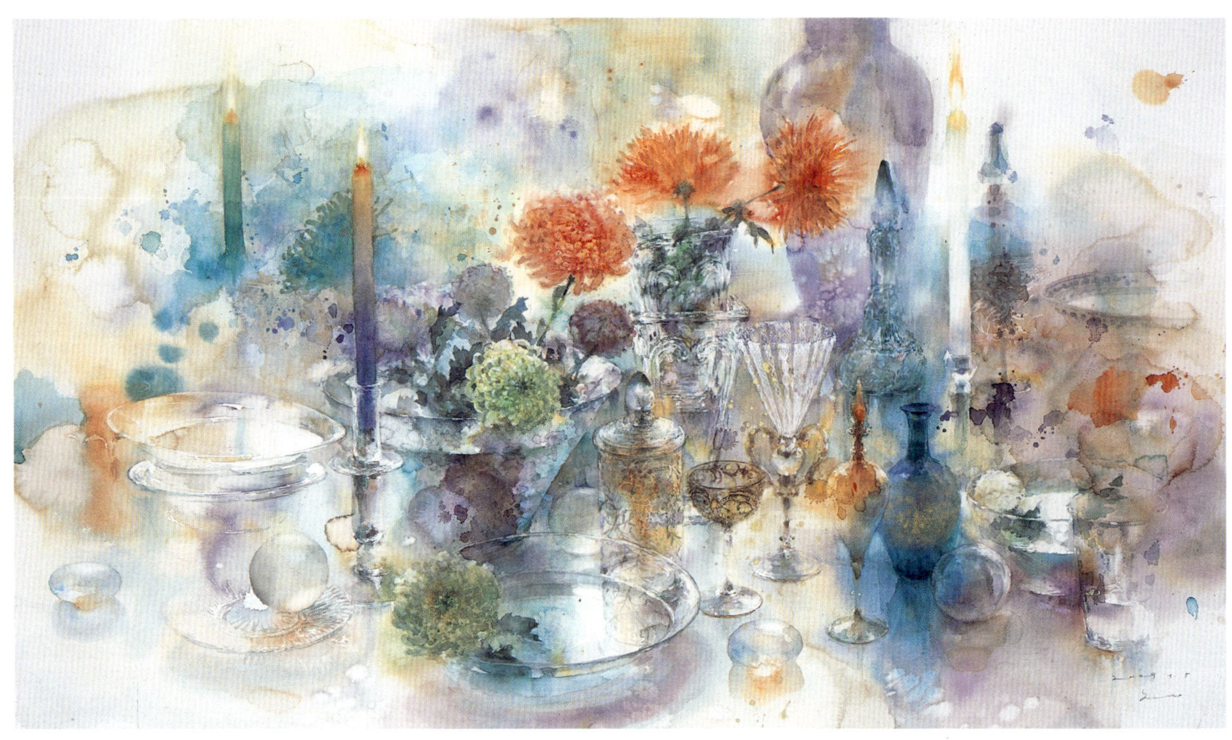

I love *Water Music* by Handel. I find that I get into a great rhythm while painting to it.

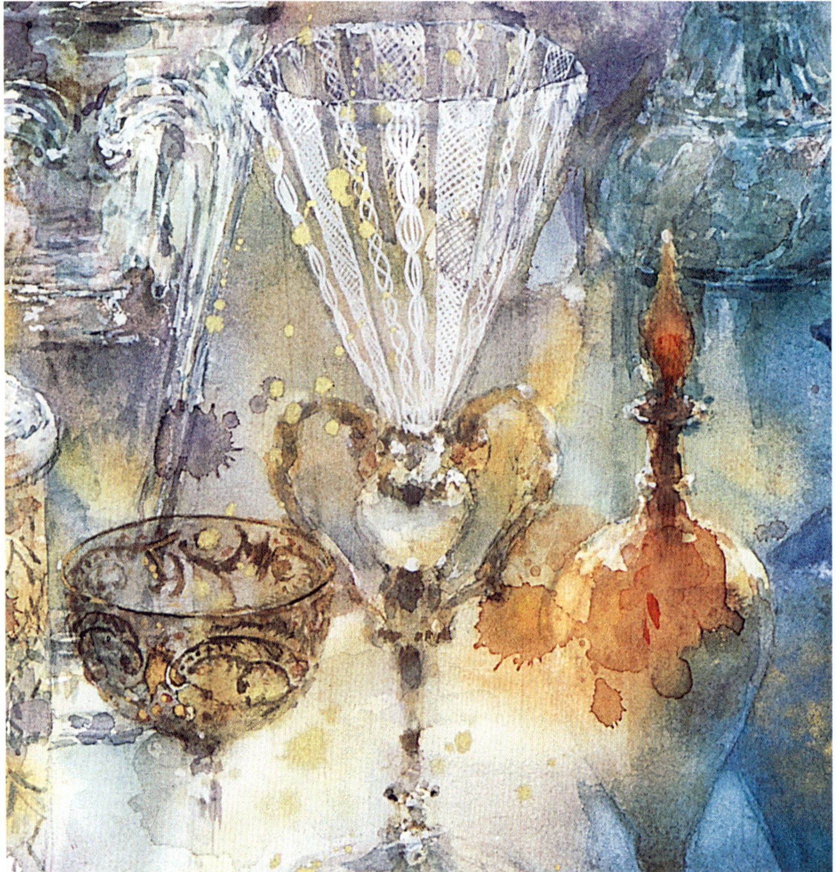

Mizu no Ue de Utau
(Singing on the Water)
28 x 46.5 in (71 x 118 cm)

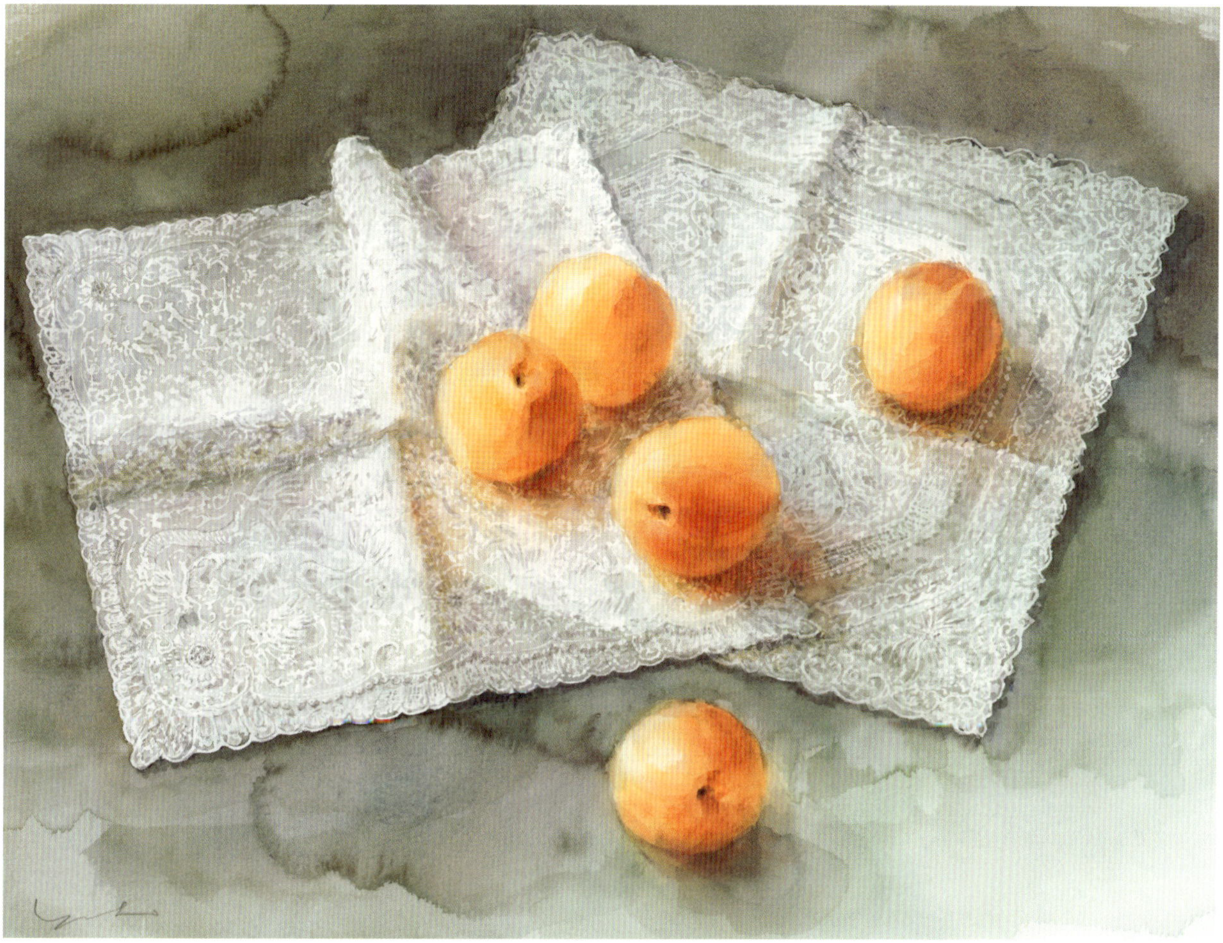

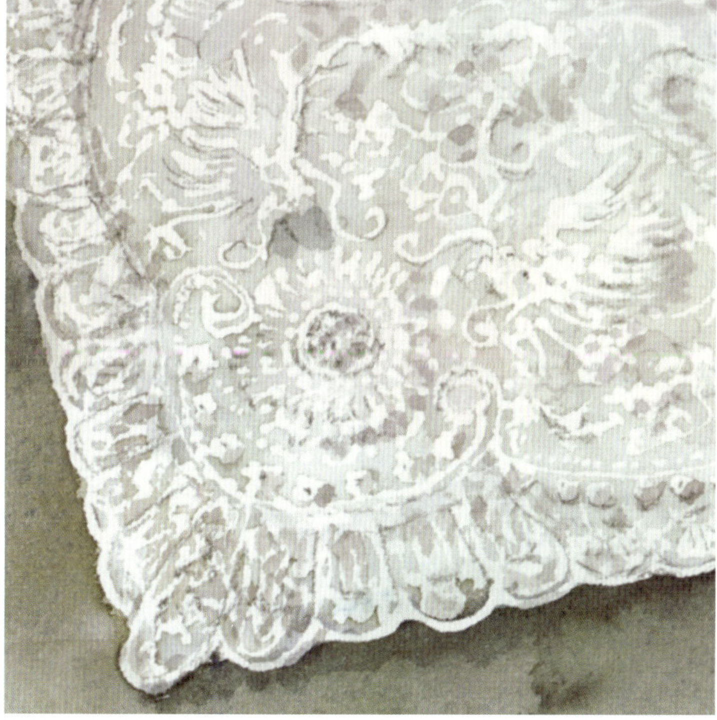

I intended this piece to look as though it were done by a Chinese artisan, so I painted it with masking ink to resemble needle work.

Anzu to Swatow
(Apricots and Swatow Lace)
15 x 19.25 in (38 x 49 cm)

Searching for Items to Use in Your Motif

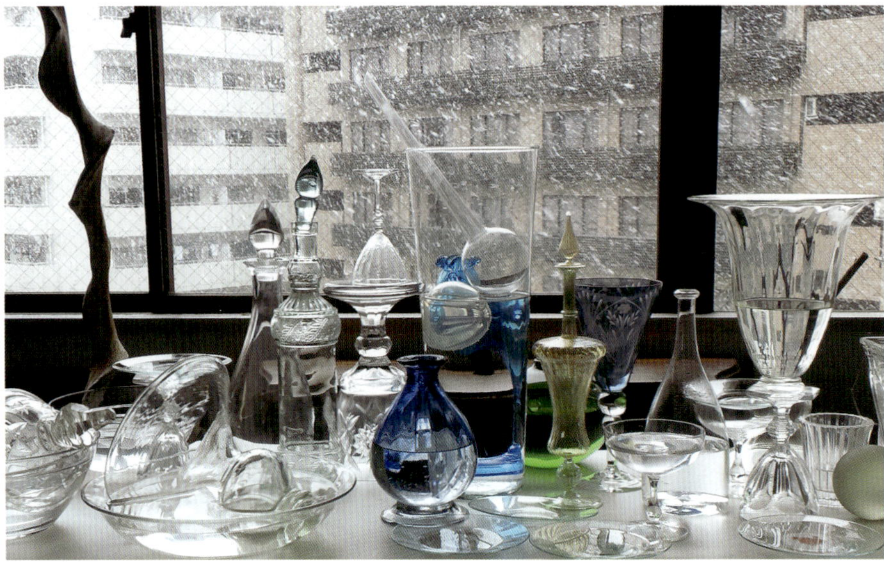

Why don't you start by collecting things that are on your mind? I wanted to paint blue glass bottles, so I asked my friends for some. As a result, little by little, empty blue glass wine bottles and Shochu bottles were brought to me. None of them were the same and, when I lined them up to paint, they looked like a crowd of people.

Even the same kinds of fruit and vegetables look different when examined individually.

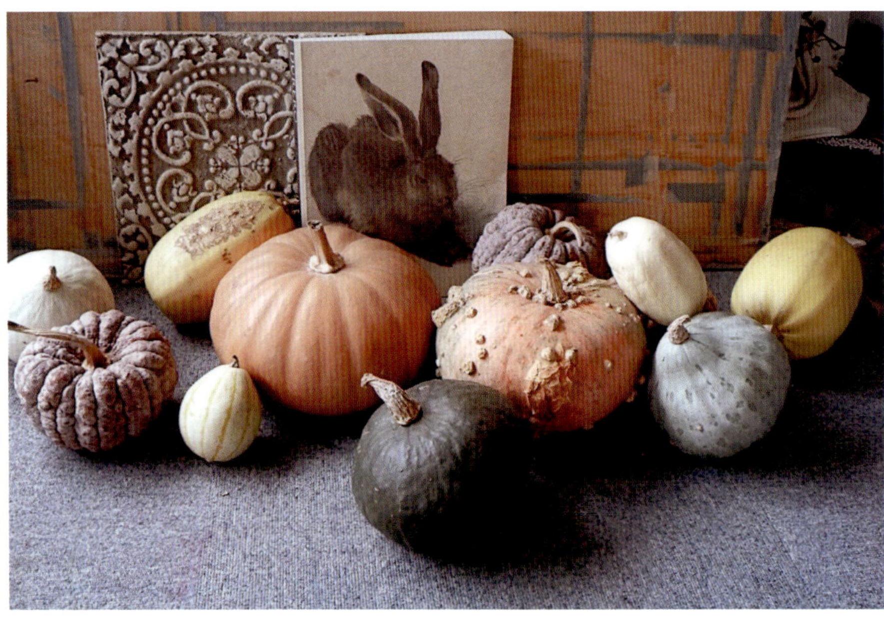

Chapter 4

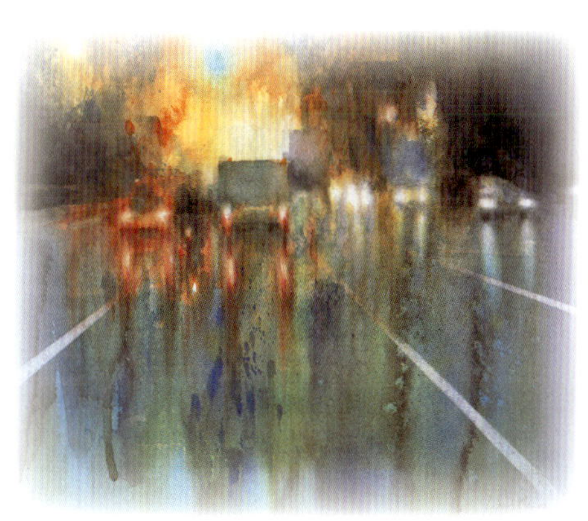

Landscapes

Drawing Venice: Photo Profiles

I rarely paint by looking at reference photos, but it is often impossible to paint an entire landscape with limited time. So, I take pictures and paint the scene after I get home.

In this chapter I summarize the method for using profiling procedures to draw perspective lines and then how to freely lay colors to complete. Through painting you can feel connected to places that you haven't even visited.

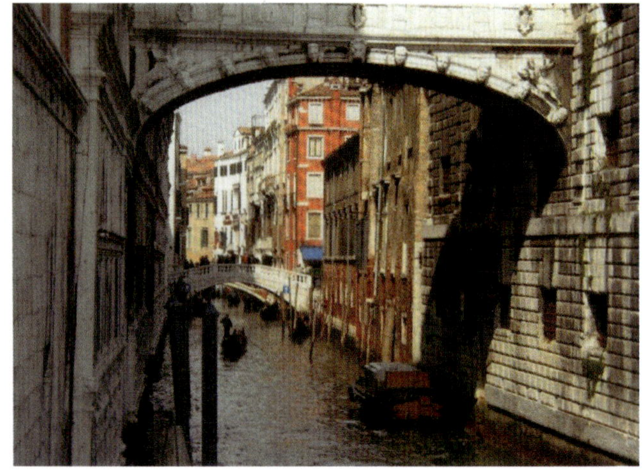

<table>
<tr><td>

Profiling

</td><td>

Profiling involves taking a monochromatic copy (or a photo) to draw in lines according to steps ① to ③.

</td></tr>
</table>

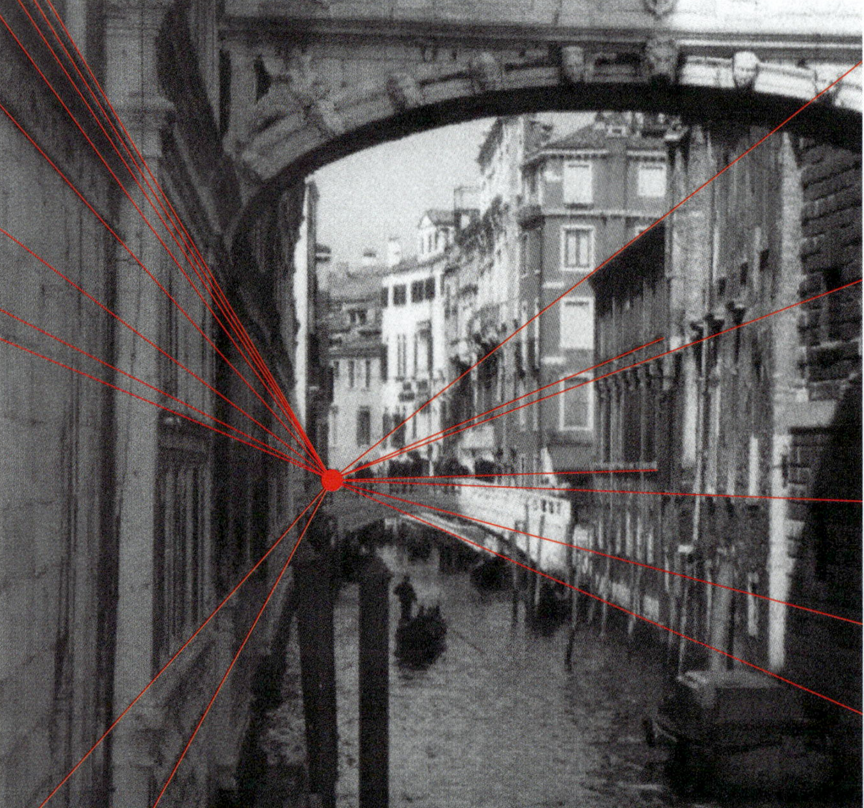

● Vanishing Point

First, locate the vanishing point.

① To locate the eye-level of the photographer, draw lines that follow the lines of the buildings toward the back. Usually they will concentrate in one spot. That is the vanishing point. This becomes the eye-level of the photographer.

Beginning to Sketch

1

Using a ruler, draw an eye-level line by looking carefully at the copy. This is the Profiling ② line.

2

From the vanishing point, draw lines like you did in Profiling ①.

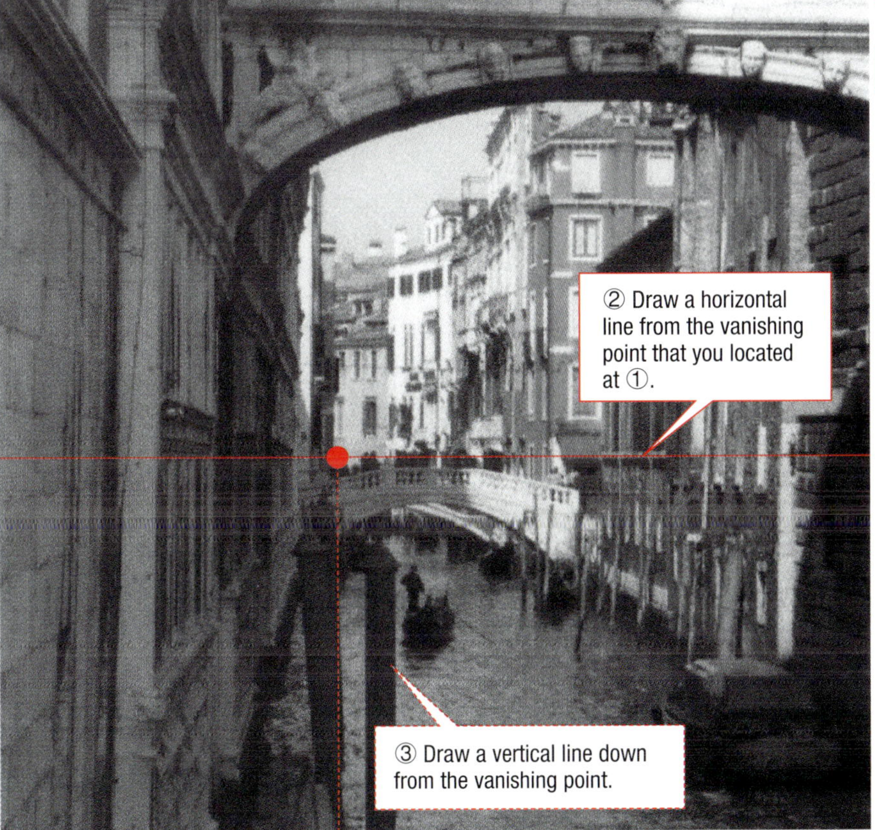

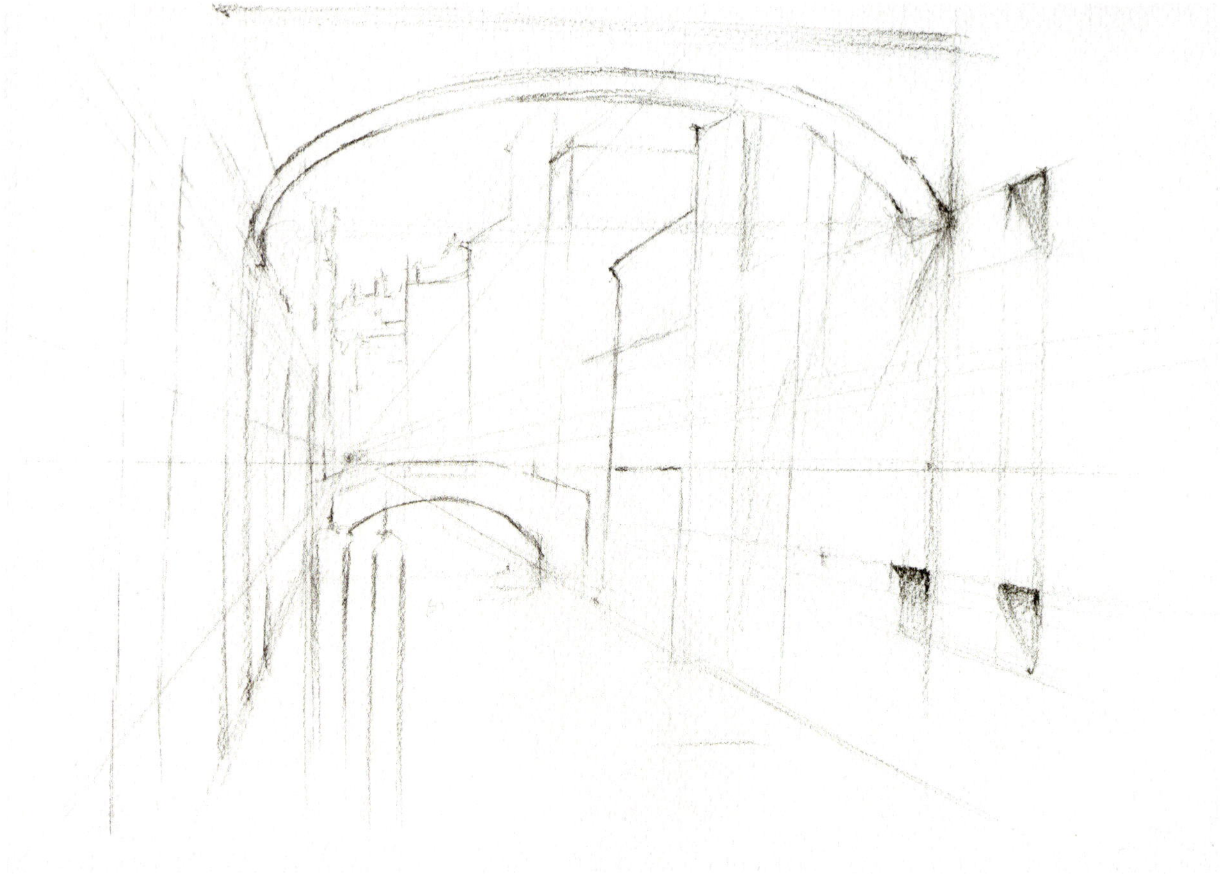

3

Capture the rough shapes of the buildings. The trick here is to not
yet draw in the details.

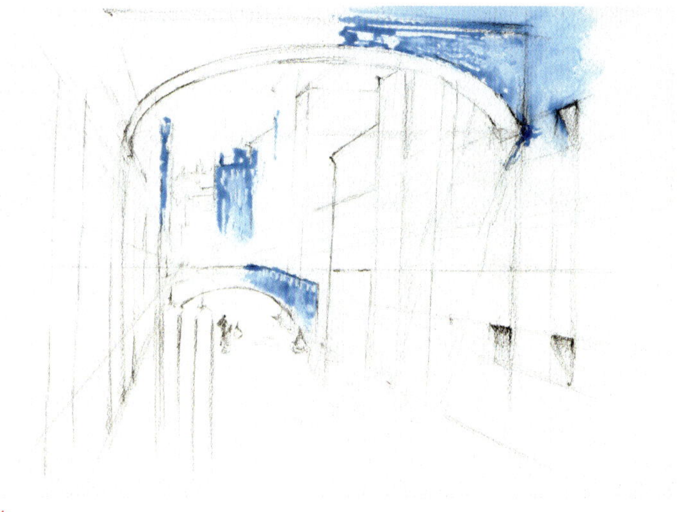

4

Apply masking ink where you intend to leave white spaces.

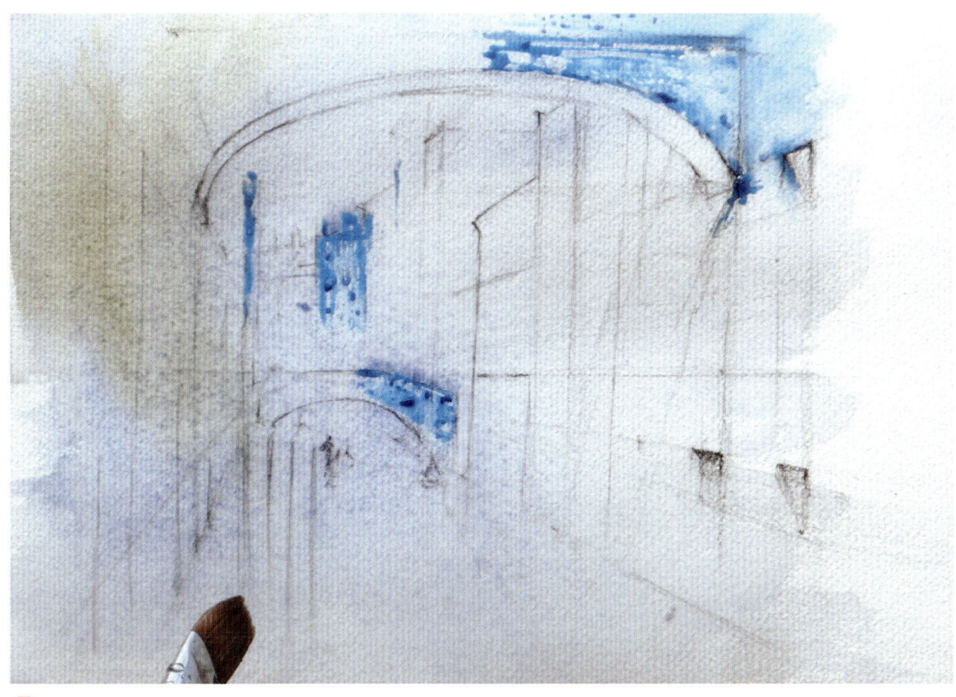

5

Stand the paper up and lay colors thinly over the entire surface.

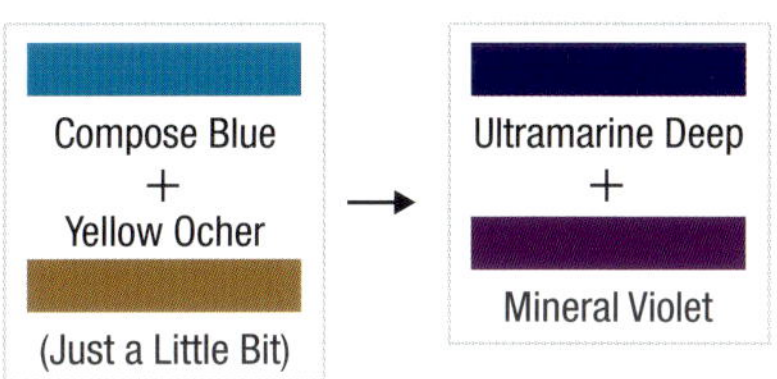

Stand the paper up and let the paints run before they dry.

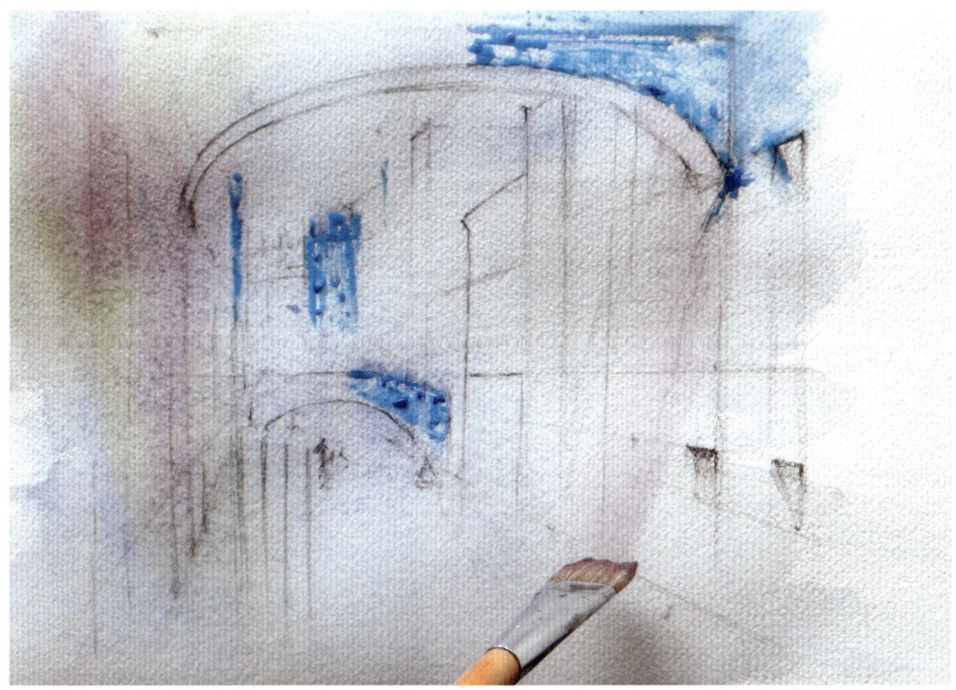

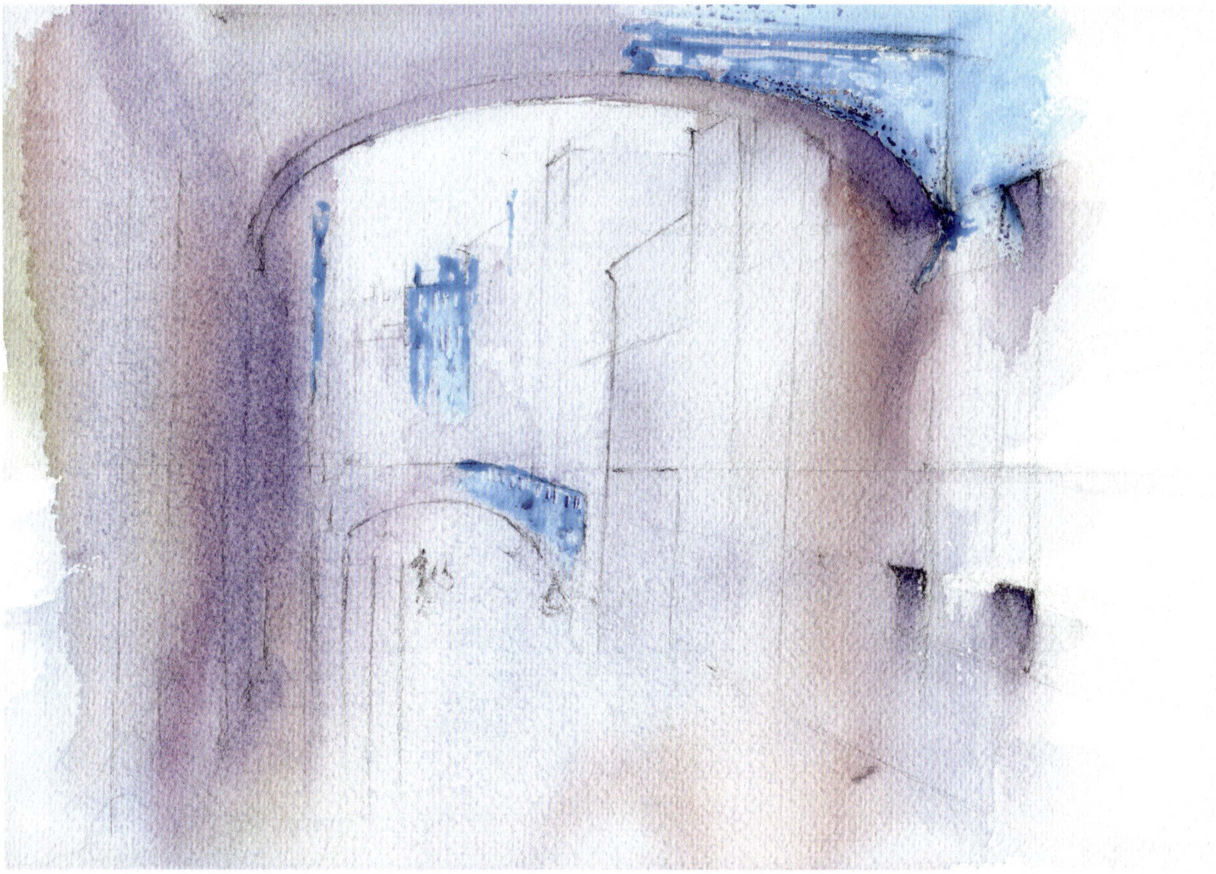

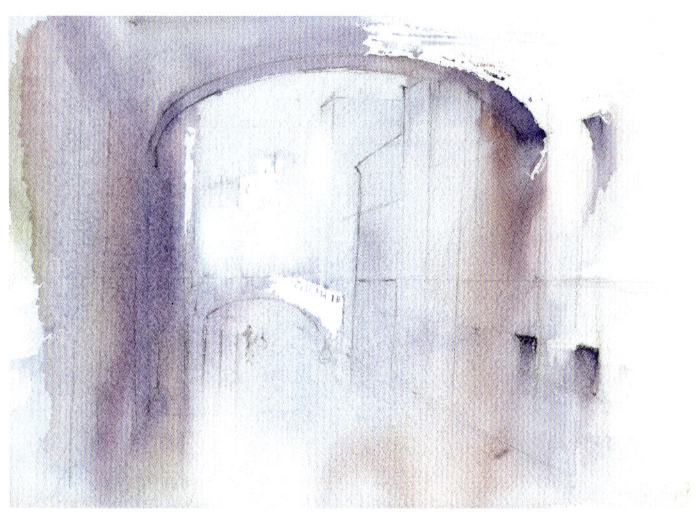

6

After laying colors on the entire surface . . .

7

Allow to dry and then remove the masking ink.

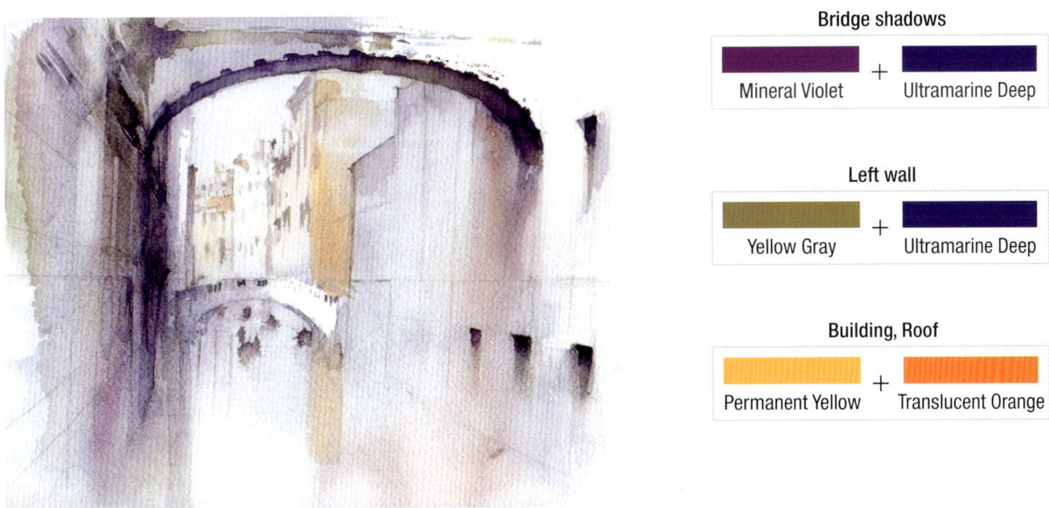

8

Paint in the shadows for the bridge and buildings.

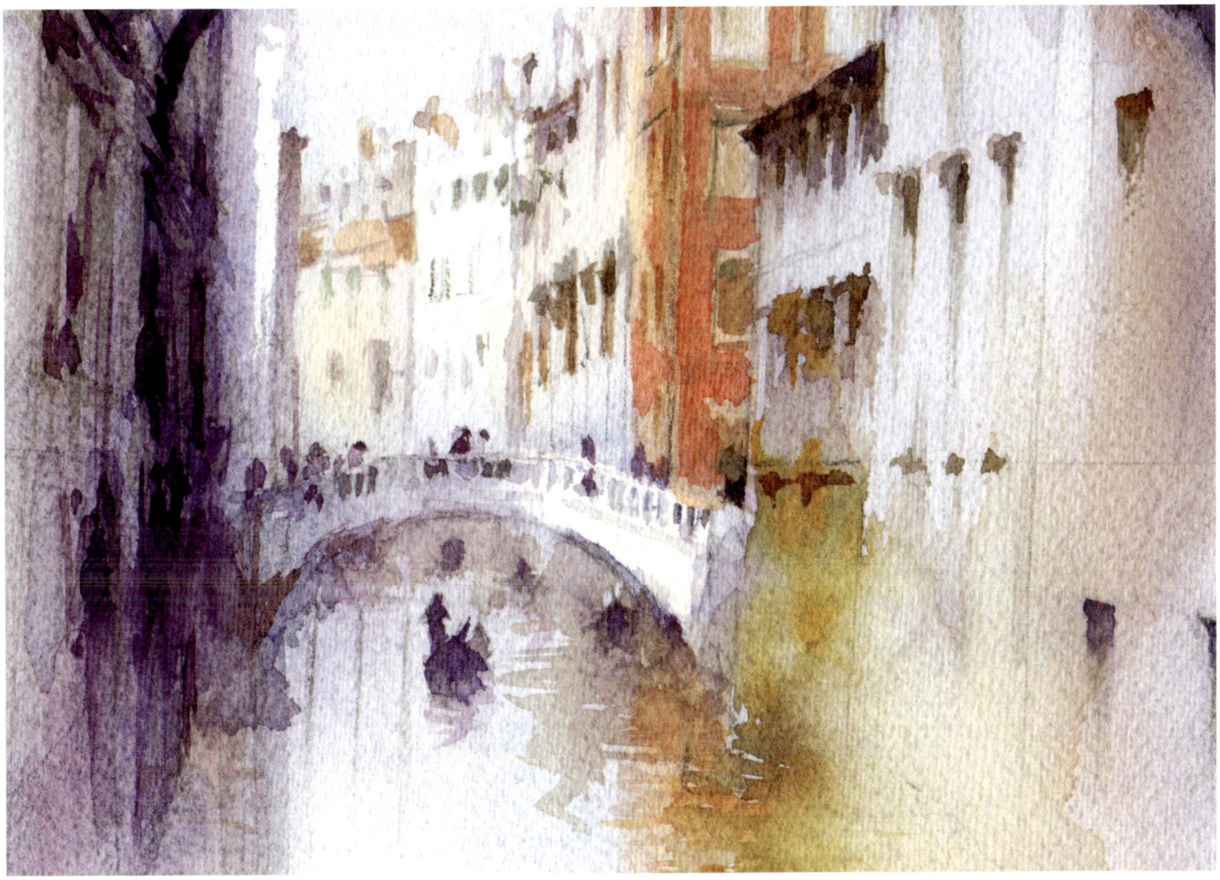

Add more shading.

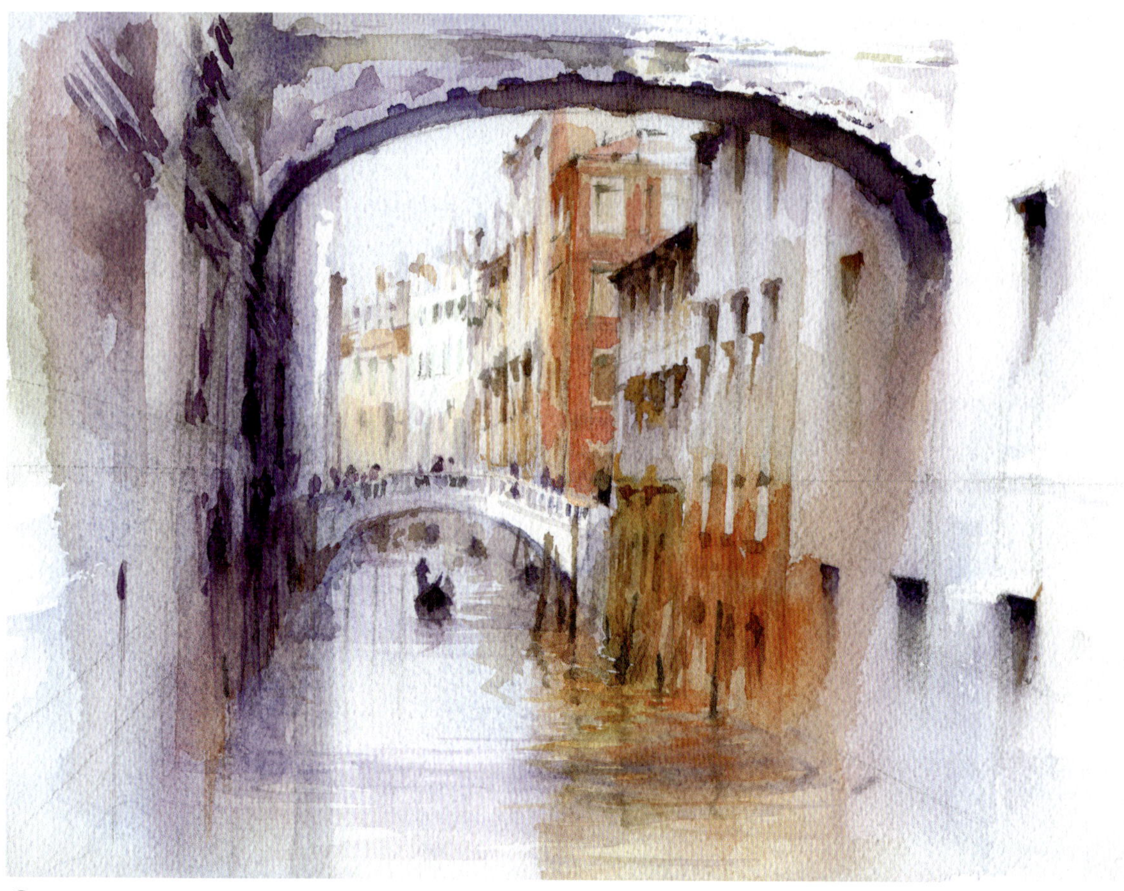

Complete

Paint in the remaining details and the shadows of the bridge to complete.

In my classes I give out monochromatic copies of a landscape photo to everyone. Then I have them begin to decipher the picture by drawing lines according to the Profiling procedures introduced in this book. They draw in those lines on a piece of paper and then start to create a rough outline. From this point forward, in addition to maintaining the basic concept of "painting from the rear," everyone lays down colors freely to complete.

When a landscape that I drew suddenly shows up on TV, it brings me a sense of closeness and I think, "I know this place. Oh, this place has such an atmosphere." In other words, we can connect to a place that we have never visited simply through painting.

If you have a favorite picture of a place that you have never visited, you should try to paint it.

What is Important in Landscape Sketching

These three points are most important:

1. Confirm the direction of light: Examine where your lighting (the sun) is coming from by the position of shadows on trees and buildings.

2. Confirm your eye-level height: Always draw your eye-level height in a landscape.

3. Decide the atmosphere of the picture you intend to depict.

I cannot forget what my friend, a Japanese-style painter, once told me. In ancient China the word *prosperous* was used to describe Chinese-style landscape paintings. When a painting was described by saying, "this painting is prosperous," it was a laudatory phrase that meant, "the painting expresses well the atmosphere found within this landscape."

It impresses us to see a painting where the concept of "the atmosphere lives within the landscape" is remarkably well depicted. No matter how realistic your painting though, even if you trace a photo exactly and capture every nuance, right down to its distorted images, you will never succeed in surpassing a photograph. Expressions such as, "It looks just like a photograph!" are not considered laudatory.

So, how should we go about painting "more freely"? Taking points 1 and 2 into consideration, it is possible to see how to use the colors to match the atmosphere in your landscape. Then, think about how to go about achieving that atmosphere, i.e., whether to place rear objects farther away, where to place emphasis, what should be omitted, and so on.

Regarding Landscape Painting that Initially Uses a Single Color

Some people say it is easiest to first examine it in light and shade. Others say that such a method does not work for them at all.

People who say that this method is easy to understand, or at least not that difficult, are those who paint while always keeping in mind light and shade. On the other hand, people who don't know where to put light and shade are most likely those who simply look at a motif by its color.

This practice of looking at light and shade is useful for landscapes, portraits, and still-life paintings.

For landscapes in particular determining where the sun is positioned and deciding the direction of light is very important. Having said that, by mastering the method of depicting light and shade precisely using a single color, you will be able to transform an ordinary landscape painting into a spacious landscape painting with greater depth.

When I start to sketch, if I think about how the sun rotates and then decide that "it is best to paint this building in the morning light," I will paint shadings on the building using the single-color method. Afterward, I will lay wall colors, roof colors, and intrinsic colors. I will explain this more in the pages that follow.

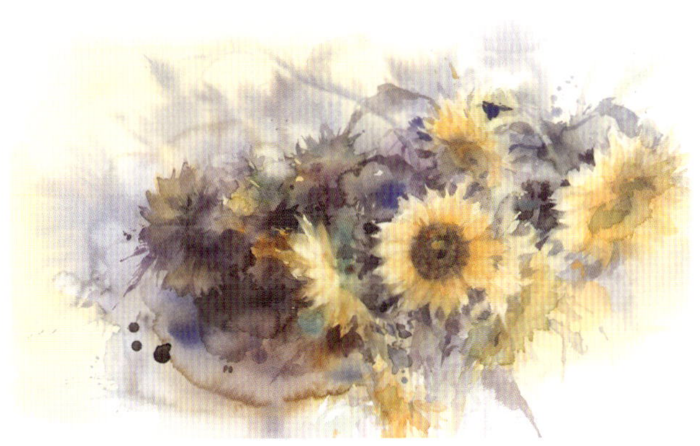

Drawing British Landscapes: Inserting Human Figures

The method for painting through shading is used here. Regardless of whether it is an open space or town scenery, even if there are people and animals, it would be disappointing not to attempt a painting just because you feel it is slightly difficult. Once you master certain tricks, it is not that bad at all.

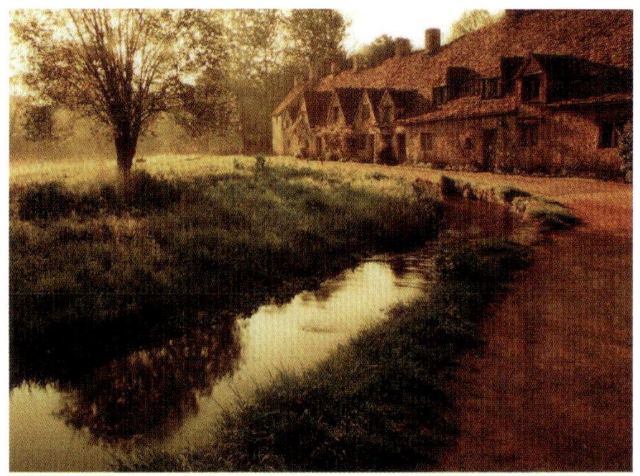

<table>
<tr><td style="border:1px solid; padding:8px;">Profiling</td><td>Use a monochromatic copy (or a photo) and draw lines according to steps ① to ③.</td></tr>
</table>

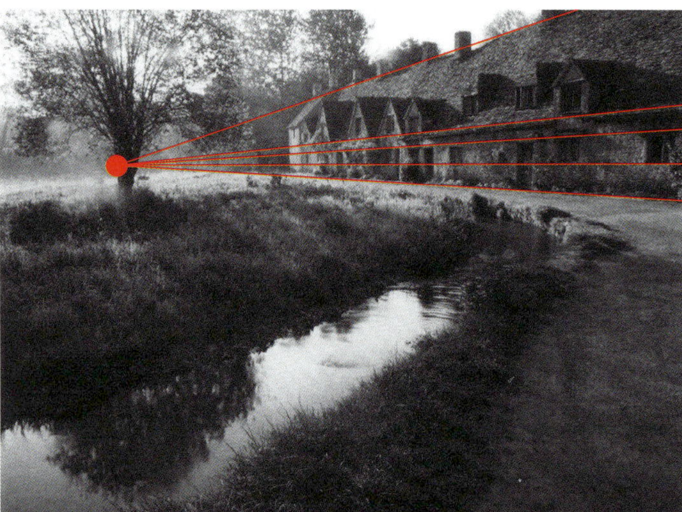

① Draw lines along the buildings to determine the point where those lines meet. The point becomes your (or the photographer's) viewpoint. In this case, it is approximately at the tree.

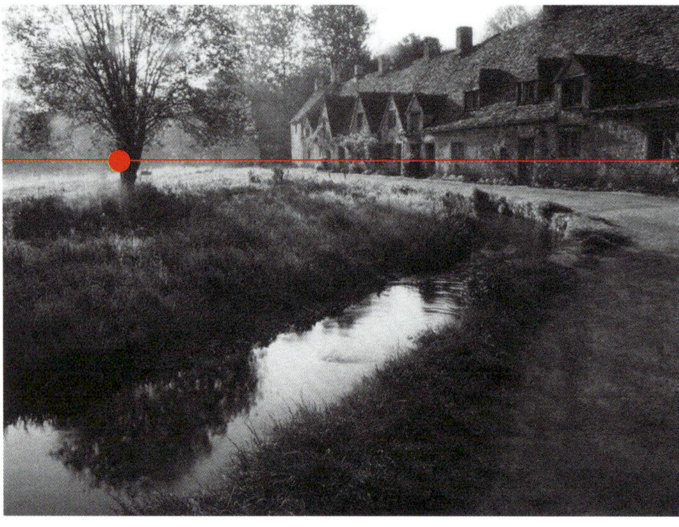

② From the point that you located in step ①, draw a horizontal line. This will be the eye-level height. This indicates that the camera was placed at a height slightly higher than the middle of the door of the building. That is about chest height for an adult. Was it taken using a tripod?

Beginning Your Sketch Lines

The tree shadow in the stream. Draw the whole thing straight down.

1

Begin to draw using the photo. Copy the viewpoint and the eye-level height onto a piece of paper using a ruler.

2

This time draw lines backward from the viewpoint in order to draw the building shape as seen in the first Profiling ①.

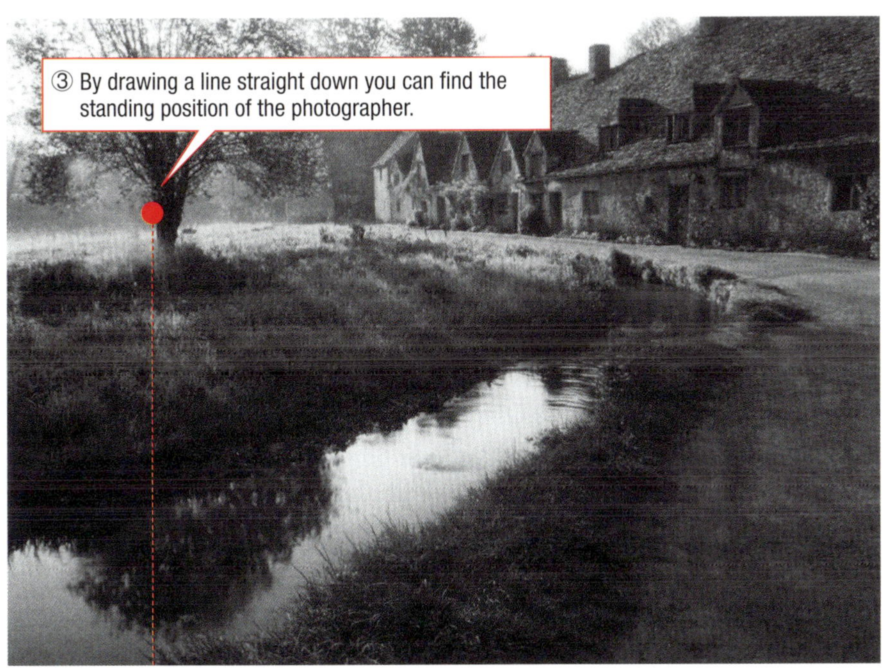

Considering the findings above we see that profiling draws the conclusion that this person is taking the photograph from behind the stream while using a tripod. At least, that is my reasoning.

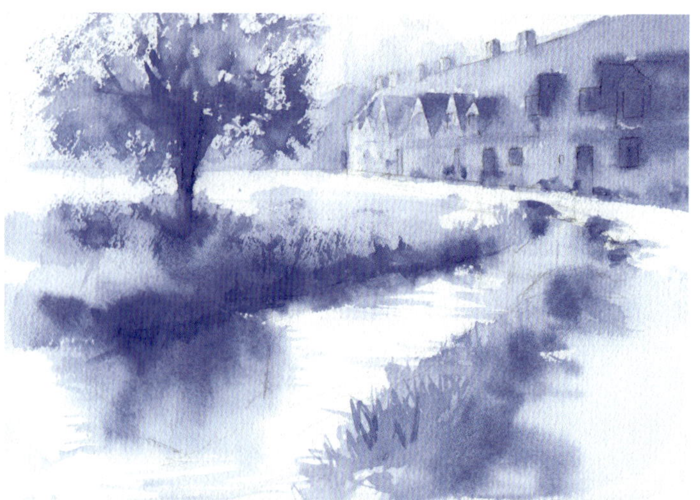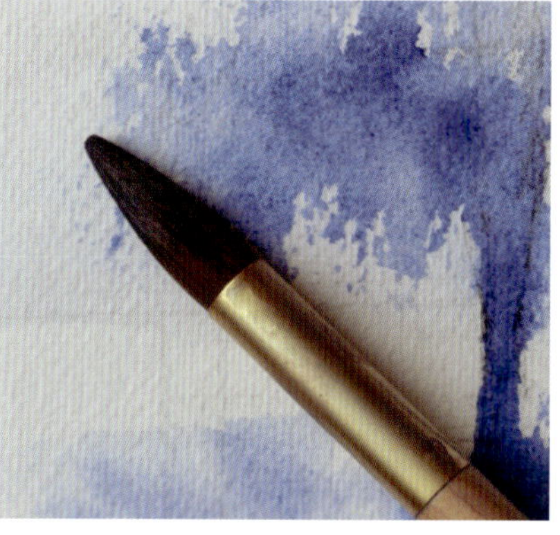

3

Copy the same shading that is seen in the photograph onto a piece of paper. In the beginning using a monochromatic copy for reference is a good practice. To get the expressions on the leaves of the tree, lay the brush down and rub it against the rough surface of the paper.

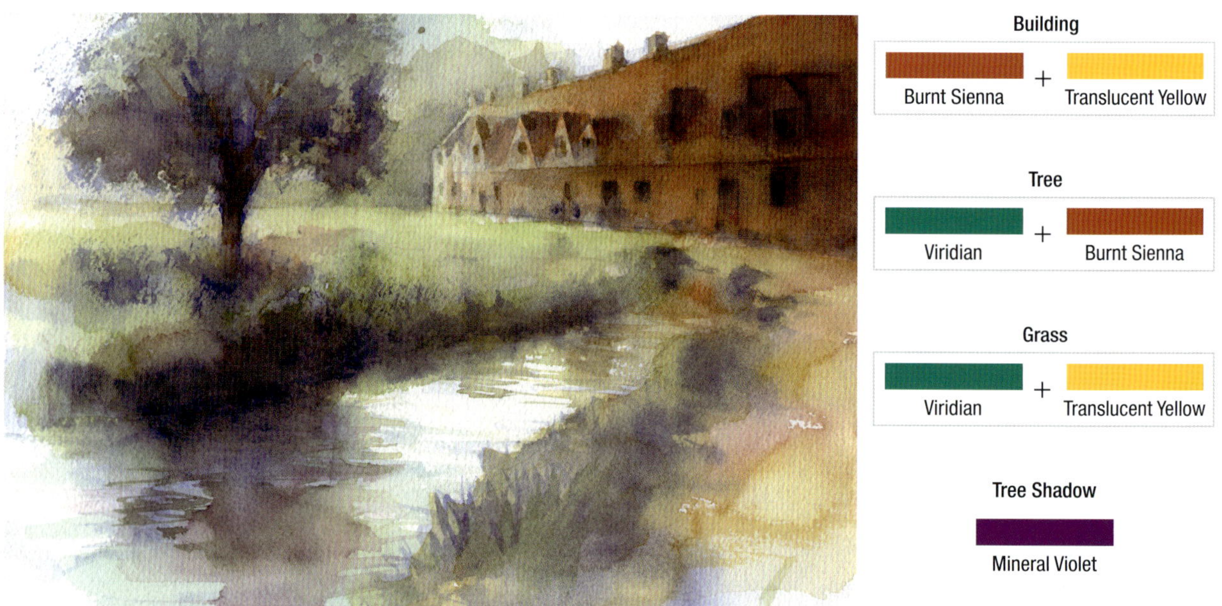

4

Let it dry completely and then lay down each intrinsic color.

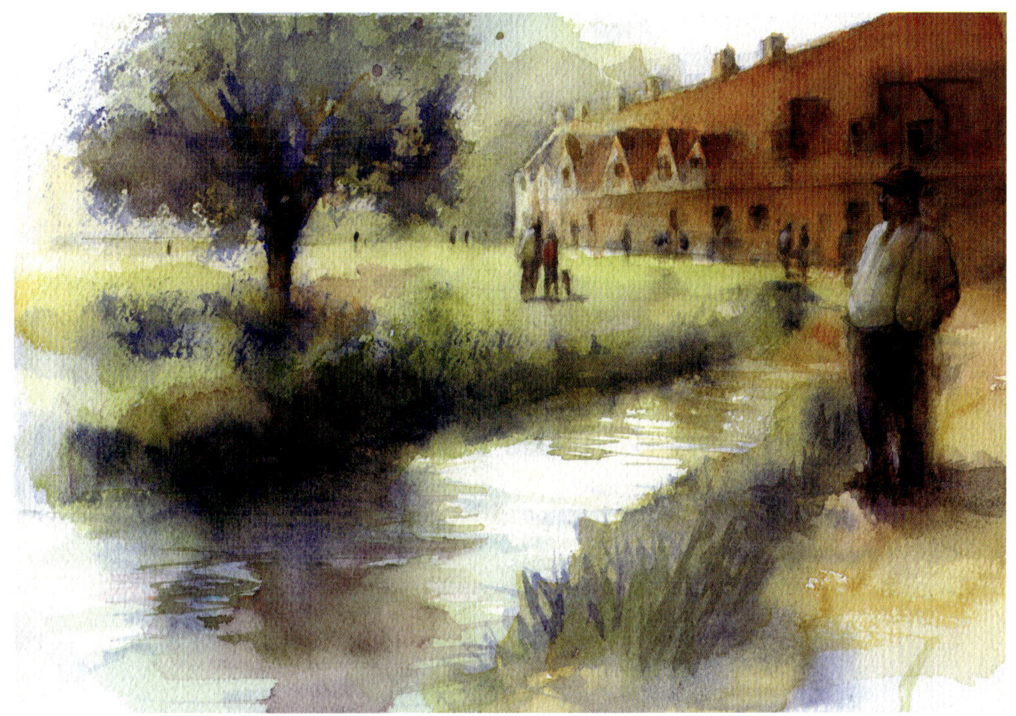

Complete

I painted the human figures just by imagining what it would be like if they were standing in this garden.

Let's remember the viewpoint (eye-level) rule.

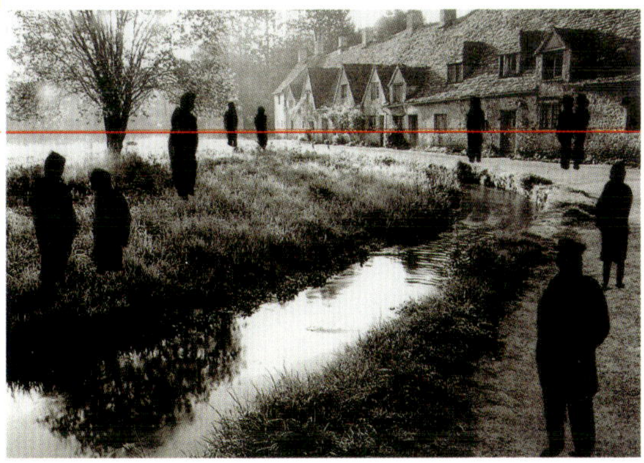

Bad Example

A human figure in the foreground is positioned lower and a human figure in background is positioned higher. Thus, the size of the human figures is inconsistent.

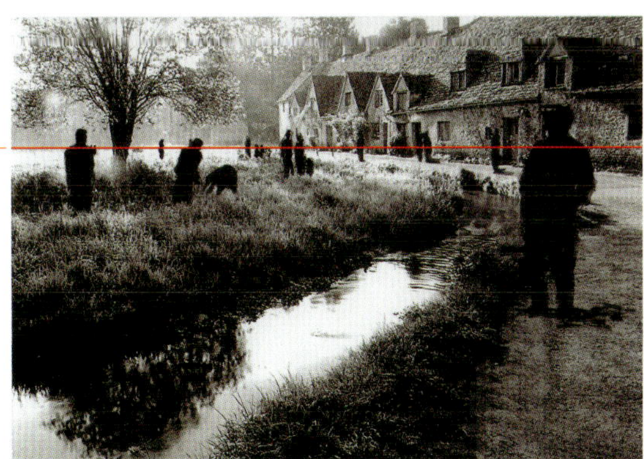

Good Example

Regardless of the position of the human figures, the viewpoint comes to approximately chest height. When drawing small children, consider their height and draw them below the viewpoint.

Birds Within Landscapes

Aside from humans, all sorts of animals exist within landscapes: someone walking a dog, other animals mixed in with a carriage, birds flying by freely, and so on. Do not simply think that it is hard to draw a bird. Once you master the tricks introduced below you will be able to capture their shape quickly.

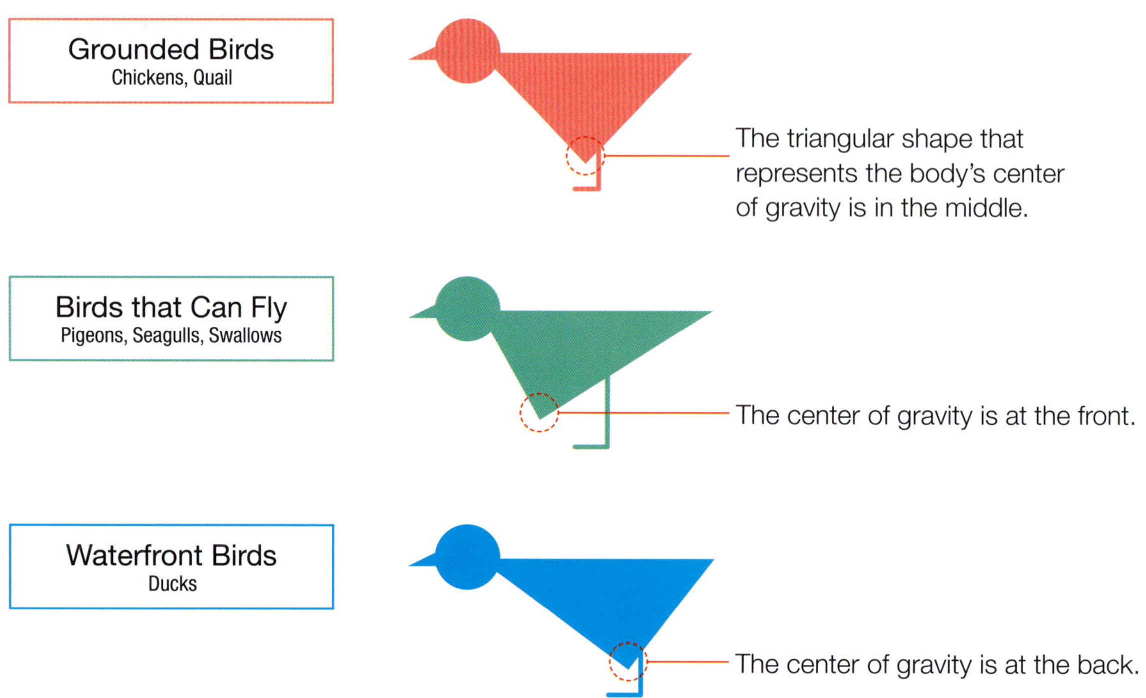

Grounded Birds

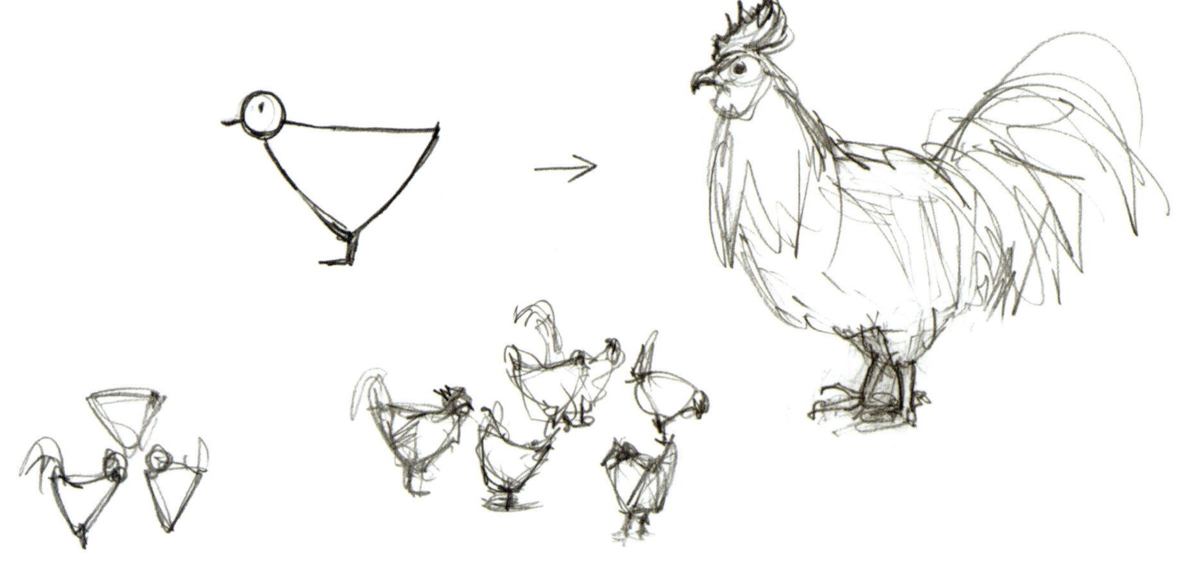

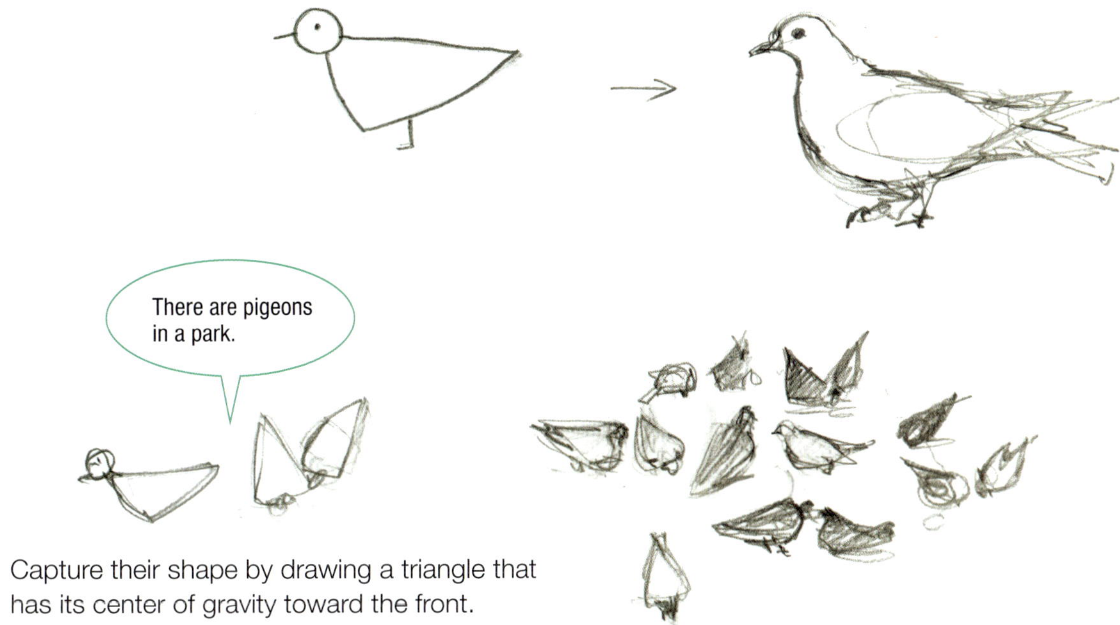

Capture their shape by drawing a triangle that
has its center of gravity toward the front.

Waterfront Birds

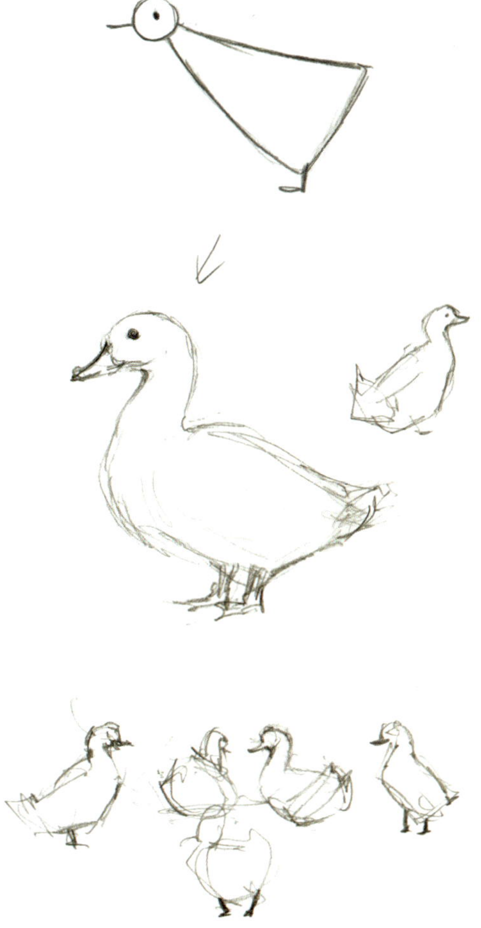

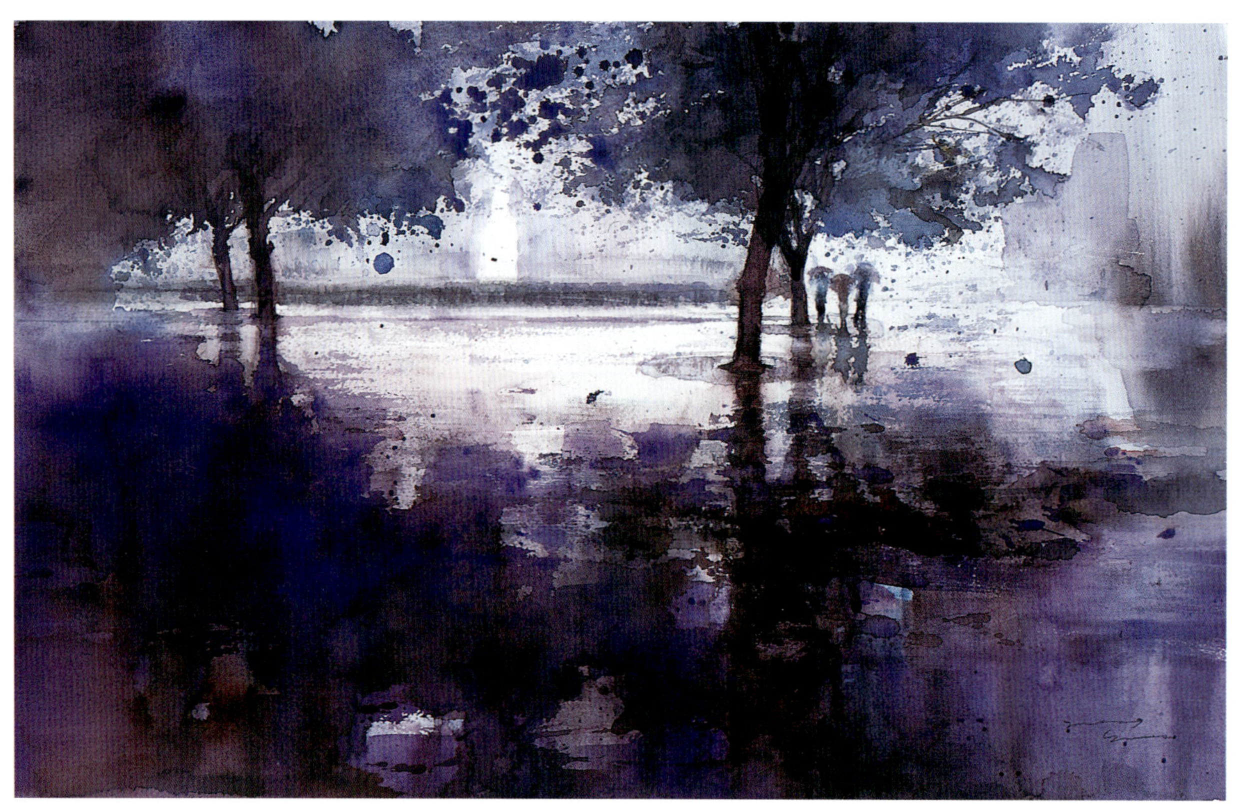

Ueno Koen (Ueno Park)
13.25 x 20.25 in (33.5 x 51.5 cm)

When I see this painting, the smell of the park and the sound from the fountain at the time I painted it comes back to me. This scenery no longer exists in Ueno. I am glad that I painted it.

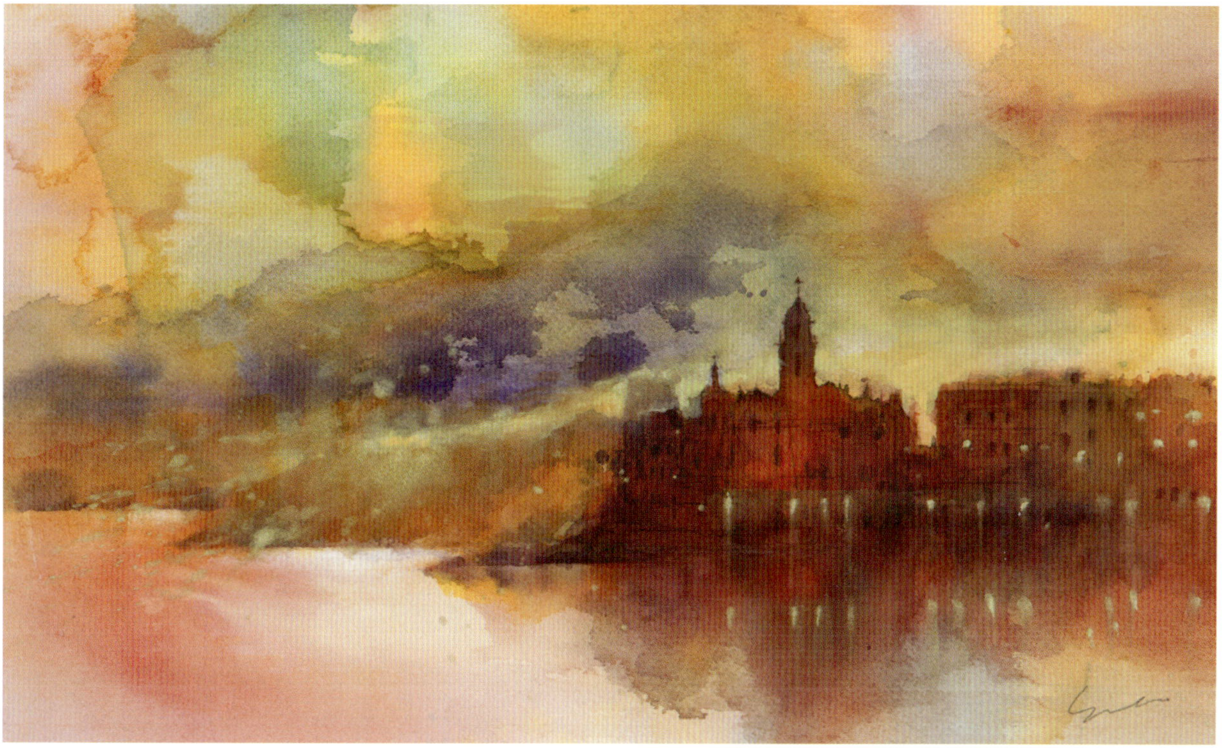

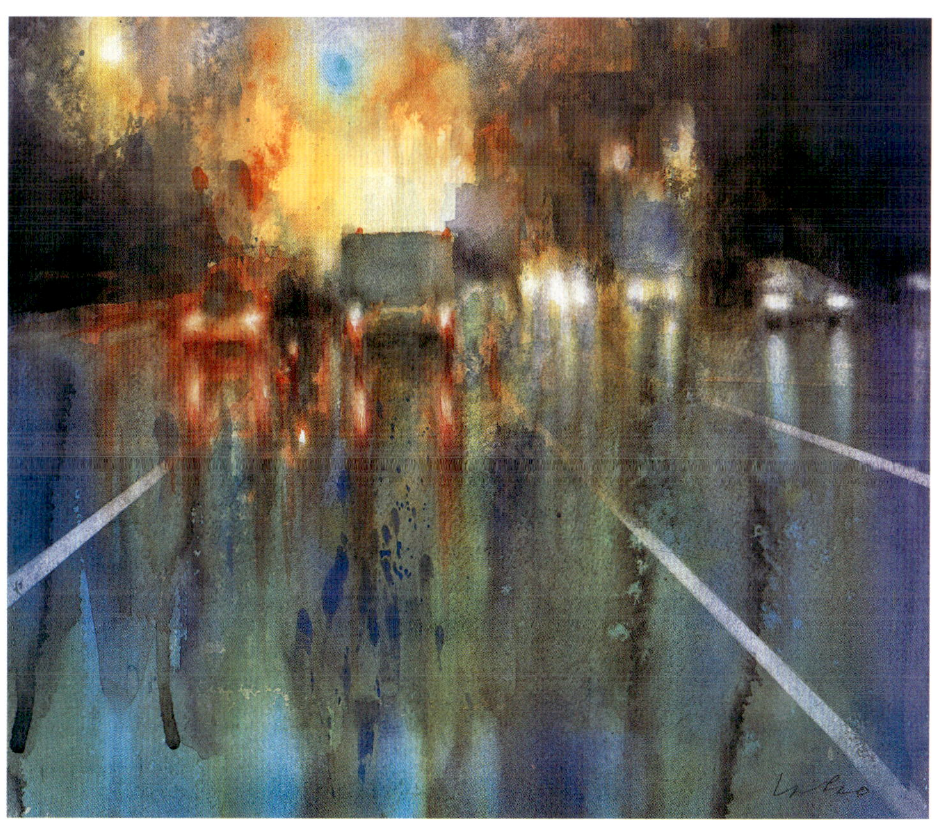

Do not paint exactly what you see. Rather, paint in a way that expresses what you desire to see.

Camogli (Camogli, Italy)
22.5 x 17.25 in (57 x 44 cm)

I painted this from a photograph that I took with a cellphone from the passenger seat of a car.

Ame (Rain)
10.25 x 11.75 in (26 x 30 cm)

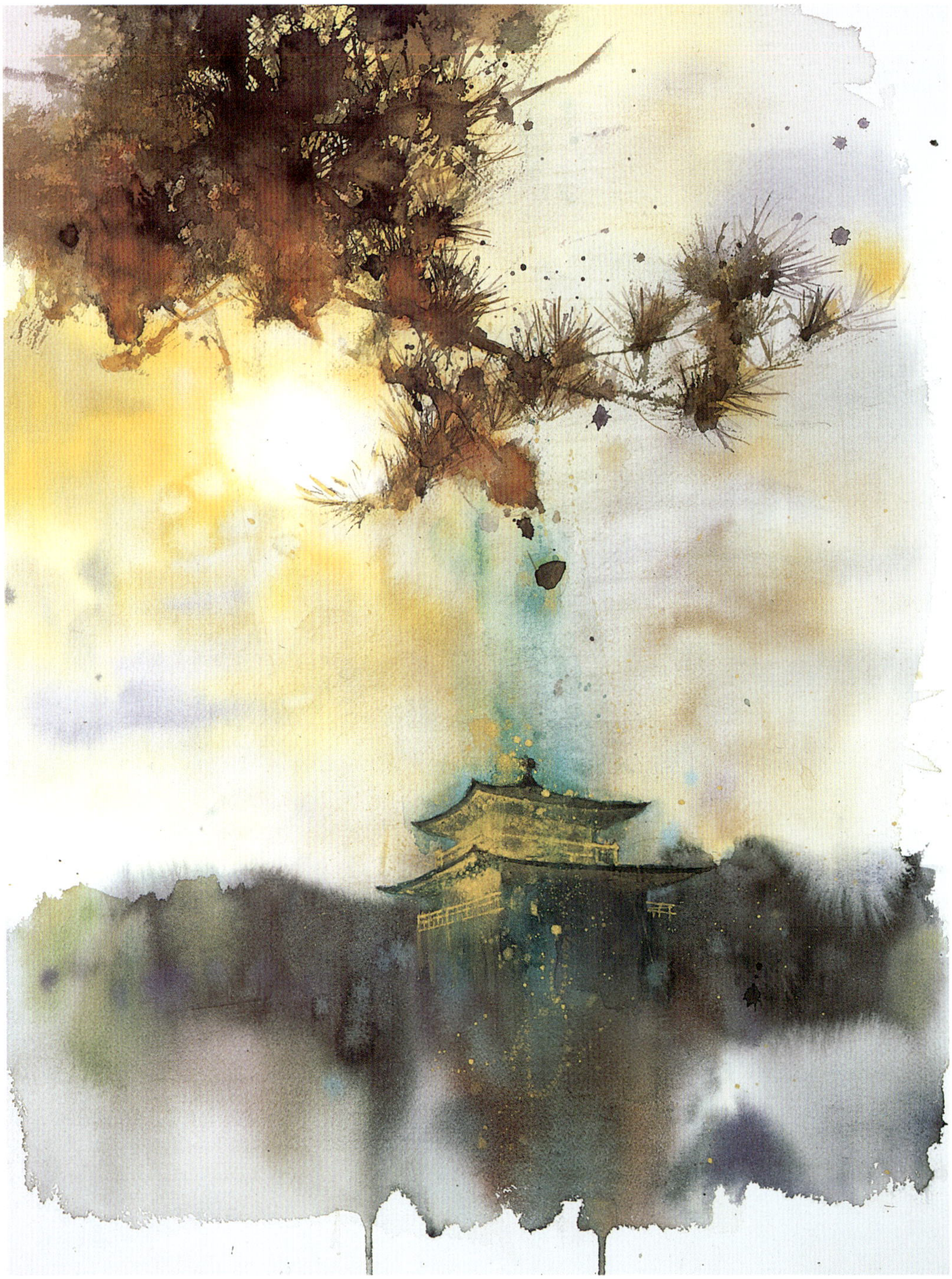

The Japanese incorporated the metallic elements of silver and gold in home decor and fashion by applying these tones in paper sliding doors, kimono and fan patterns, and other everyday items.

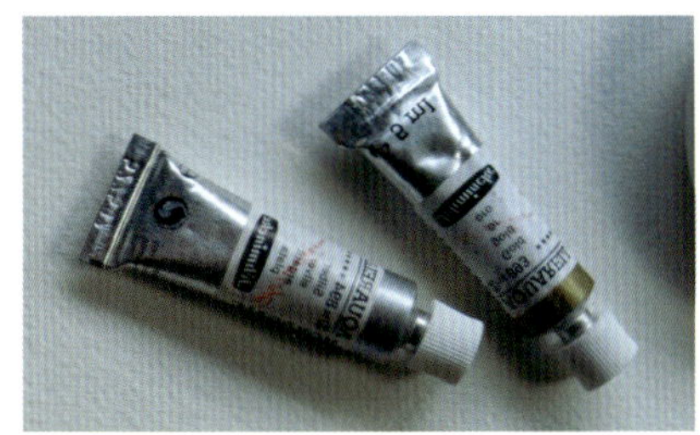

Kinkakuji (The Golden Pavilion in Kyoto)
23.25 x 17.25 in (59 x 44 cm)

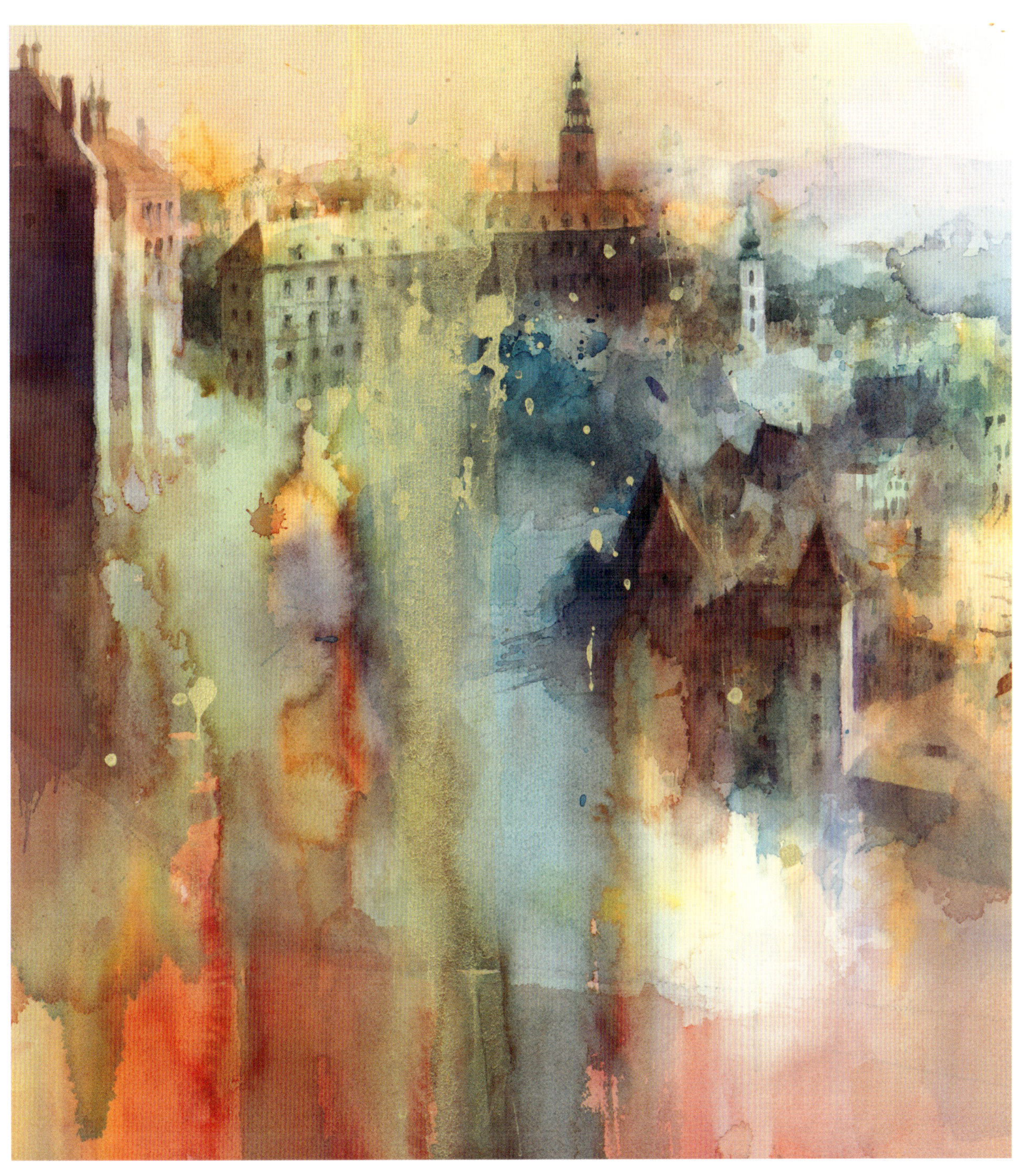

While I was painting this I was slightly afraid, as if I were
being sucked into the overwhelming space.

Český Krumlov
(Český Krumlov, Czech)
19.75 x 22.5 in (50 x 57 cm)

Things to Keep in Mind

As a watercolor enthusiast it is truly a delight to see the growing number of people engaging in painting. At the same time, there are increasing occasions when I hear things that make my ears tingle. I would like to talk about proper manners for landscape sketching and for when you invite models to be painted.

Recently, increasing number of temples and important cultural properties have begun to prohibit sketching and photography. I asked the reason for this and received the following answers: Water used for watercolors has been improperly disposed of, painters were taking up space by setting up their equipment on benches for long periods of time, painters put a tripod or an easel in restricted areas, and so on. So, you should always take your water home with you or drain it in a nearby bathroom. Also, it is okay to sit on a bench but take just enough space for you to sit. If you pay attention to these points you should be able to sketch without inconveniencing others.

In addition, given that beginners may not be aware of the proper manners when asking someone to model for them, I would like to touch upon these manners. While a model is posing for you, do not leave your studio. You should lock the door and prohibit access to your studio while a model is posing, especially when they are posing nude. Of course the same applies for posing in a costume. Photography of nudes or costumes is prohibited. In cases where you wish to take a photograph you must ask the model for permission first and then go ahead only if they sign a waiver. Usually, professional models charge extra for photographs. While a model is posing it is considered bad manners to not concentrate on drawing them or to talk to them, or otherwise engage your model. For long breaks it is proper to serve beverages and snacks to your model. Please do not forget to show your appreciation.

This might all seem a bit nitpicky but the aforementioned manners are quite important and you should definitely keep them in mind.

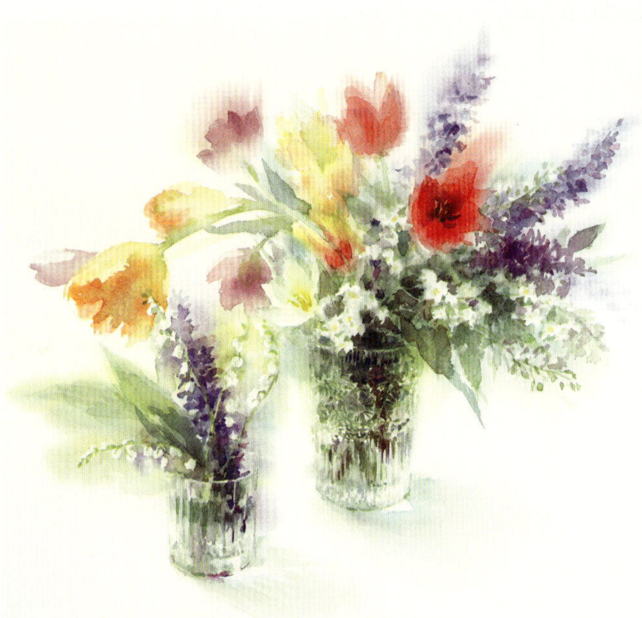

Chapter 5

Portraits

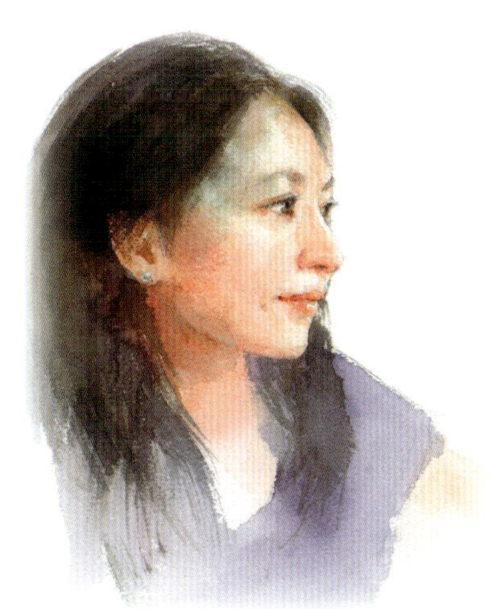

Profiles

I like painting in profile. I feel awkward when I am face-to-face and very close to someone. However, when I paint a profile I can get fairly close to someone without getting nervous.

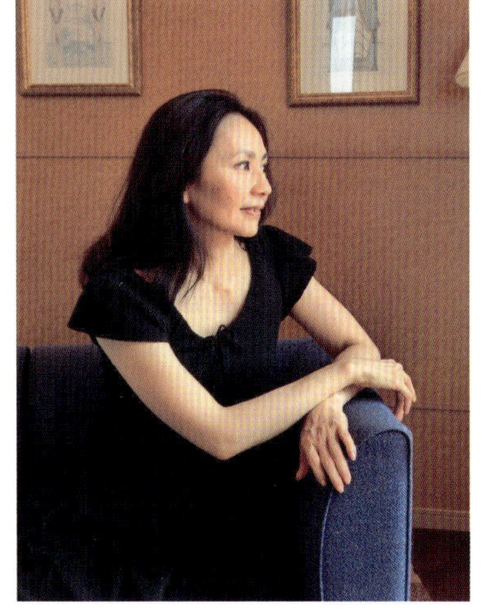

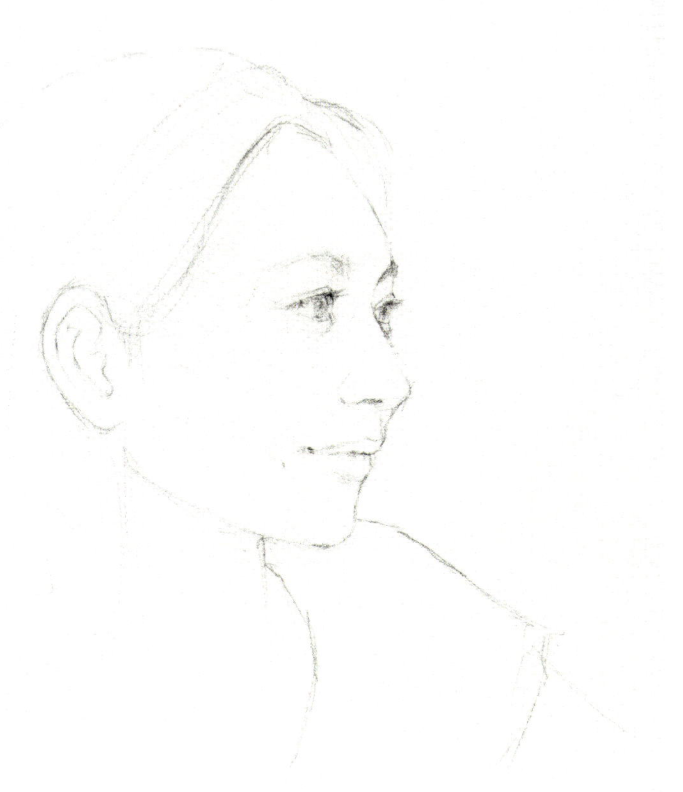

1
Sketch the profile with a pencil.

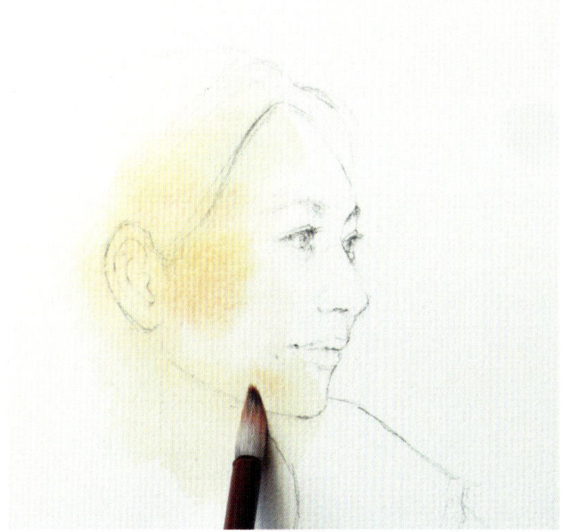

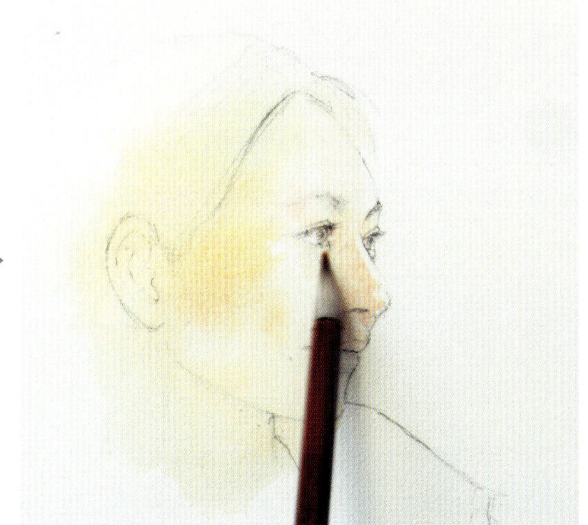

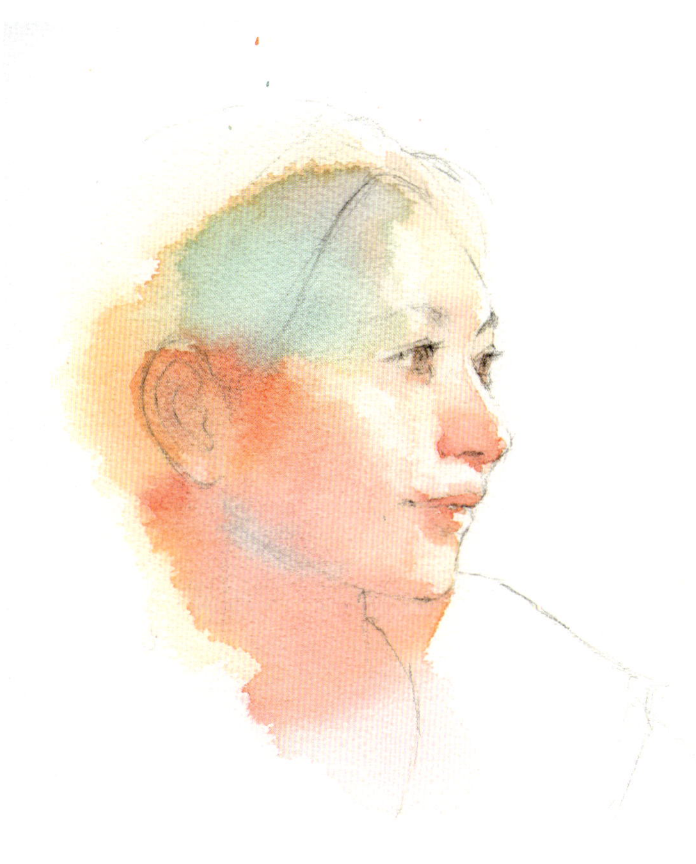

2

Where the model's skin is thin it looks bluish, even though it is labeled "flesh color." I did the underpainting a little boldly. The skin continues under the model's hair so lay colors under the hair and not just on the face.

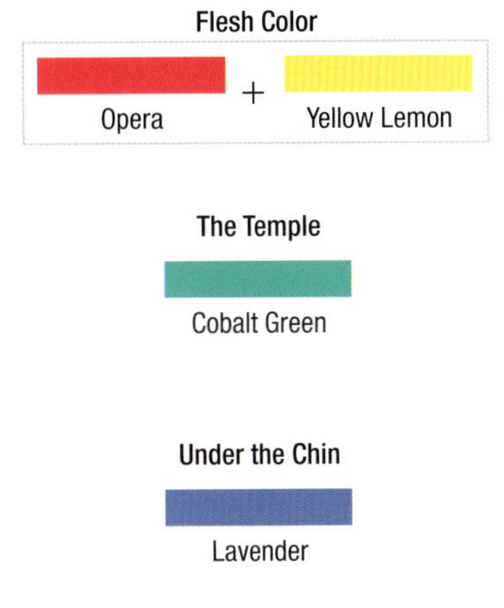

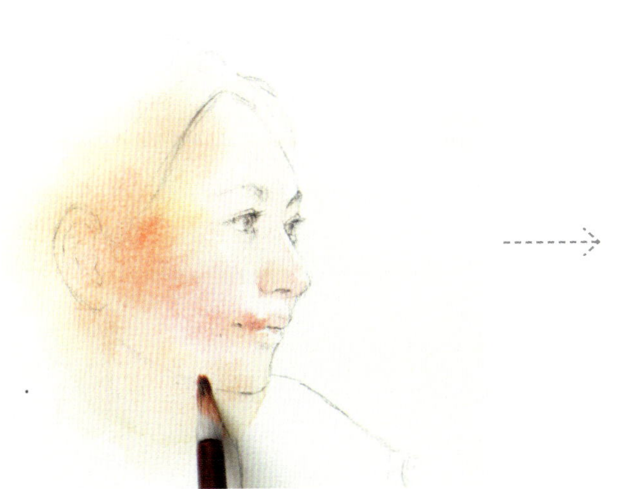

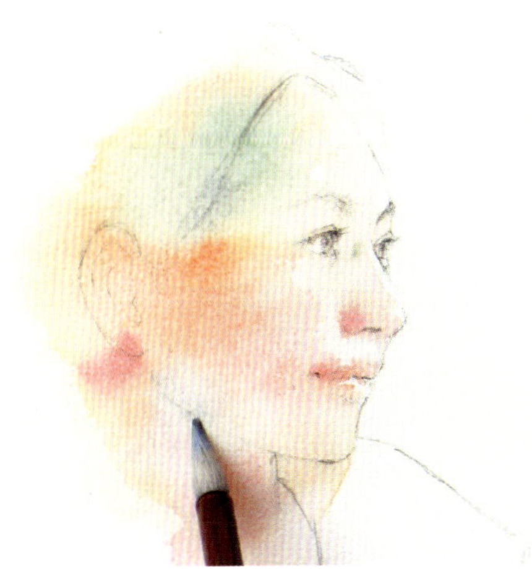

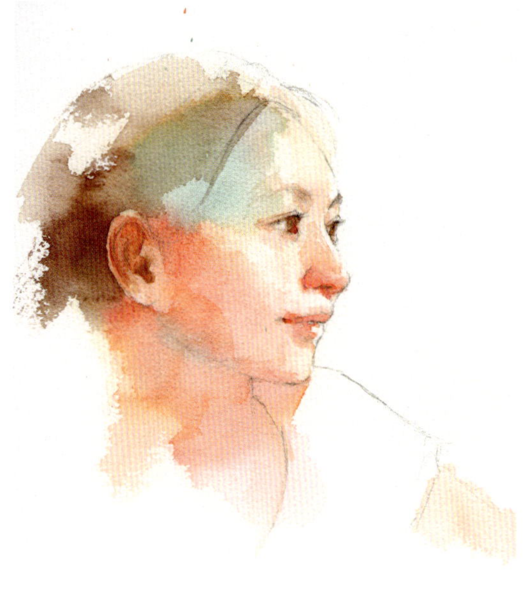

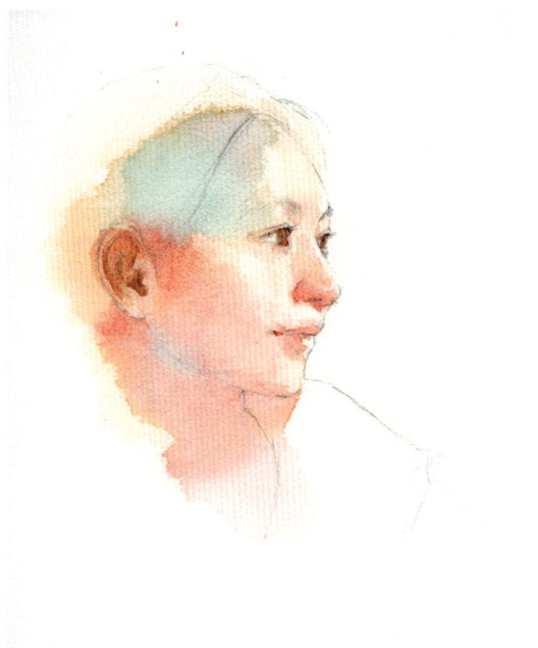

3

The basic form for an ear is fixed. It is very helpful to remember this basic form.

Hair Color

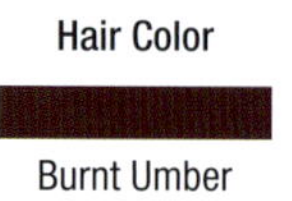

Burnt Umber

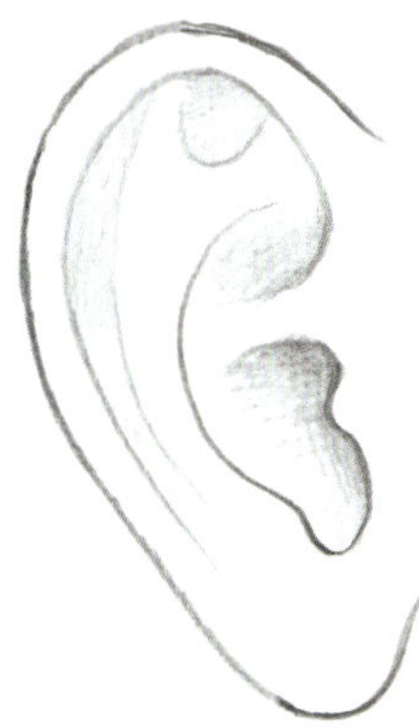

4

After confirming the position of the cheekbone, add shading accordingly.

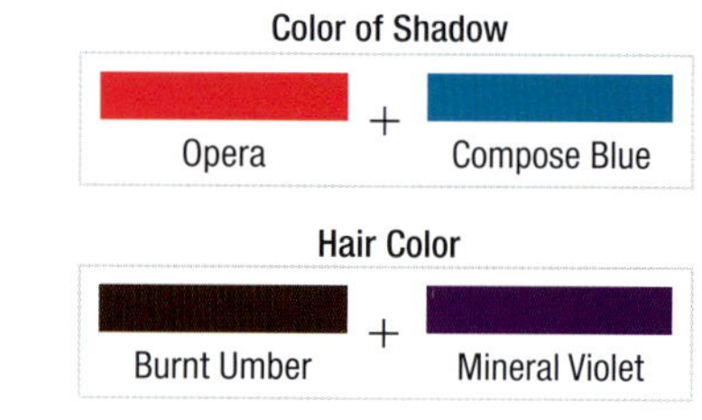

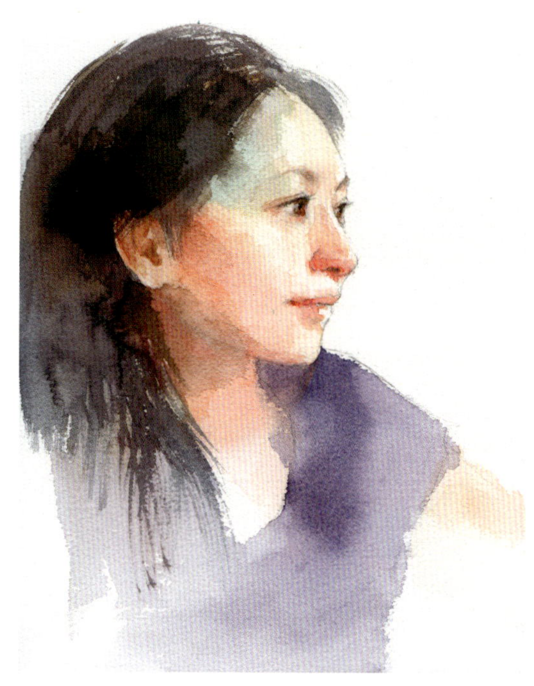

5

Be careful to balance the color of the hair when painting.

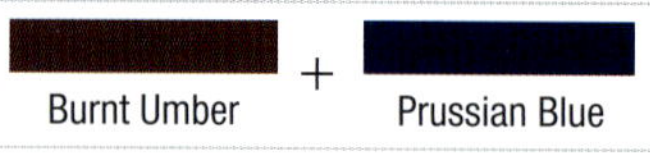

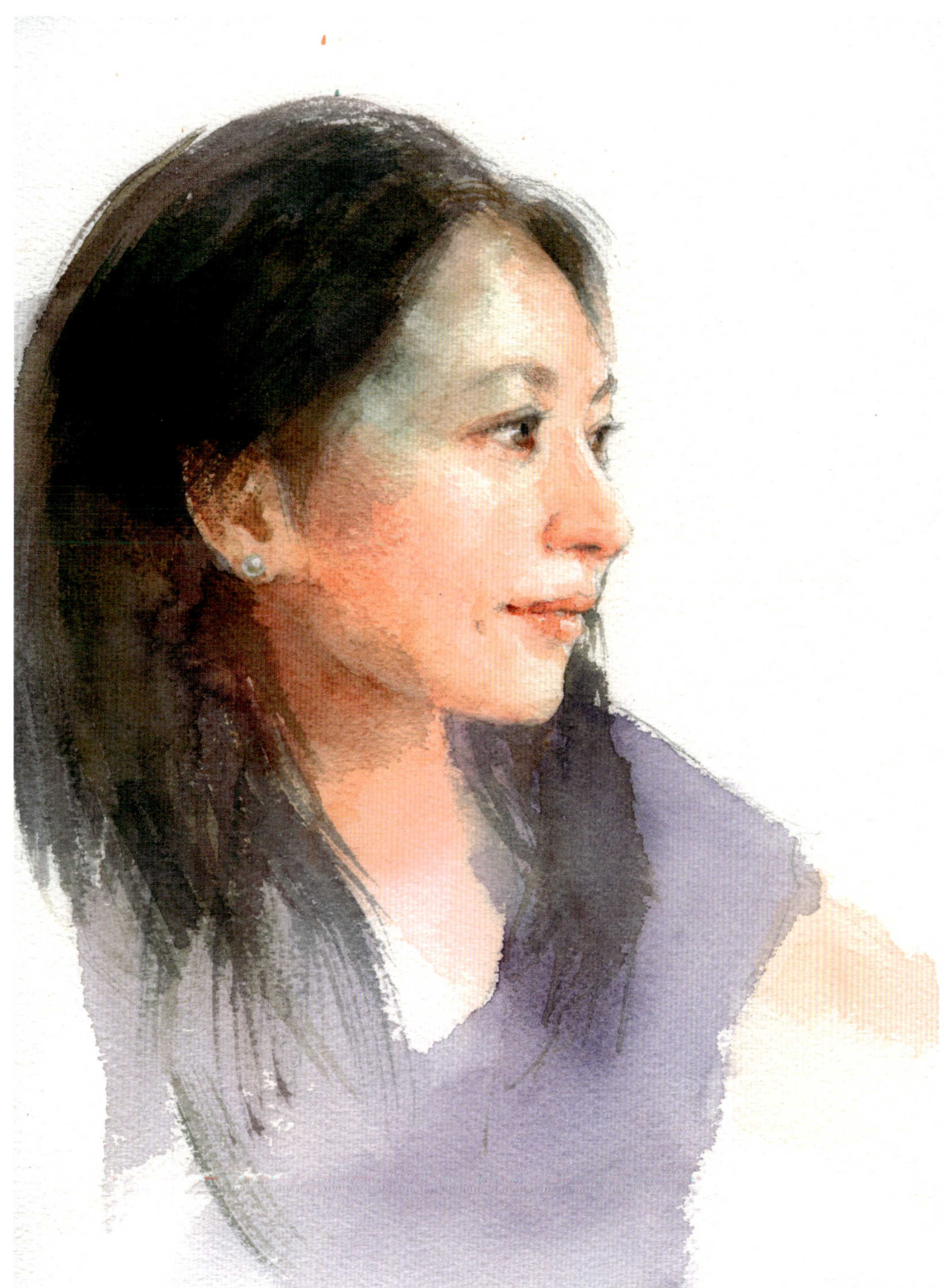

Complete

The female model I asked to pose for this portrait is a novelist. She had just published a novel, *Umi to Shinju* (*The Sea and Pearls*), so I added a pair of pearl earrings to the portrait at the end.

Hand Expressions

The three steps for drawing hands:

1. Grasp the general contour first.
2. Draw the position of each knuckle.
3. Fill out each finger individually.

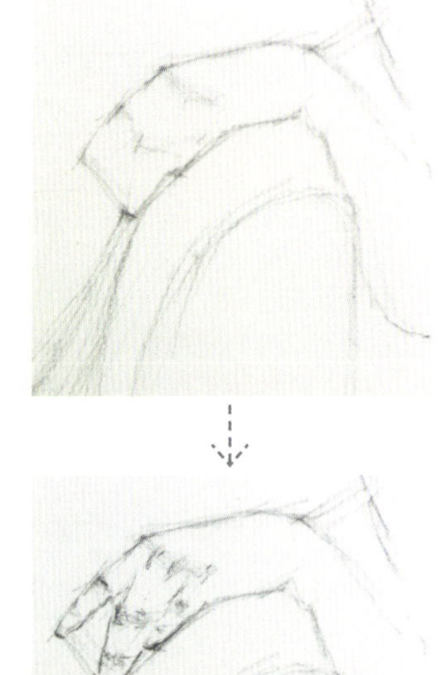

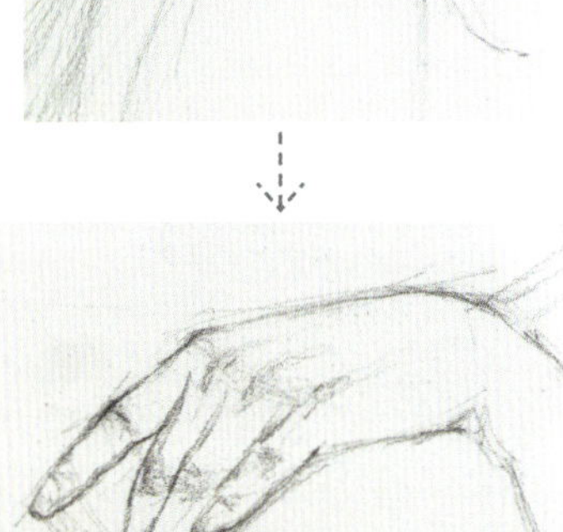

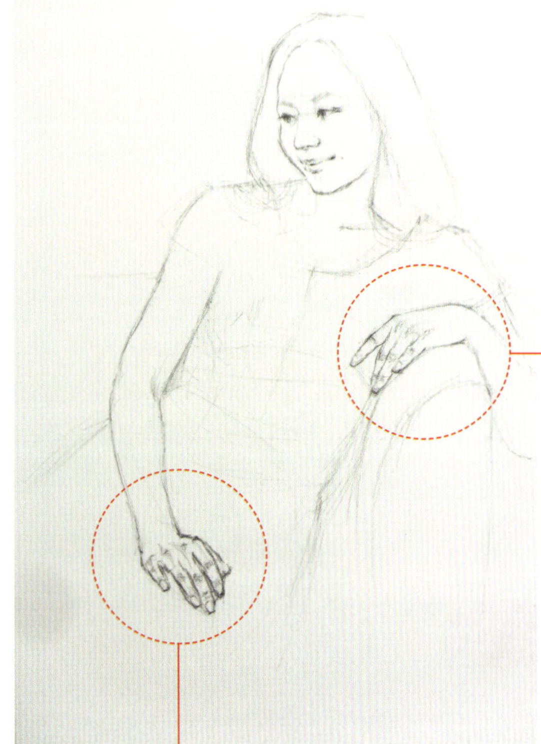

The finished rough outline.

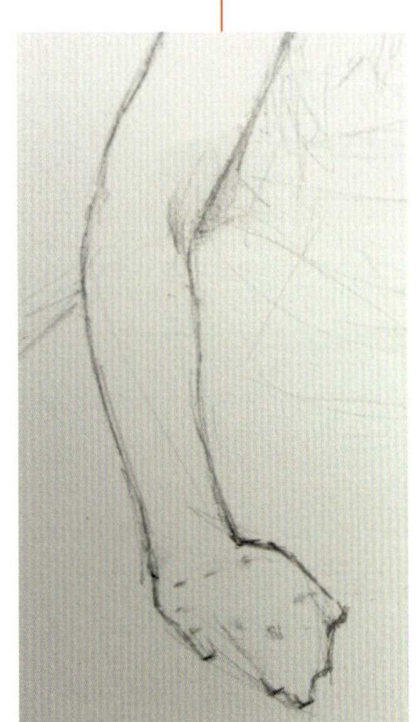

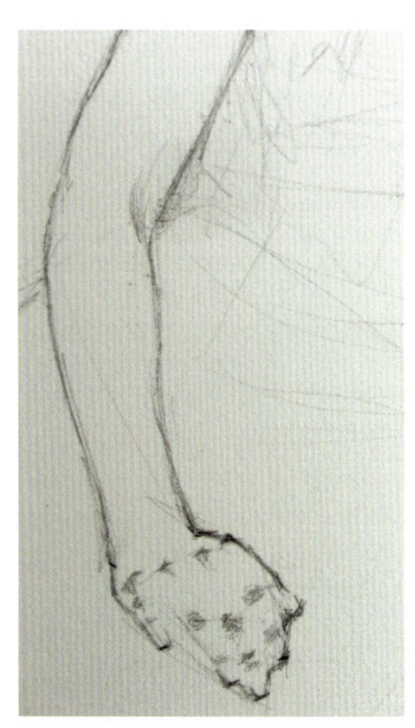

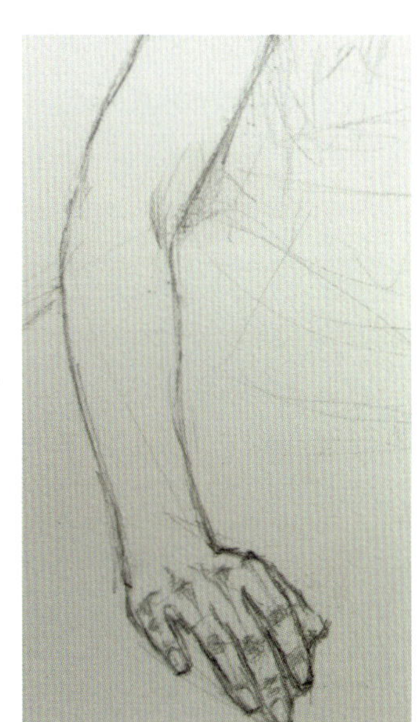

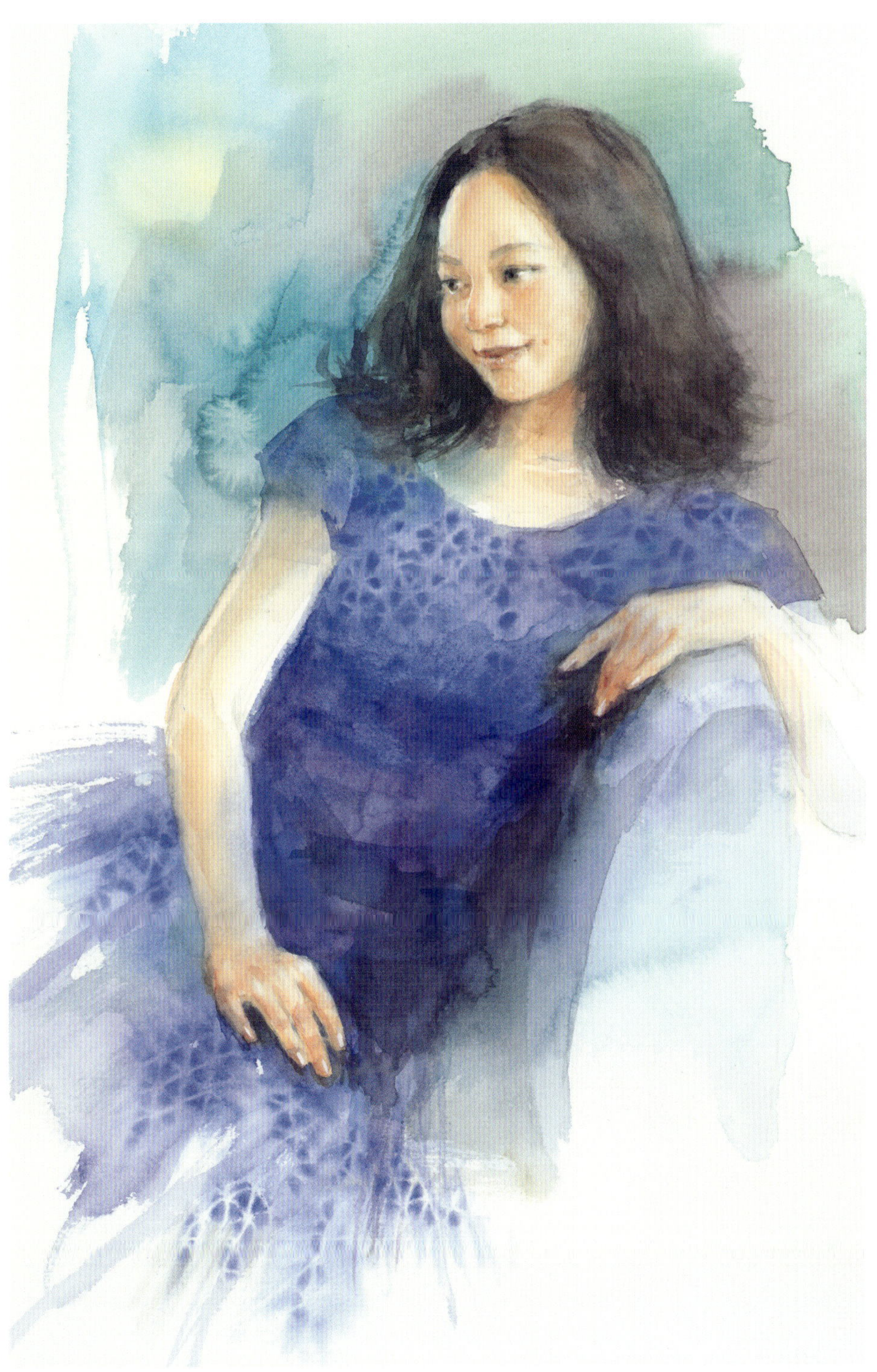

Something good must have happened to our model. She remains silent but exudes joy from her fingers and her lips.

Ajisai no Hito (Lady in a Hydrangea Dress)
19.75 x 13 in (50 x 33 cm)

Shading

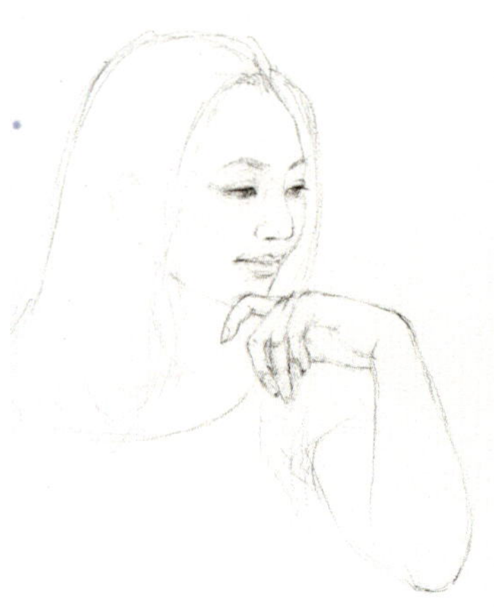

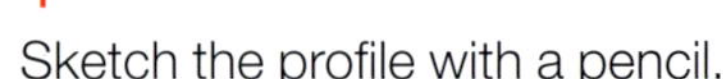

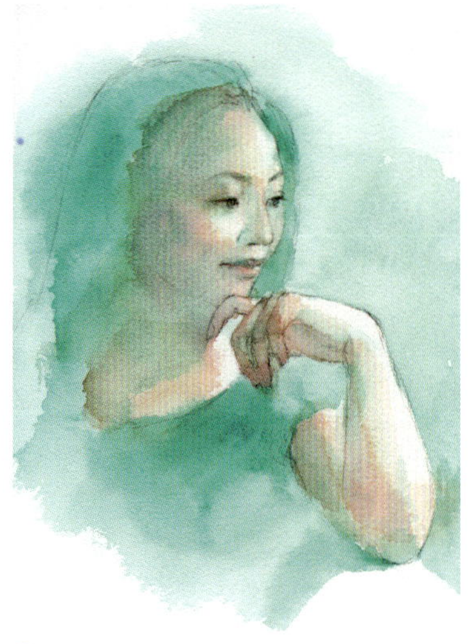

1

Sketch the profile with a pencil.

2

This time we will try to shade using a single color.

Using Cobalt Green only, add feeling to your painting.

Note

Please don't feel like you should hesitate to use bluish colors for the face. This method of shading is meant to replace a world that appears to be monochrome. It might seem bold to use green here, but just remember to add shading precisely to the face.

3

After letting the green base dry, lightly lay down the flesh colors.

Though you want to portray a flesh color that is thin, try your utmost to use only a little water. Be careful to prevent the paint below from bleeding through and mixing with the flesh color.

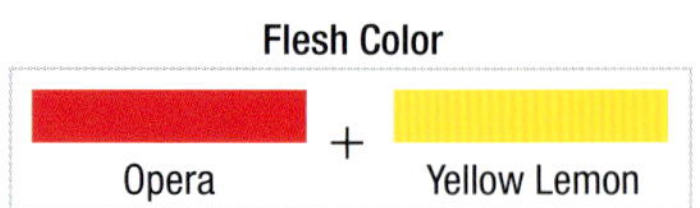

A fundamental watercolor concept states: "start by painting colors that are bright."

I think that this concept is basically fine, but I would also say that sometimes it is better to ignore such concepts. For example, in this lesson we first painted the flesh color in green. I have also painted blue flesh color first and then laid a thin flesh color on top of that. Actually, laying a bright color on top of a dark color is possible. If somebody tells you that it doesn't work you should try to figure out the reason why. Occasionally we should regress to that child in us who wants to do it anyway even after we have been told not to. Give new things a try!

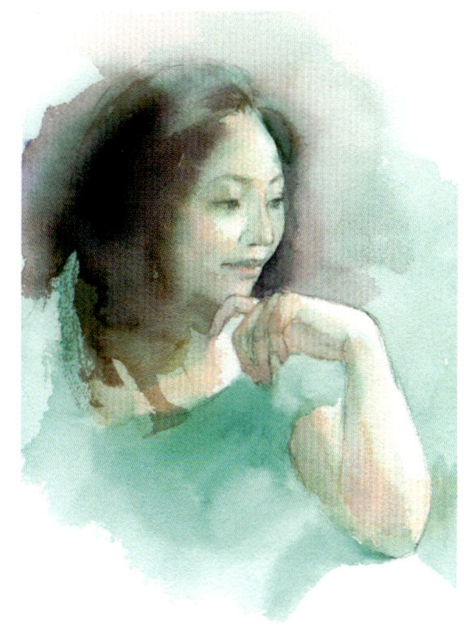

4

First, I painted this so that it
would run on purpose.

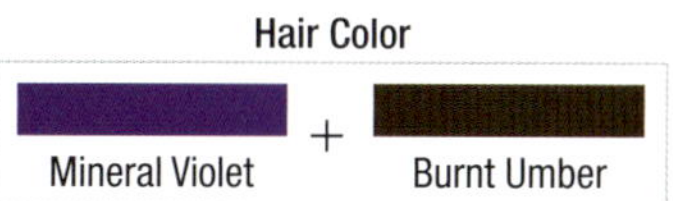

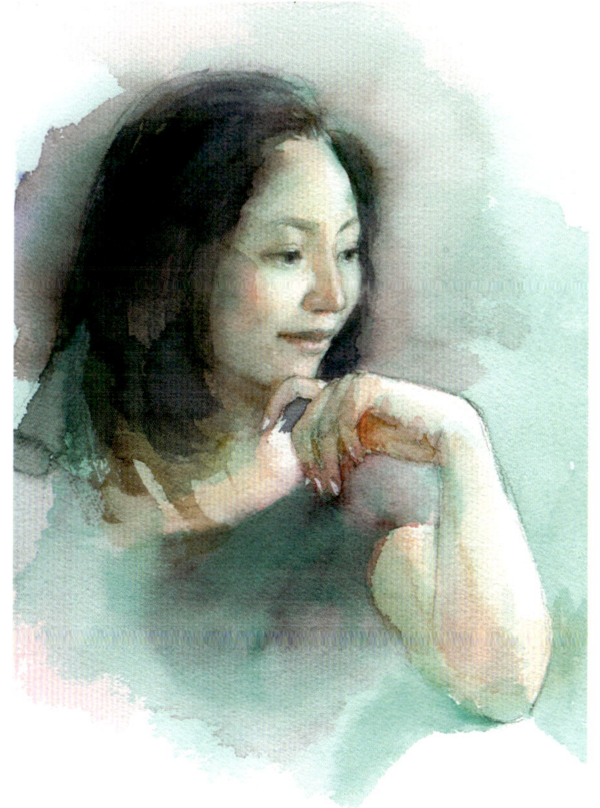

Complete

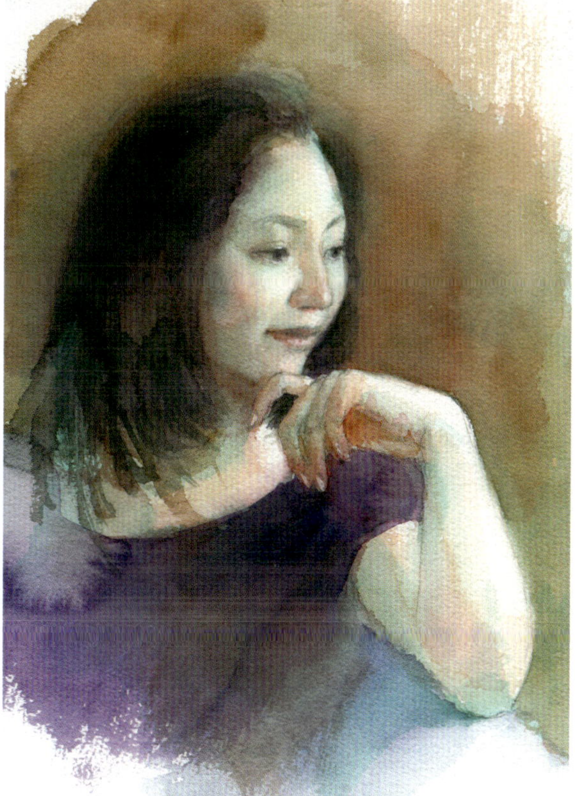

Here I tried painting the background a little darker.
Since all of our colors have Cobalt Green as a
common color it is okay to layer any of them as a
background color at the end.

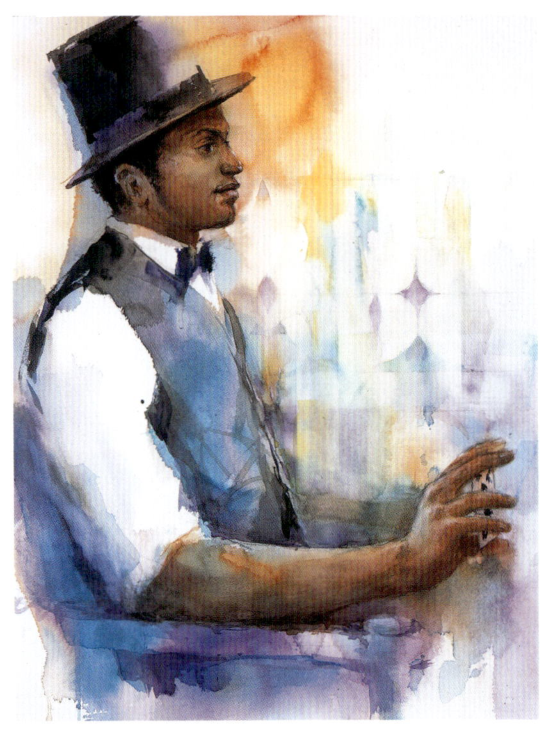

Poker Face (1)
18.5 x13 in (47 x 33 cm)

As an actor, our model was able to give us various expressions as each card was dealt.

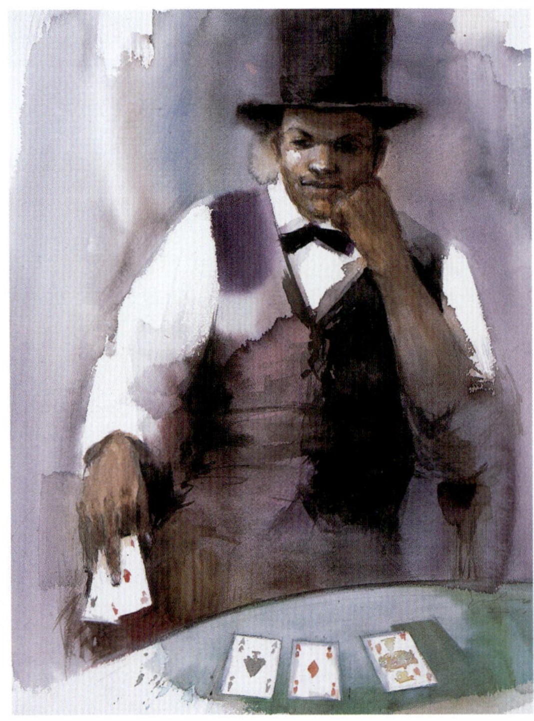

Poker Face (2)
22 x 16.5 in (56 x 42 cm)

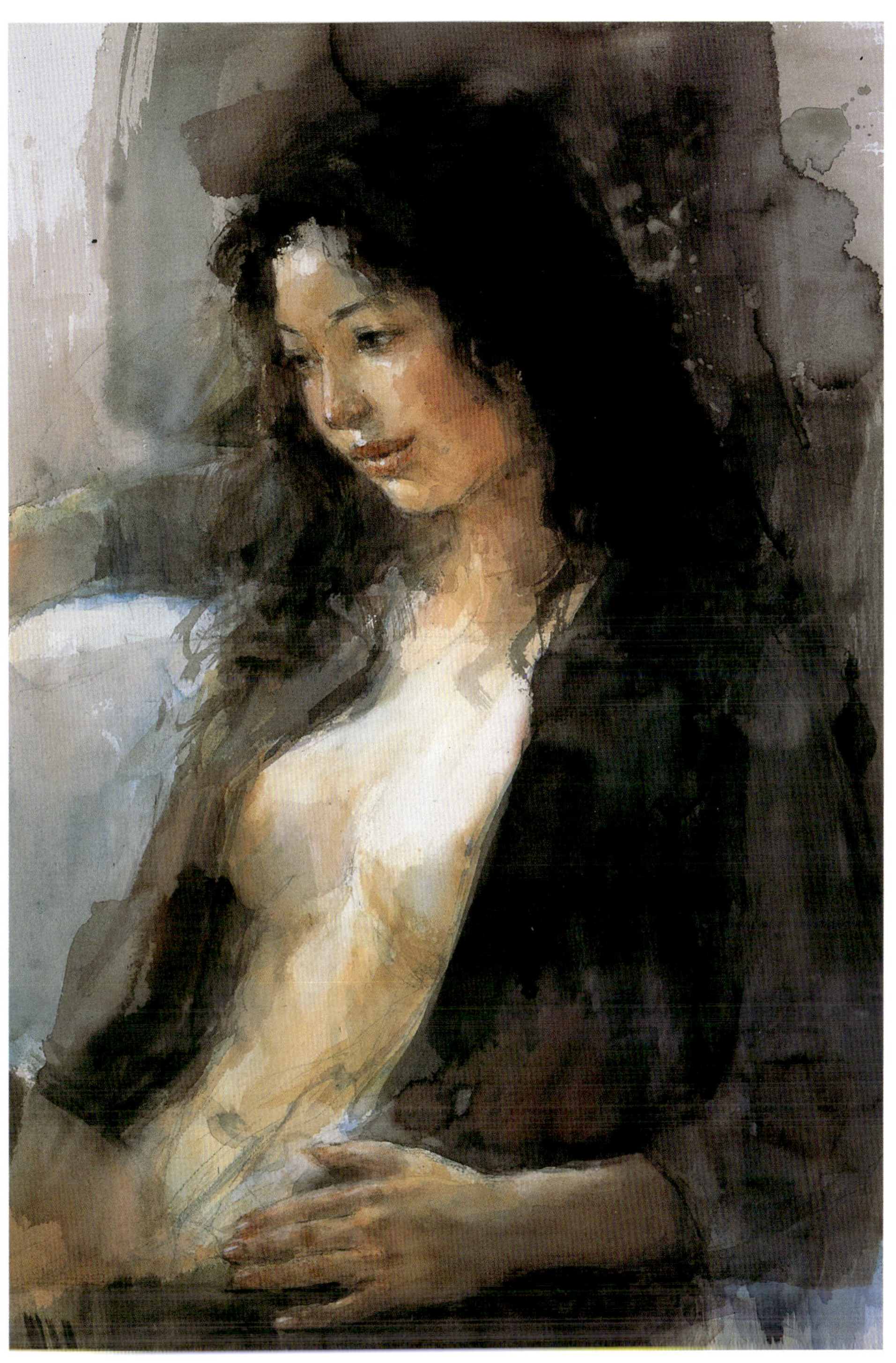

This beautiful model came to my studio. I said, "I'm sorry that you had to come on such a rainy day. Did you get soaked?" She replied, "No worries, I love rainy days."

Ame no Sukina Hito (Rain Lover)
22.75 x 15.5 in (58 x 39 cm)

Clothing 1: Uneven Patterns

Paint female clothes with striking colors and designs. Use a primer to create the uneven patterned lace and then begin to paint.

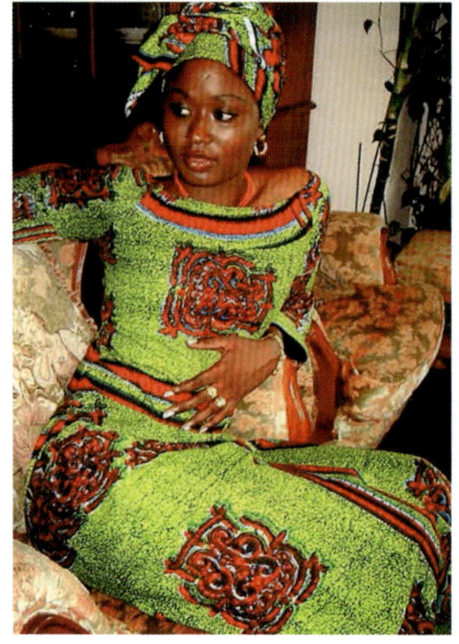

A Senegalese dancer friend.

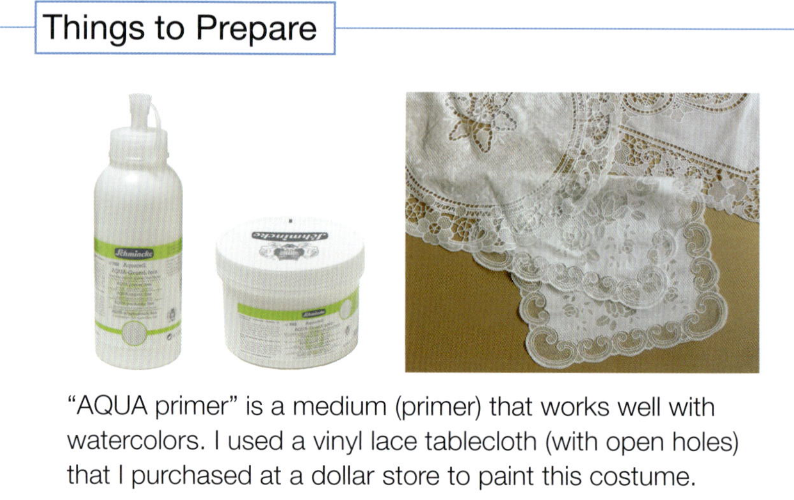

"AQUA primer" is a medium (primer) that works well with watercolors. I used a vinyl lace tablecloth (with open holes) that I purchased at a dollar store to paint this costume.

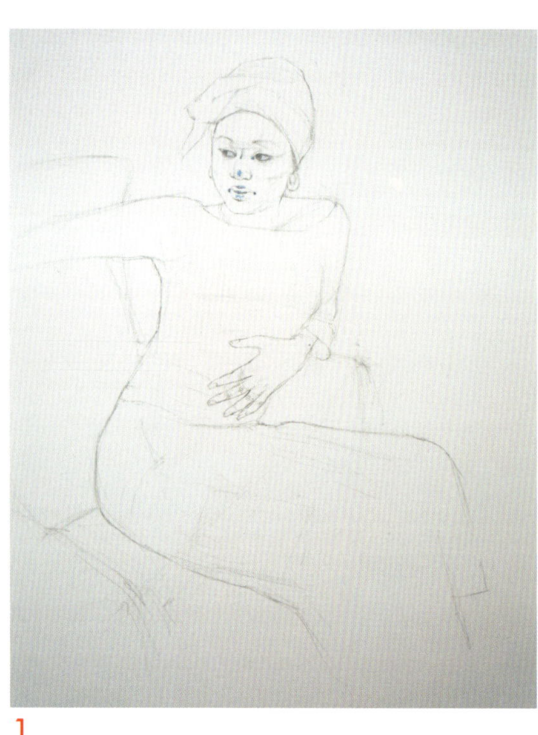

1

Sketch the profile with a pencil.

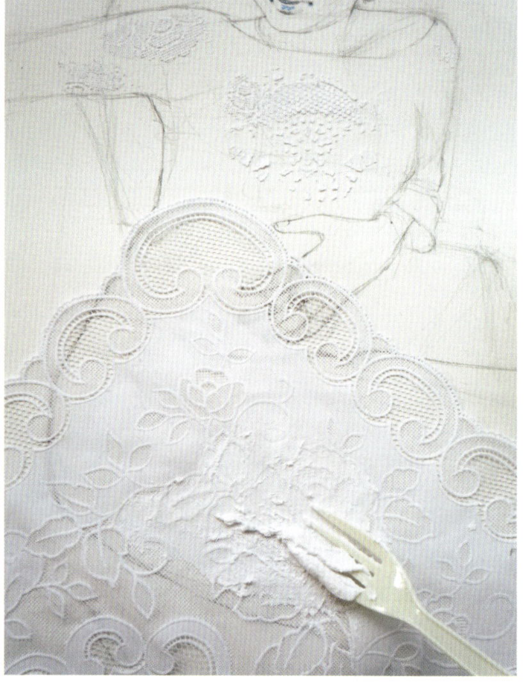

2

Place the vinyl tablecloth where you want the pattern and then apply primer over it.

The primer will penetrate the open holes of the tablecloth and make uneven patterns.

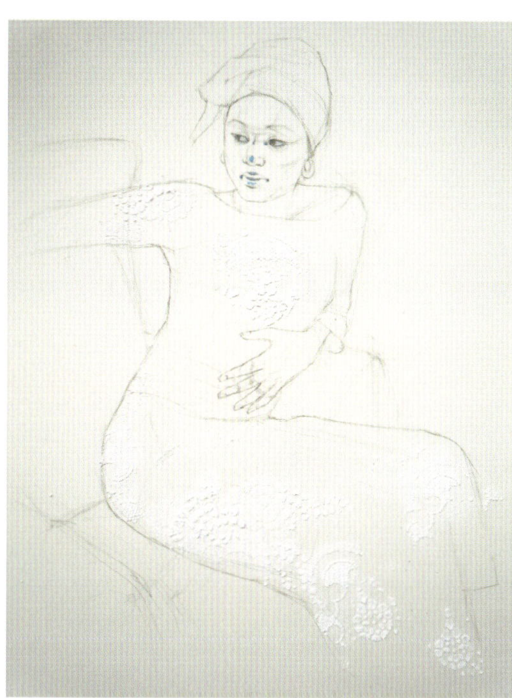

3

Dry the primer using a dryer.

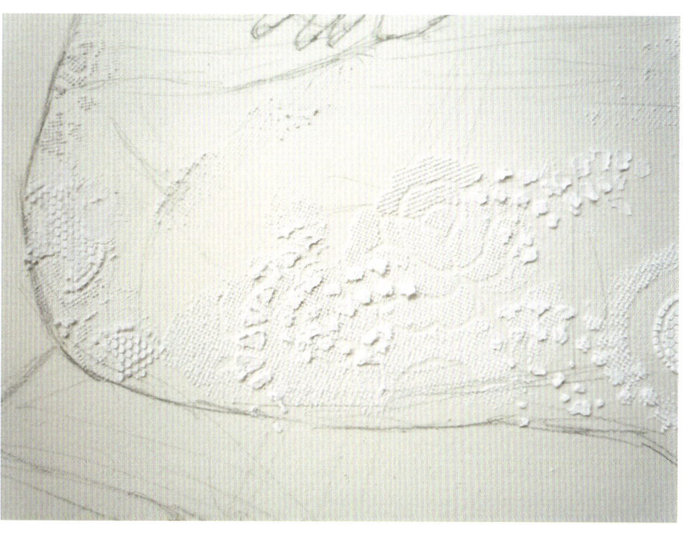

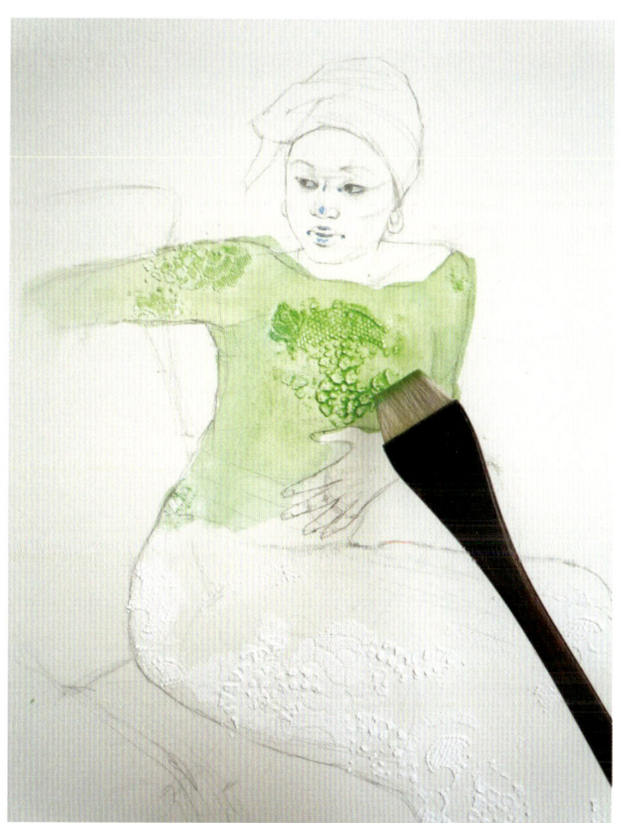

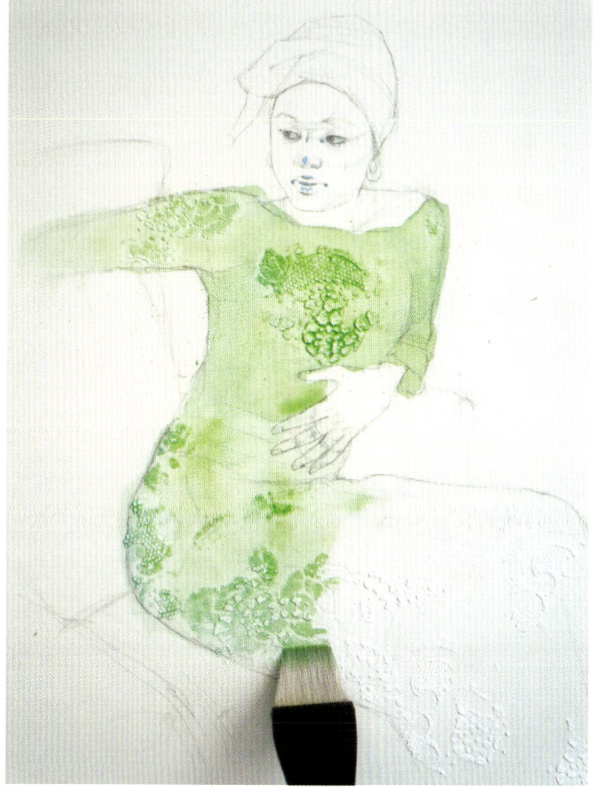

4

Add color to the clothes with a hake brush.

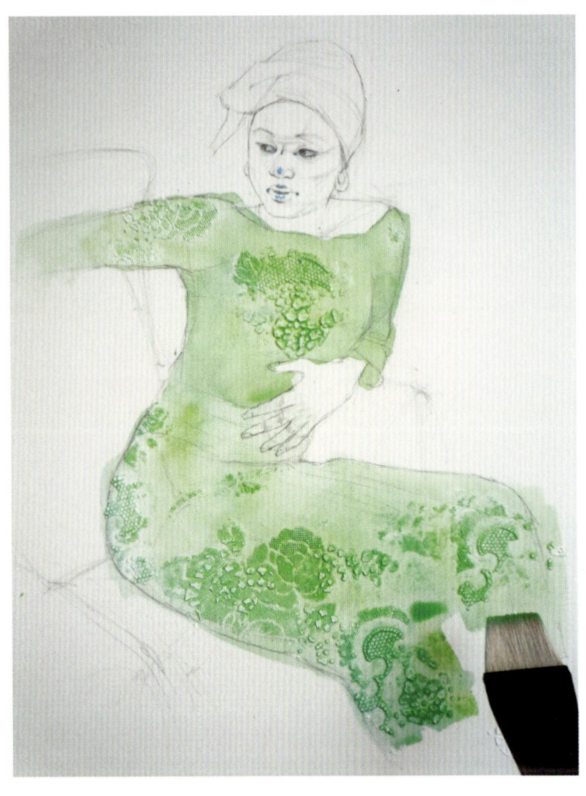

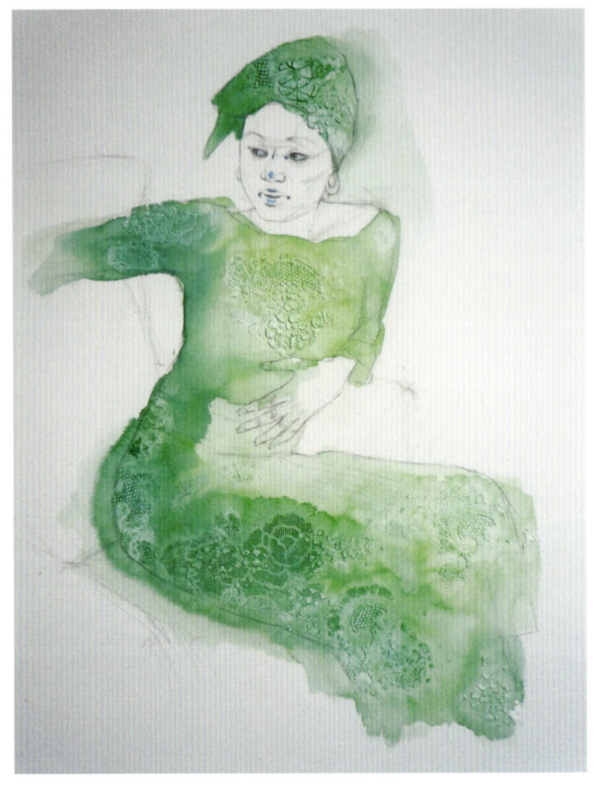

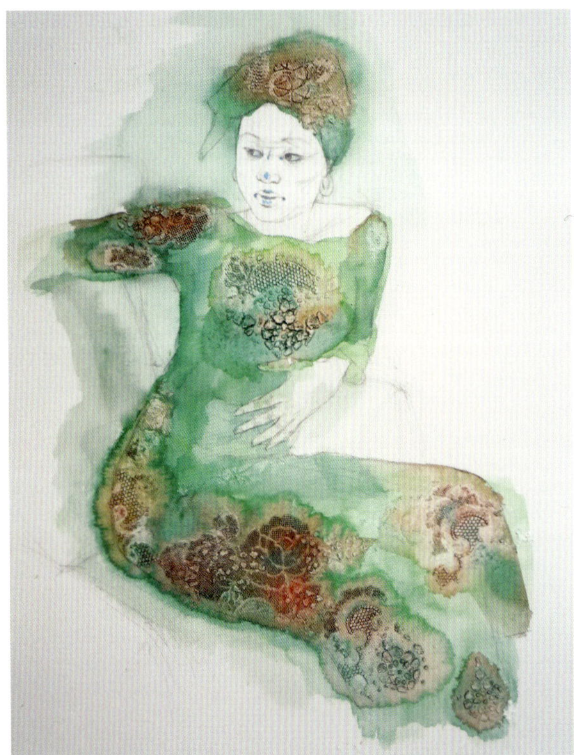

5

Add shading all over the clothes with watercolors.

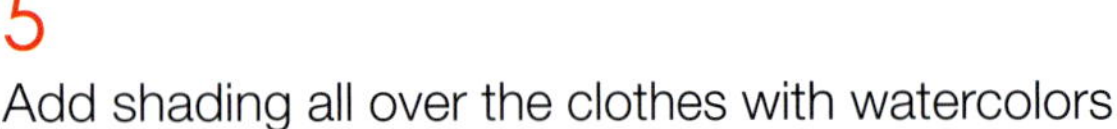

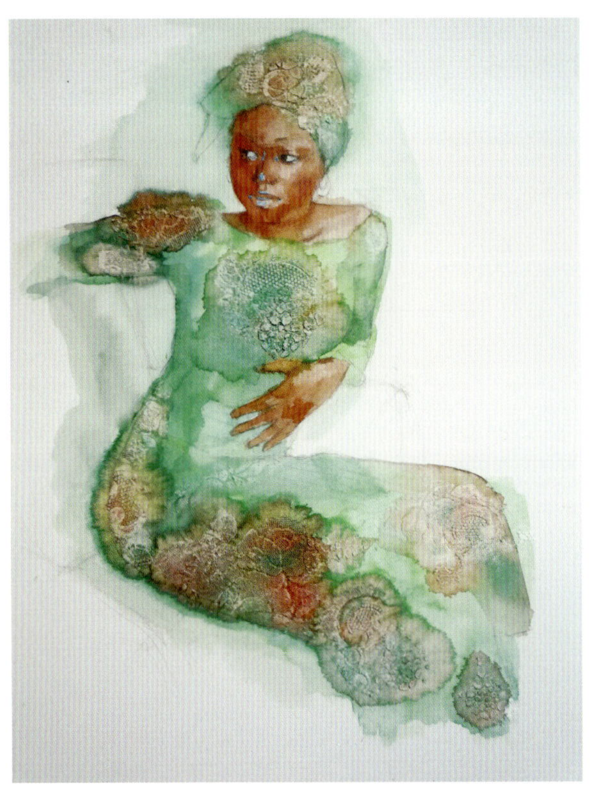

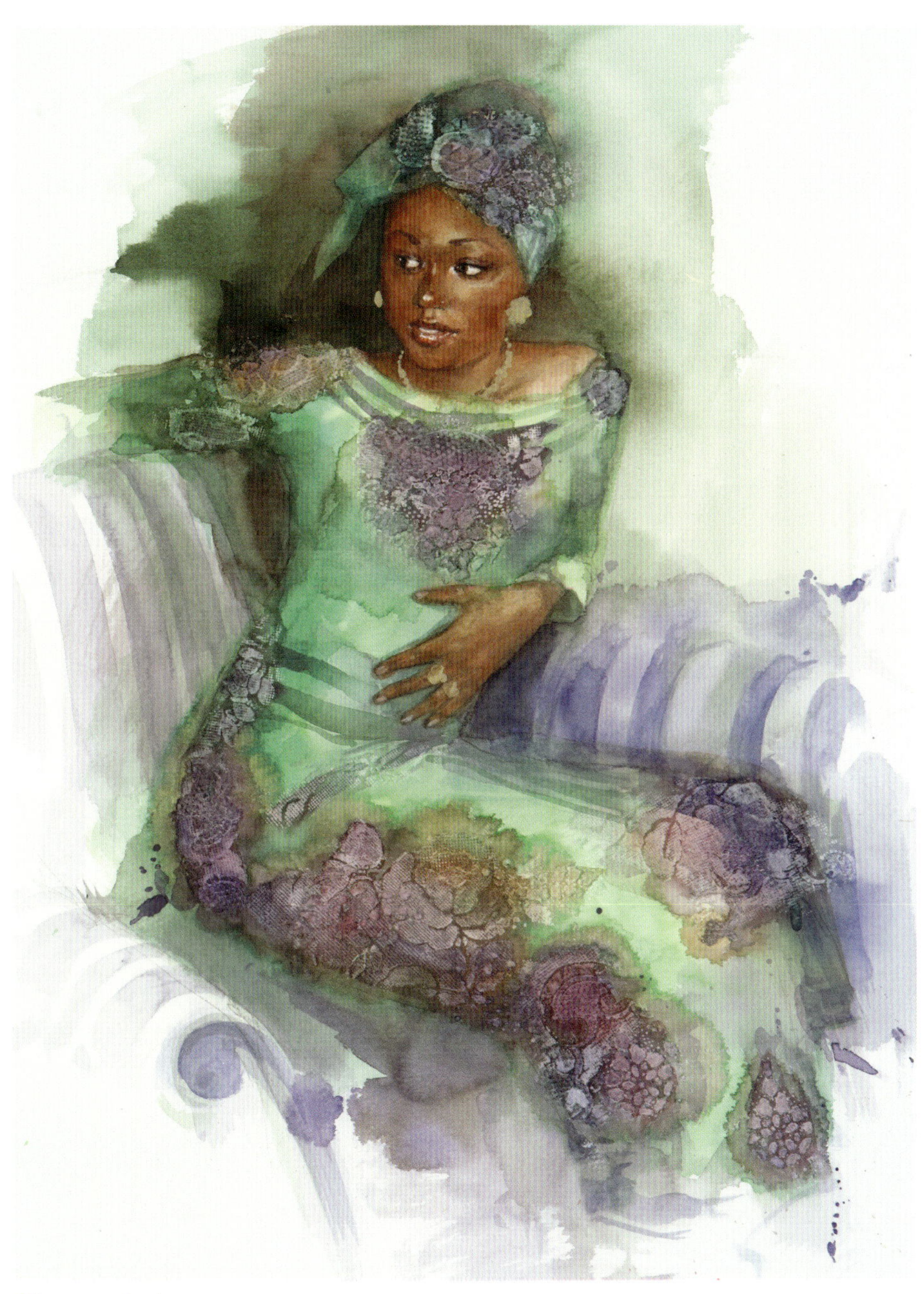

Complete

Clothing 2: Gold Patterns

I used gold leaf to paint this gold embroidery–decorated national costume.

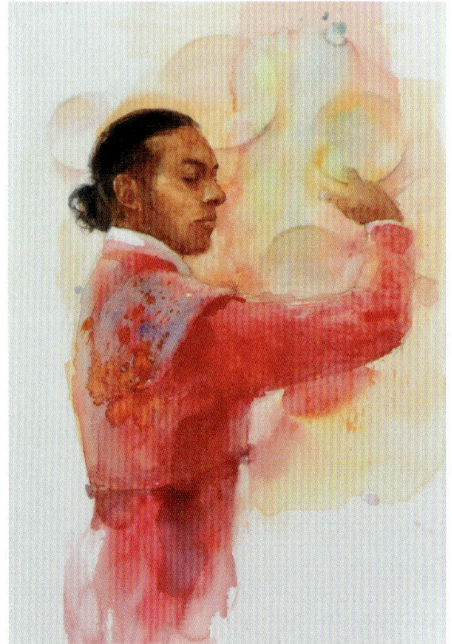

After laying down the various colors it was almost finished.

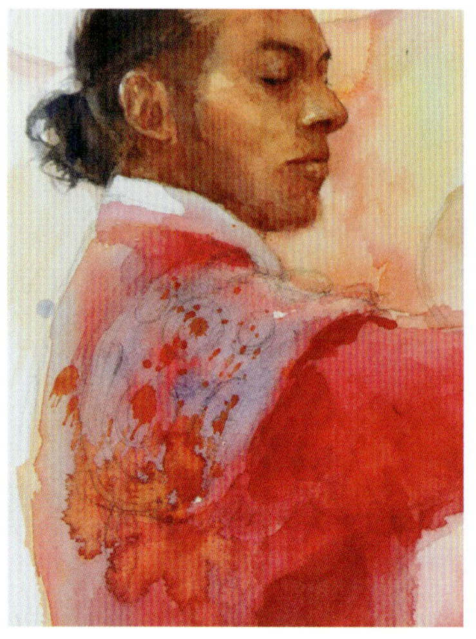

I added patterns to the shoulders.

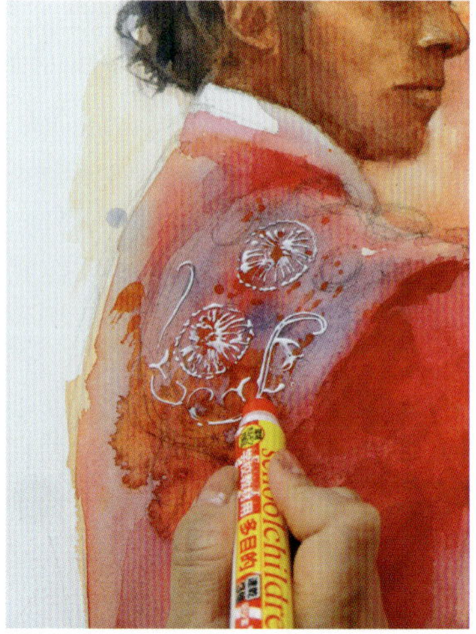

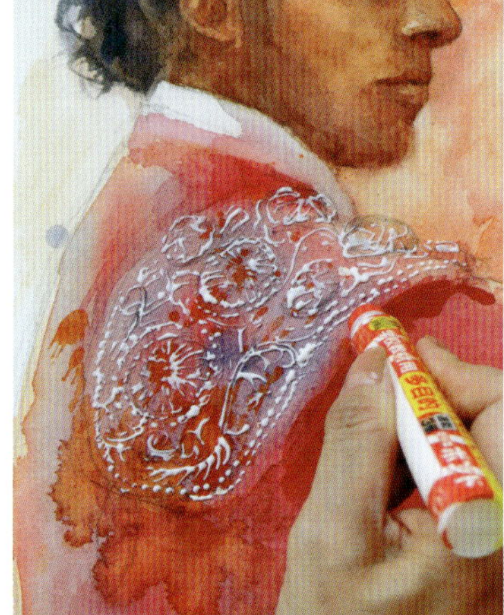

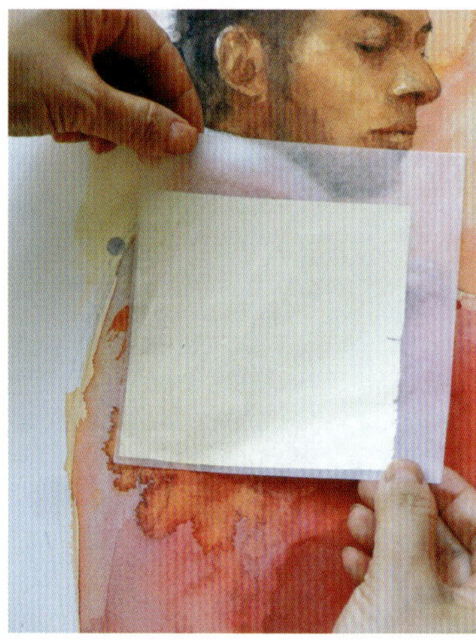

Preparing Gold Leaf

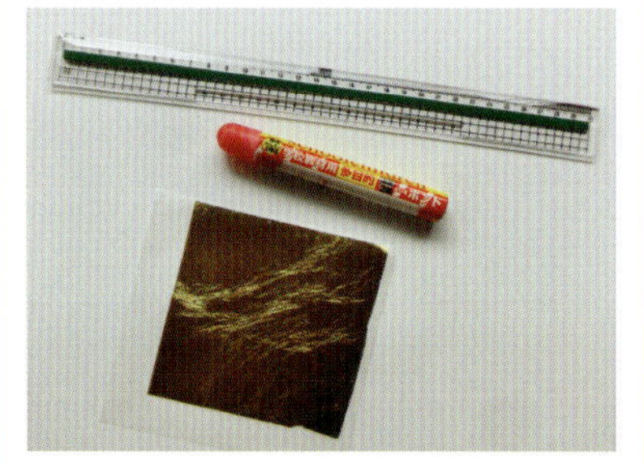

Gold Leaf / Akashigami (Waxed Paper) / Quick Dry Glue Pen / Ruler

Preparation

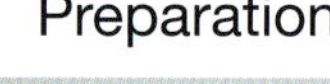

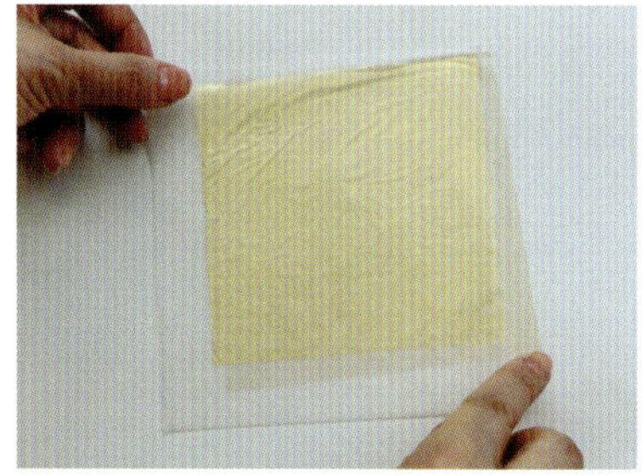

1

Put akashigami (waxed paper) on the backside of the gold leaf.

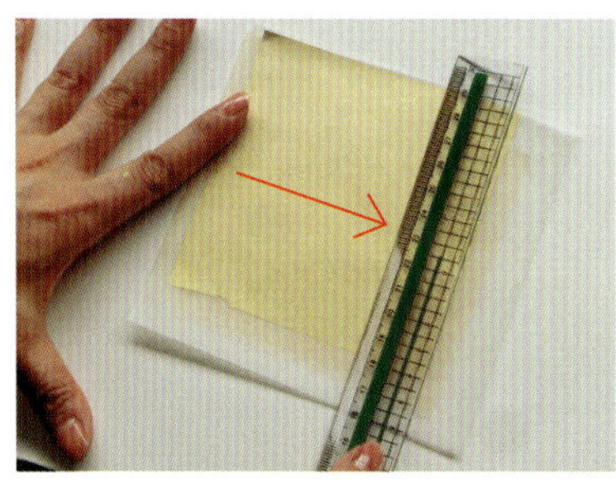

2

Press a ruler lightly against the akashigami (waxed paper) and smooth it out.

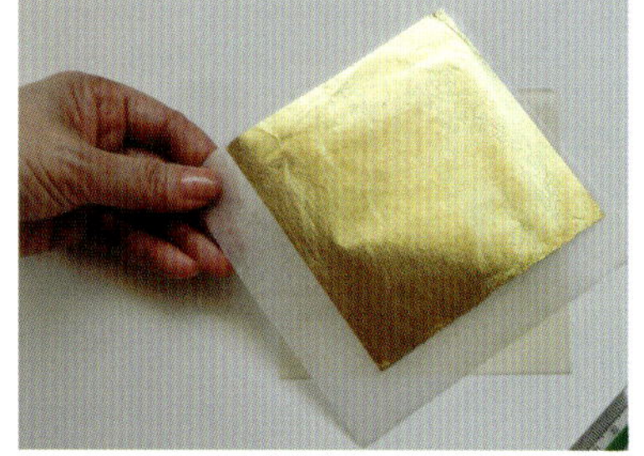

3

Now, the gold leaf is attached to the akashigami (waxed paper). The above photo shows the gold leaf from the front.

Draw the pattern using a fast-drying glue pen and then, before the glue dries, apply the gold leaf attached to the akashigami (waxed paper).

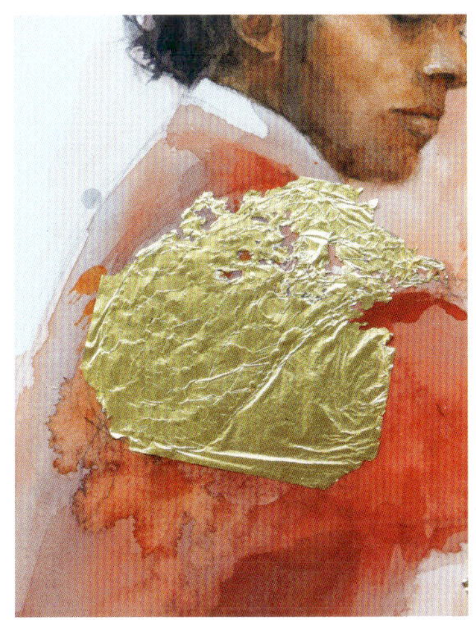 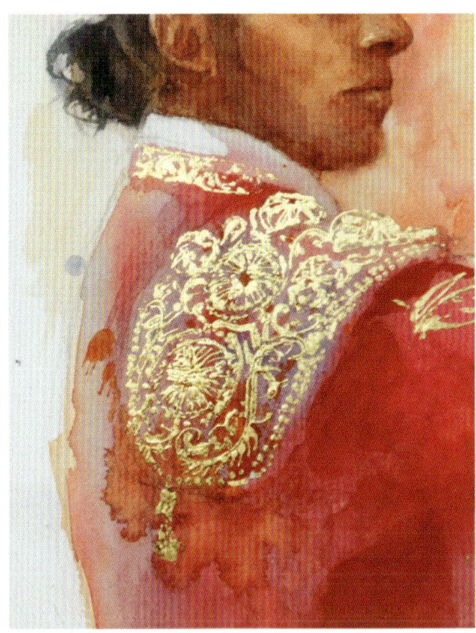

Leave it for about one hour to dry and then brush off excess gold leaf using a feather brush.

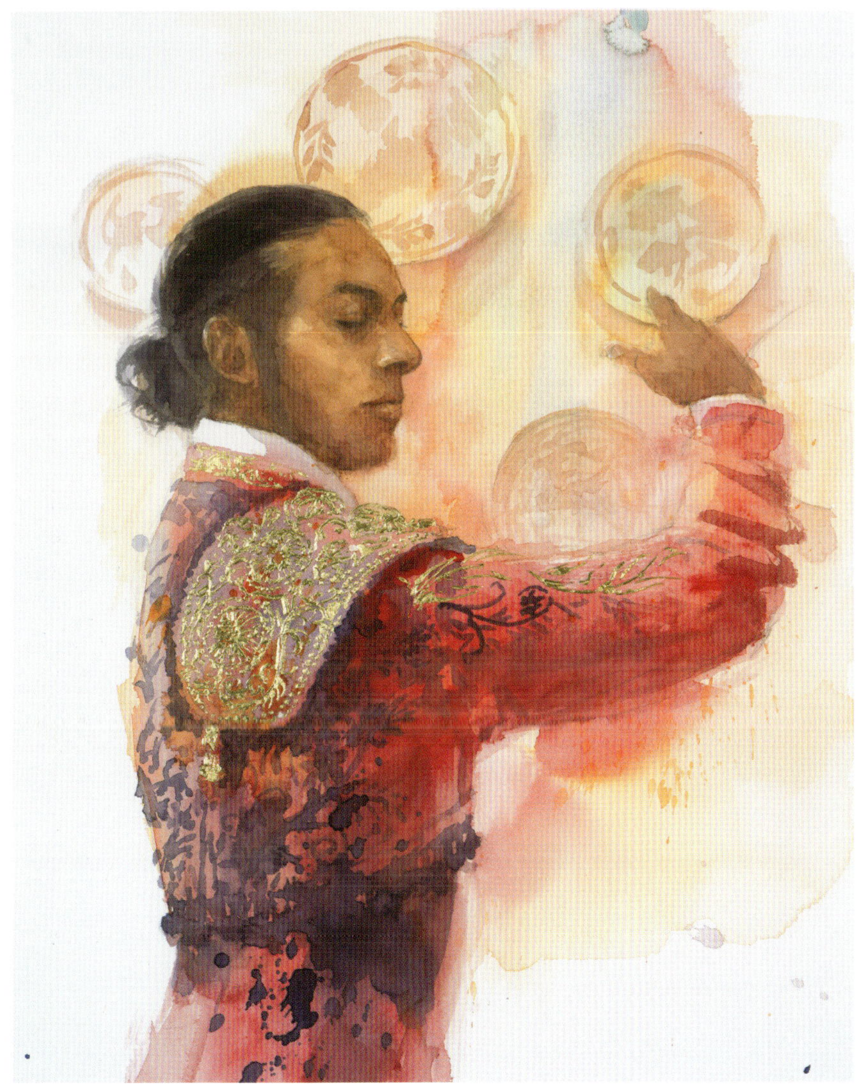

Billy
21.25 x 17 in (54 x 43 cm)

Flowers and Human Figures

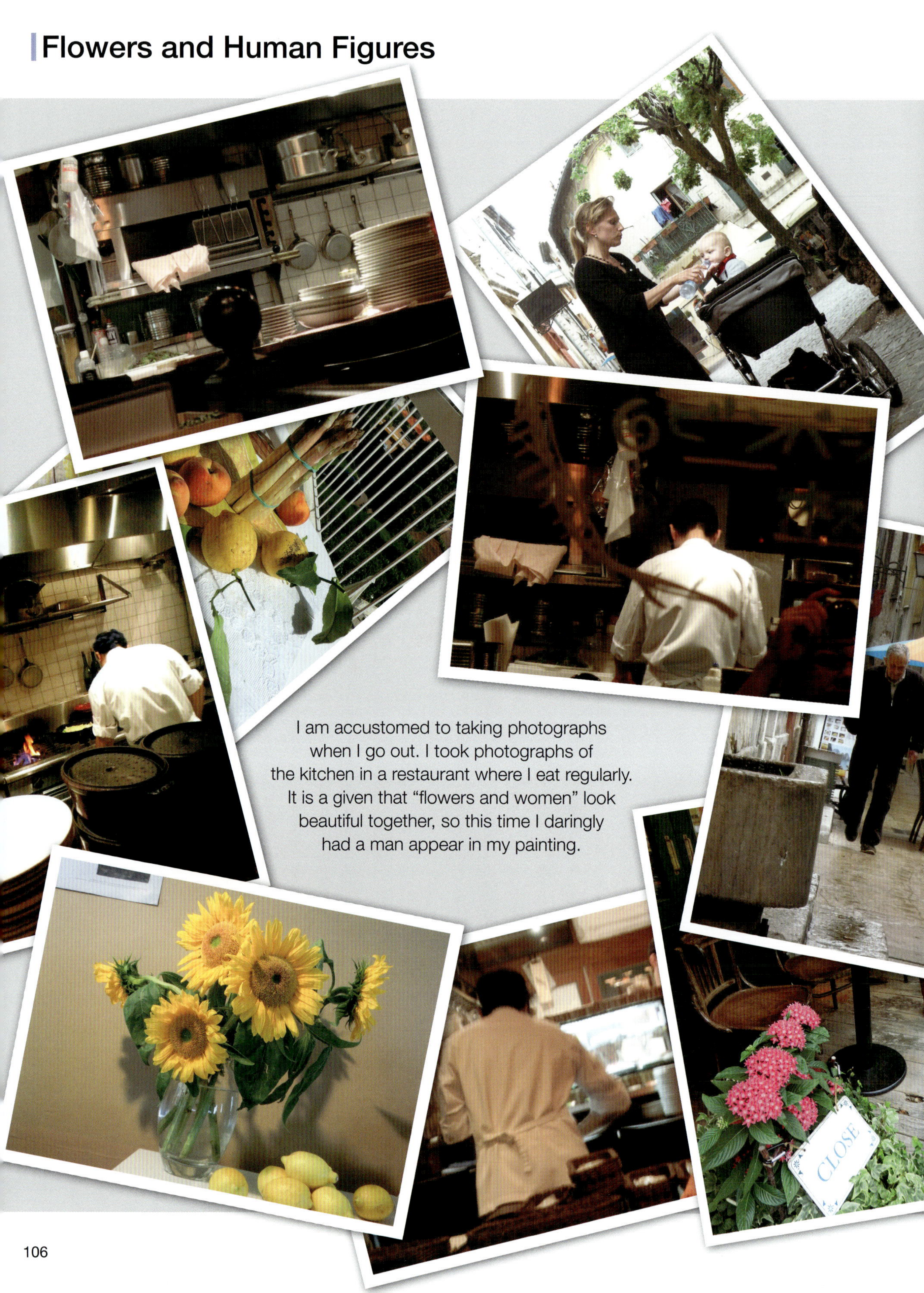

I am accustomed to taking photographs
when I go out. I took photographs of
the kitchen in a restaurant where I eat regularly.
It is a given that "flowers and women" look
beautiful together, so this time I daringly
had a man appear in my painting.

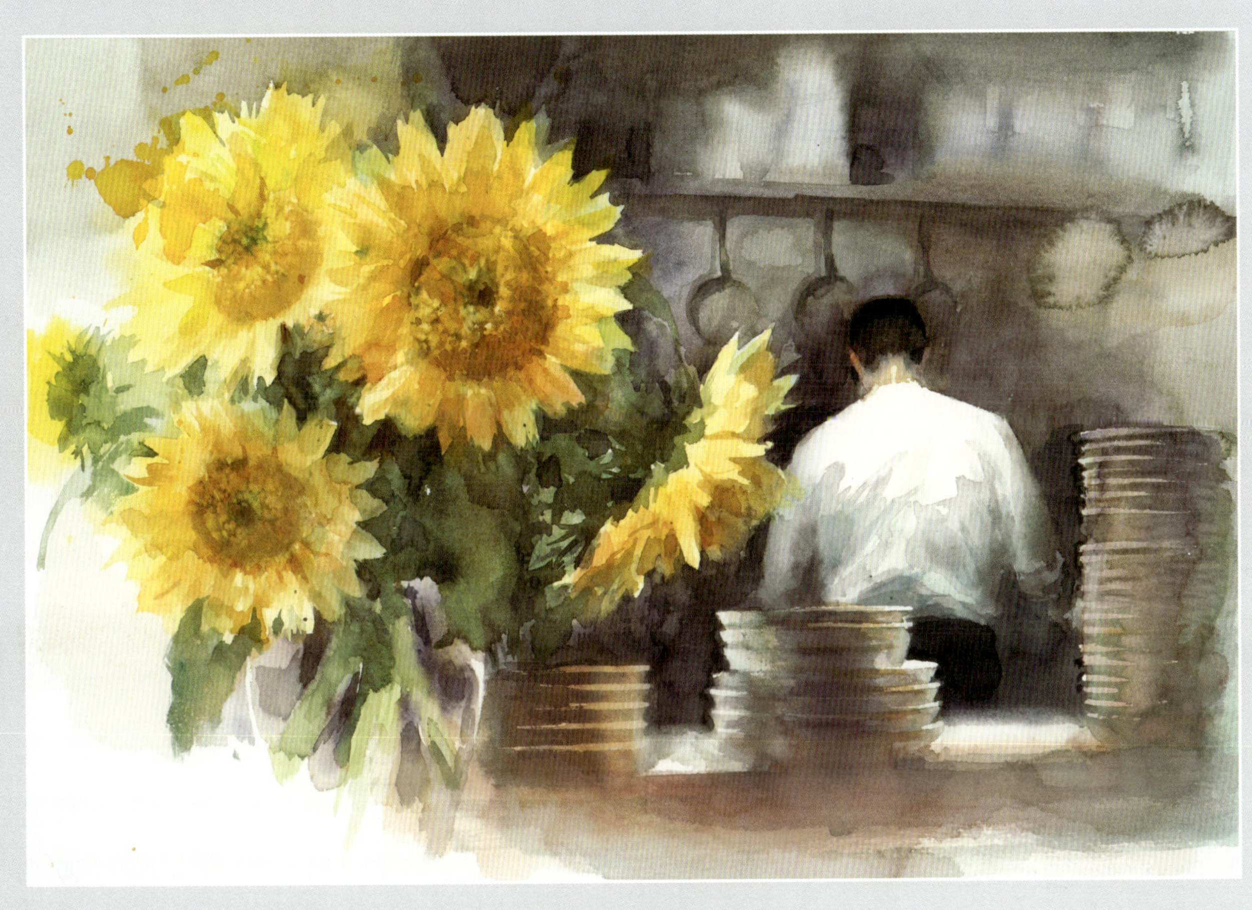

Girasole
14.25 x 19.75 in (36 x 50 cm)

Roses in a vase: that alone is enough for a quality painting. But this time let's be a little more playful.

Let's imagine—what if these flowers were placed in a café or what if they were in the lobby of a small hotel somewhere abroad? It's as if those roses, in that vase in front of my eyes, are traveling all over the world. Isn't it fun to imagine?

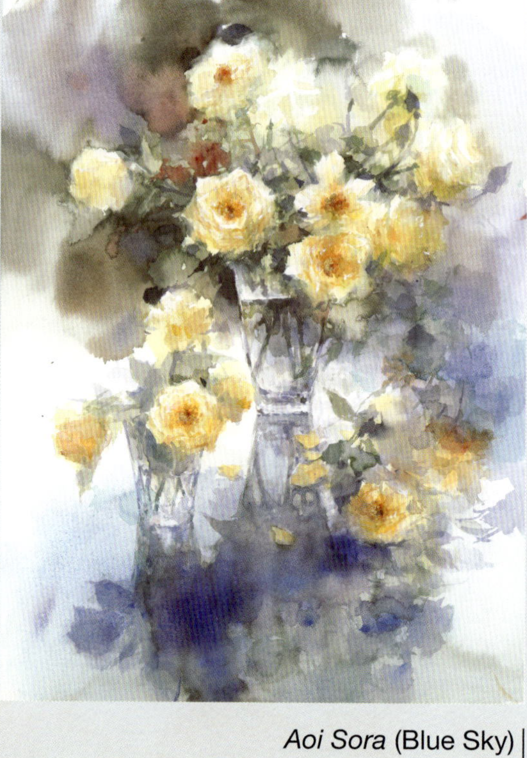

Aoi Sora (Blue Sky)
29.25 x 21.75 in (74 x 55 cm)

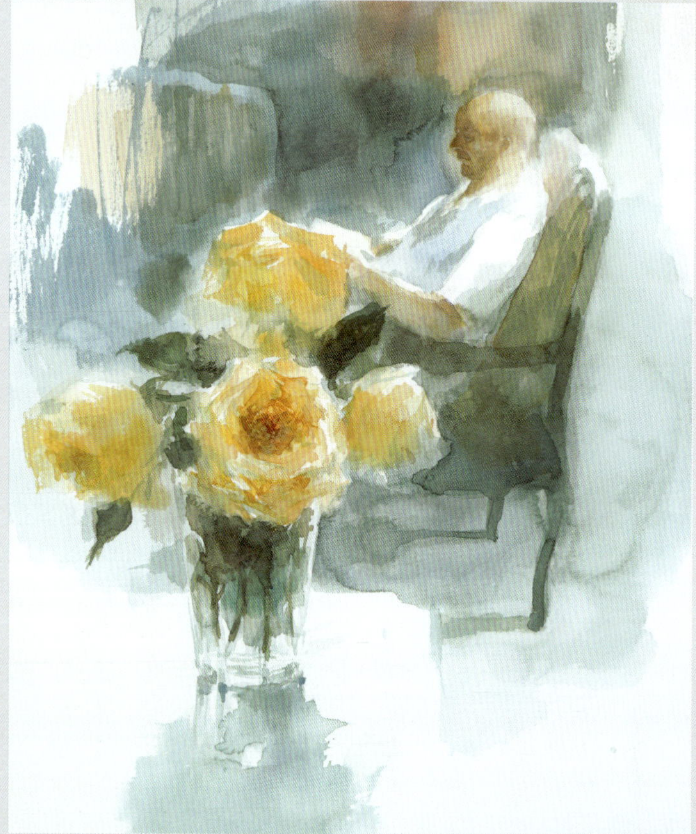

I painted these two paintings at the same time.

Peninsula
19.75 x 14.25 in (50 x 36 cm)

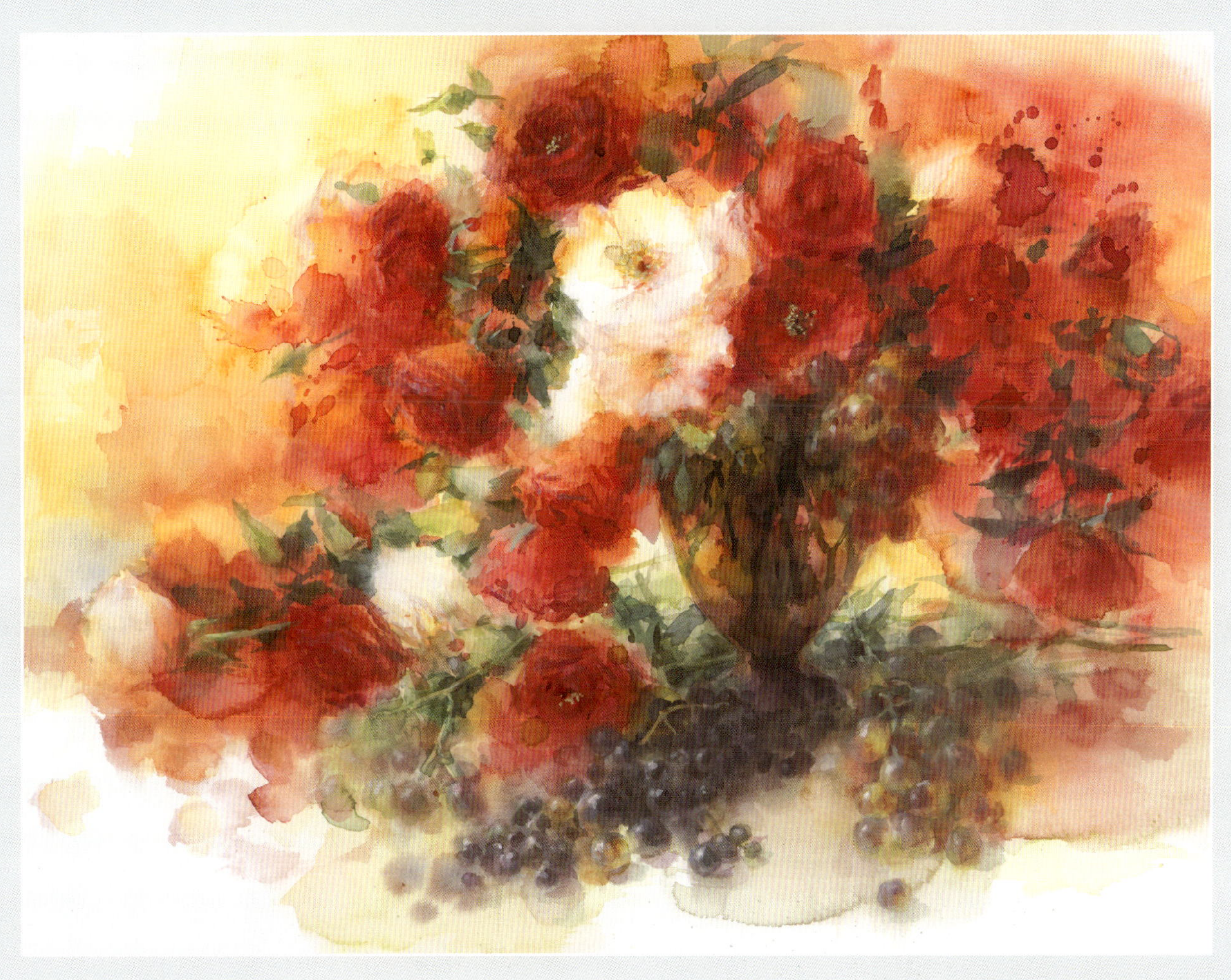

Tegami o Yomu Hi (A Day for Reading Letters)
20.5 x 26.25 in (52 x 67 cm)

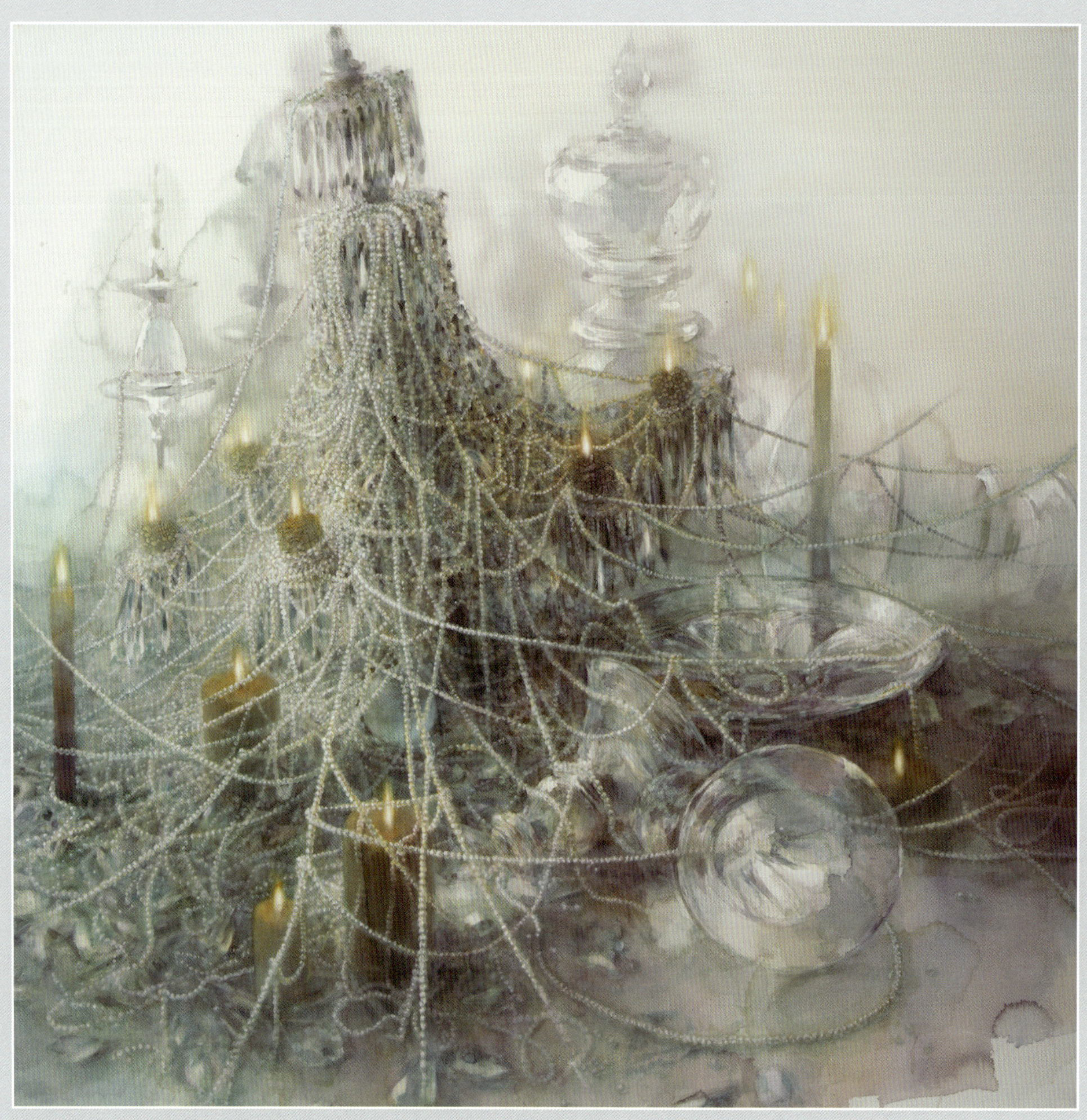

Yume no Ato (After a Dream)
36.5 x 35.75 in (93 x 91 cm)

It is said that a palette reflects your mind; you should always keep it tidy. Though I completely agree, I must apologize because my palette is actually this messy. If it is easier for you to use, you should not mind whether your palette is clean or dirty. What's important is that, when you want to paint, your palette has all the necessary colors. It's that simple.

Though there are countless shades of paint, I mainly use red, blue, a little bit of yellow, and additionally some green, purple, and brown. Most of them are Schmincke watercolors. I line up a variation of the three primary colors—red, yellow, and blue—and then I use colors that I make by mixing the primaries together. Given that my own tastes can be fickle, I sometimes find that some mixed colors that I once used frequently no longer appeal to me. I often use gold and silver and I also add in some platinum.

Watercolors go with anything and are very compatible with Japanese painting materials. You could say that watercolors are very "lenient" paints.

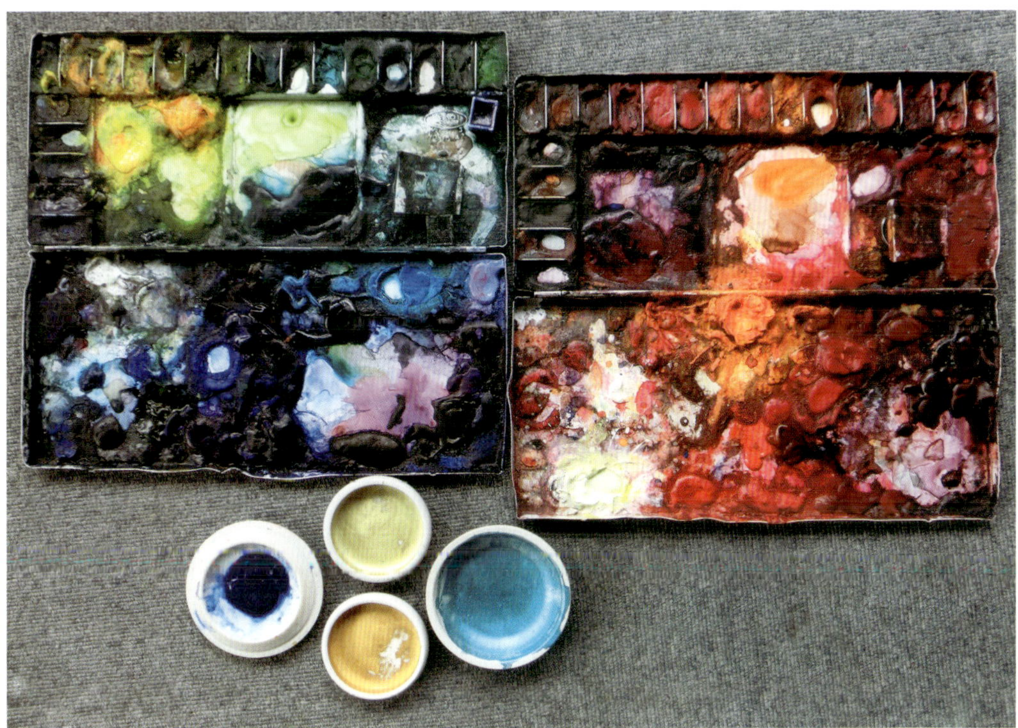

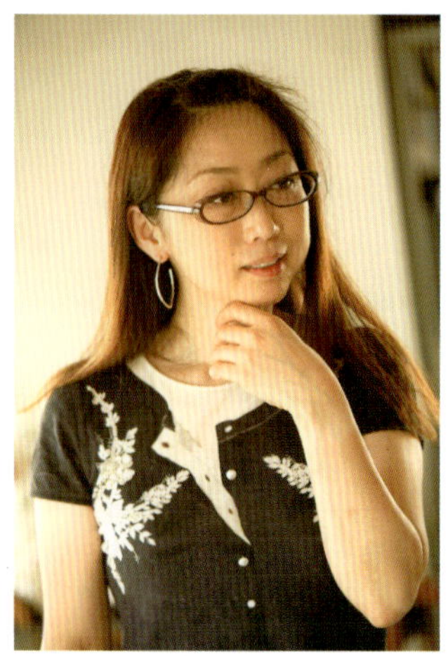

Yuko Nagayama

Born in 1963 in Tokyo, Japan, Nagayama graduated from Tokyo University of the Arts in 1985 with a major in oil painting. She studied under Hiroshi Karase in the Graduate School at Tokyo University of the Arts, and graduated in 1987. She received the Ataka Award and the Ohashi Award.

She works in watercolor, mixed media, and collages, but it is her original watercolor painting methods, in particular, that are recognized both domestically and internationally. One of her paintings graced the cover of *L'Art de l'Aquarelle*, a French watercolor magazine, that also featured an article on her demonstrations. In addition to watercolors, Nagayama uses gold, platinum, and Japanese-style paints, which create wonderfully original translucent paintings, and the watercolor magazine *Amazing Palette* highlighted this unique palette.

In Japan, Nagayama is known to be a pioneer of performing watercolor-painting demonstrations that have been popular since 2006. Initially she did her demonstrations at her private gallery without any advertising. However, her presentations, which let the audience members share in the depth and scope of watercolor expression, have become well-known through word of mouth, and nowadays she gives many sold-out lectures. But to this day, Nagayama still enjoys preparing motifs and performing demonstrations at her private gallery, without any advertising. For more information, visit www.nagayamay.com.

You Can Paint Dazzling Watercolors in Twelve Easy Lessons
by Yuko Nagayama

First designed and published in Japan in 2012 by
Graphic-sha Publishing Co., Ltd.
1-14-17 Kudankita, Chiyoda-ku, Tokyo 102-0073, Japan

English edition published in the United States of America in 2019 by
Harper Design
An Imprint of HarperCollins*Publishers*
195 Broadway
New York, NY 10007
Tel: (212) 207-7000
Fax: (212) 207-7654
harperdesign@harpercollins.com
www.harpercollins.com

Distributed throughout the world, excluding France, by
HarperCollins*Publishers*
195 Broadway
New York, NY 10007

ISBN 978-0-06-287776-5

Library of Congress Control Number: 2014937992

Printed in China

Second Printing, 2024

Creative staff
Photographs: Yasuo Imai
Book design: Yoshiaki Takagi, Haruna Okubo (Indigo Design Studio)
Editor: Mari Nagai (Graphic-sha Publishing Co., Ltd.)

English edition
English translation: Kevin Willson
English edition layout: Shinichi Ishioka
Production and management: Kumiko Sakamoto (Graphic-sha Publishing Co., Ltd.)